How Judaism Became a Religion

How Judaism Became a Religion

AN INTRODUCTION
TO MODERN JEWISH THOUGHT

Leora Batnitzky

PRINCETON UNIVERSITY PRESS

PRINCETON AND OXFORD

Copyright © 2011 by Princeton University Press

Published by Princeton University Press
41 William Street, Princeton, New Jersey 08540

In the United Kingdom: Princeton University Press
6 Oxford Street, Woodstock, Oxfordshire OX20 1TW

press.princeton.edu

Library of Congress Cataloging-in-Publication Data
Batnitzky, Leora Faye, 1966–
How Judaism became a religion : an introduction to modern
Jewish thought / Leora Batnitzky.
p. cm.
Includes bibliographical references and index.
ISBN 978-0-691-13072-9 (hardcover : alk. paper) 1. Judaism—
History—Philosophy. I. Title.
BM157.B38 2011
296.09—dc22   2011012703

British Library Cataloging-in-Publication Data is available

This book has been composed in Sabon

Printed on acid-free paper. ∞

Printed in the United States of America

1 3 5 7 9 10 8 6 4 2

To Jonathan, Gabriel, and Eli

Ben Zoma said: Who is wise? One who learns from everyone.
Mishnah Avot 4:1

It is better to know some of the questions than all of the answers.
James Thurber

CONTENTS

ACKNOWLEDGMENTS

THIS BOOK grew out of an undergraduate course that I have taught for the last decade at Princeton University called Jewish Thought and Modern Society (REL 242). First and foremost, I am grateful to the students who have taken the course over the years for thinking about the question that animates this book: Is Judaism a religion? Three other occasions went a long way in helping me to conceive and write this book: an invitation about twelve years ago from Mark Larrimore to give a lecture on Moses Mendelssohn in his course Approaches to the Study of Religion, a Sophomore Initiative Grant in 2004 from Princeton that allowed me to rework REL 242 around the question of whether Judaism is or is not a religion, and a long series of conversations with Olga Litvak about how to include eastern European thinkers in REL 242. Early discussions with Michele Rosenthal and Diane Winston about this project were also a great boon.

Allan Arkush, Yaacob Dweck, Martin Kavka, Alan Mittleman, Sam Moyn, David Novak, Eli Sacks, Ken Seeskin, and Jeff Stout each offered extensive comments on (and in Allan's case, corrections to) the manuscript at various stages. I am enormously grateful for their intellectual generosity. I would like especially to thank Eli Sacks for producing the annotated suggested reading lists following each chapter. Thanks are also due to Jessica Fechtor for her suggestions for readings for chapter 7, and to Alyssa Quint for her helpful comments on chapters 6 and 7. All of these colleagues have greatly enriched this project. All errors, of course, remain my own.

On both an institutional and human level, I continue to feel fortunate to be a part of the Department of Religion at Princeton. I would like particularly to thank my colleagues Eric Gregory, Martha Himmelfarb, Peter Schäfer, Jeff Stout, and Cornel West for helping me think about many of the issues and figures discussed in this book, even if at times they did not know they were doing so. The manuscript also benefited at various stages from Gabriella Wertman's editorial and technical assistance as well as Michele Alperin's editing of the penultimate manuscript. Thanks are also due to Lorraine Fuhrmann, Pat Bogdziewicz, Baru Saul, and Kerry Smith for their continued assistance on all matters.

At Princeton University Press, Fred Appel guided this project along with patience and good advice. I'd also like to thank Nathan Carr and

Diana Goovaerts for their help in the publication process as well as Cindy Milstein for her careful copyediting of the final manuscript.

My family has been a constant source of support and (happy) distraction. I thank my husband, Bob, for his enthusiasm and advice about this project. While I was writing this book, our sons, Jonathan, Gabriel, and Eli, were mostly good sports when I told them, perhaps a few too many times, that I needed just a couple more minutes. I appreciate their patience and even more so I hope that someday they will be interested in the issues in this book. I dedicate the book to them.

How Judaism Became a Religion

INTRODUCTION

IS JUDAISM A RELIGION? Is Jewishness a matter of culture? Are the Jews a nation? These are modern questions, and this book tries to explain why this is the case. More specifically, this book tells the story of how and why the idea that Judaism is a religion was invented in the modern period, and the many conceptual tensions that followed from it.

Like the notion of Jewish religion, the modern concept of religion more generally is not a neutral or timeless category but instead a modern, European creation, and a Protestant one at that. The etymology of the term "religion" remains disputed, with some arguing that it comes from the Latin "to bind," while others contend the root word is "to reread," and still others "to be careful." As the distinguished scholar of religion Jonathan Z. Smith notes, the word "religion" was used in its Roman and early Christian settings as a noun (religio), an adjective (religiosus), and also an adverb (religiose), and all of these uses were related to the performance of ritual practices. In the sixteenth century, colonialists began to use the term specifically with reference to non-Christian ritual practices. Yet by the eighteenth century, religion did not refer mainly to ritual practice or performance but instead to personal belief or faith.[1]

From the eighteenth century onward, modern Jewish thinkers have been concerned with the question of whether or not Judaism can fit into a modern, Protestant category of religion. After all, Judaism has historically been a religion of law and hence practice. Adherence to religious law, which is at least partially, if not largely, public in nature, does not seem to fit into the category of faith or belief, which by definition is individual and private. It is the clash between the modern category of religion and Judaism that gives rise to many of the creative tensions in modern Jewish thought as well as to the question of whether Judaism and Jewishness are matters of religion, culture, or nationality. As we will see, internal Jewish disagreements about the category of religion mirror internal Jewish debates about not only theological and philosophical matters but also about, for instance, modern Yiddish literature and Jewish nationalism. At the same time, we will see that the story of the invention of Jewish religion anticipates many current debates about the nature of contemporary society, such as the separation of church and state, the nature of modern views of tolerance and pluralism, and questions about religion's place in the public square.

To appreciate the novelty of the idea of Jewish religion, we need to understand a bit about the nature and structure of medieval and early modern Jewish communities. Prior to modernity, which I will define in the pages that follow as the acquisition of citizenship rights for Jews, Judaism was not a religion, and Jewishness was not a matter of culture or nationality. Rather, Judaism and Jewishness were all these at once: religion, culture, and nationality. The basic framework of organized Jewish life in the medieval and early modern periods was the local Jewish community, which was an autonomous legal body that had jurisdiction over the Jewish population in a particular area. Many such communities were spread throughout Europe, and any given community existed only by virtue of the permission of some external authority, usually the nobility or royalty, who would offer the community protection in return for taxes and the performance of some useful function. Increasingly throughout the Middle Ages, Jews functioned as tax collectors or were involved in other financial enterprises, since they were often banned from artisan trades, farming, military service, and owning land.

While a local Jewish community's existence depended on the whims of others, premodern Jewish communities also had a tremendous amount of political autonomy. Jewish communities were self-governing, and each community had its own set of bylaws administered by laypersons who, among other things, elected a rabbi for the community, who had jurisdiction over matters of ritual law while also giving credence to the laws of the community as a whole. Each community had its own courts as well as its own educational, health, economic, and social services systems. The community was also responsible for law and order, and had the right to punish its members in a variety of ways, including exacting fines, imprisonment, and corporal punishment.

Local Jewish communities often varied greatly from one another. Yet despite local differences, premodern Jews imagined themselves as one united people (as *klal yisrael*, "the collective people of Israel"). Rabbis and scholars engaged one another on matters of Jewish law, or thought across communities; many economic activities occurred across communities; and perhaps most significantly, Jewish communities frequently came to each other's aid in times of need by, for instance, providing money to help communities rampaged by violent riots. On a theological level, Jews had a common messianic hope that all the Jewish communities dispersed around the world would be reunited in the land of Israel in the days of the Messiah.

For members of the Jewish community who had transgressed its laws, one of the greater punishments was excommunication, and appreciating why will help to illuminate the nature of an individual Jew's identity in the premodern world. Excommunication applied not to individuals only but extended to their entire family too. Excommunicated individuals could not marry or engage in economic activity within the community, nor could they be buried in the communal cemetery. Without converting to Christianity or Islam, an excommunicated individual would have nowhere to go. Excommunications were usually for short periods, but sometimes they extended indefinitely.

The famous Jewish heretic and philosopher Baruch Spinoza (1632–77) was excommunicated from the Amsterdam Jewish community in 1656. According to the community record book, Spinoza was excommunicated for his "evil opinions and acts." These opinions and acts were not specified, but given his later writings, one can get a general sense of them. In his philosophical work, Spinoza denied the creation of the world, the immortality of the soul, a providential God, the election of the Jewish people, and the continued relevance and meaning of Jewish law. His "evil acts" likely consisted in his refusal to follow Jewish law. The fact of Spinoza's excommunication testifies to the political power of the premodern Jewish community, yet his refusal to convert to Christianity and ability to live an independent life free of any religious community, to the dismay of both the Jewish and Calvinist communities of Amsterdam, undercut the Jewish community's power. In this, Spinoza also anticipates Jewish modernity, in which Jewish communities do not exercise political power over individual Jews.

In his *Theologico-Political Treatise*, published anonymously, Spinoza makes an argument about Jewish law to which many modern Jewish thinkers would later respond. In an attempt to raise doubts about the truth of revealed religion generally, Spinoza is particularly critical of any notion of religious law that supports the idea of a personal, supernatural God who communicates God's will to people. To discredit this understanding of religious law, Spinoza contends that the laws of the Hebrews—that is, the Jews—were pertinent only in the context of their original, political meaning: "ceremonial observances ... formed no part of the Divine law, and had nothing to do with blessedness and virtue, but had reference only to the elections of the Hebrews, that is ... to their temporal bodily happiness and the tranquility of their kingdom, and ... therefore they were only valid while that kingdom last[ed]."[2] Because the ceremonial law no longer corresponds to a political kingdom, Spinoza's argument concludes that Jewish law is not divine law and that postbiblical Jewish law is meaningless.

As Spinoza knew full well, and as his excommunication shows, Jewish law did not disappear in the postbiblical period. In fact, what we call "Judaism" and "Jewish law" today developed postbiblically. Jewish law and Judaism are useful targets for Spinoza since criticizing them would not offend his Christian readers but instead would allow his more philosophical readers to draw the implications of his arguments for themselves. Spinoza, following Thomas Hobbes, anticipates (and hopes for) a time when a unified, sovereign state would be the only type of political authority. Within just two centuries, much of Spinoza's vision would come to pass, and it is in the context of the emergence of the modern nation-state that Moses Mendelssohn (1729–86) would invent the idea of Jewish religion—the subject of chapter 1.

• • •

With this brief overview, we can now begin to understand why the question of whether Judaism and Jewishness refers to a religion, nationality, or culture is a particularly modern one. It simply was not possible in a premodern context to conceive of Jewish religion, nationality, and what we now call culture as distinct from one another, because a Jew's religious life was defined by, though not limited to, Jewish law, which was simultaneously religious, political, and cultural in nature. Jewish modernity most simply defined represents the dissolution of the political agency of the corporate Jewish community and the concurrent shift of political agency to the individual Jew who became a citizen of the modern nation-state. The fundamental question for much of modern Jewish thought in its many variations is: What value is there to Judaism in a time in which Jews don't have to be defined as Jews, at least from the perspective of the modern nation-state? It is this question that motivates different attempts to define Judaism in terms of religion, nationality, or culture.

Within the following chapters, major Jewish philosophers and thinkers will be covered, including Mendelssohn, Abraham Geiger, Samson Raphael Hirsch, Heinrich Graetz, Nahman Krochmal, Hermann Cohen, Joseph Soloveitchik, Yeshayahu Leibowitz, Martin Buber, Franz Rosenzweig, Emil Fackenheim, Abraham Isaac Kook, Zvi Yehudah Kook, Emmanuel Levinas, Solomon Maimon, Israel Salanter, Sholem Yankev Abramovitsh, Sholem Aleichem, Perez Smolenskin, Moses Hess, Leon Pinsker, Theodor Herzl, Ahad Ha'am, Hayim Nahman Bialik, Michah Josef Berdiczewsky, Mordecai Kaplan, and Leo Strauss.[3] Although there is significant secondary literature and controversy surrounding each of these figures, the story told here does not for the most part delve into it. Yet to allow interested readers to pursue some of this literature further, a selective, annotated reading list follows each chapter. While in no way meant to be comprehensive, the suggested readings also include relevant thinkers (such as Abraham Joshua Heschel and Isaac Breuer, just to cite two examples) and subjects that fall outside the orbit of this book. As is clear from the names of the Jewish thinkers mentioned above, Jewish men largely tell the story of the Jewish religion's invention and conceptual aftereffects, without much self-consciousness about the role of women and gender in modern Jewish life and thought. While issues of feminism and gender are beyond this book's scope, the suggested readings following chapters 4, 7, and 9 recommend books that may be of especial interest to readers wanting to pursue this subject further.

The book as a whole is structured in two parts. The first section, "Judaism as Religion," comprises five chapters that track the development of the modern argument that Judaism is a religion from the eighteenth century to today. The second part, "Detaching Judaism from Religion," is made up of four chapters focusing on rejections of the contention that Judaism is a religion, also moving from the eighteenth century to today. These parts are both organized thematically, but also follow a more or less historical chronology. The conclusion of the book then turns briefly to ultra-Orthodox Judaism. Within the story of how Judaism became a religion and its aftermaths, ultraorthodoxy can be understood as a wholesale rejection of the modern attempt to divide human life into different spheres (such as religion, nationality, and culture), and thereby as a refusal to engage the question of whether Judaism is or is not a religion. The book ends with a discussion of a U.S. Supreme Court case in 1994 involving the ultra-Orthodox Satmar Hasidim (*Board of Education of Kiryas Joel Village School District v. Grumet*) that captures the conceptual tensions arising from defining Judaism as a religion (or not).

Given the scope of this book, three important clarifications are in order:

First, important historical work has been published recently on early modern Jews in an effort to correct our understanding of how Jews became modern. My concern in this book, however, is primarily with Jewish conceptualizations of whether Judaism is a religion or not. The argument that Judaism is a religion developed in the German Jewish context, and for this reason the first part of the book concentrates largely, though not exclusively, on German Jewish thinkers.

A number of factors might explain why the idea that Judaism is a religion was invented in the German Jewish intellectual and political framework, and not elsewhere. To begin with, German Judaism produced a highly intellectualized tradition of thought that mirrored its German cultural and philosophical surroundings. The idea of Jewish religion was born in the context of the Jewish response to the German Enlightenment (discussed in chapter 1). One of this book's central assertions is that the idea of Judaism as a religion emerged together with the modern nation-state. The German Jewish invention of the idea of Jewish religion was also a cultural and political reaction to the gap between the ideal of full Jewish integration into the German state, and a far more incomplete and vexed political and cultural reality (explored in chapter 2). This may explain why self-conscious conceptualizations of the idea of Jewish religion did not occur in England and France, where the processes of Jewish emancipation were far more complete.

The second half of the book turns mainly, although not exclusively, to eastern European and American Jewish thinkers who reject the idea that Judaism is a religion. By the end of the eighteenth century, Western Europe had moved away from the feudal and corporate structure of medieval Europe, toward unified and sovereign states. The Habsburg, Ottoman, and Russian empires, in contrast, had absorbed all the previously independent countries of eastern and central Europe, and feudal institutions were reinstated. As a result of the economic and political turmoil of eastern and central Europe generally, Jewish communities changed dramatically from within. Eastern European Jewish individuals, like their premodern ancestors, nevertheless were still defined legally, politically, and theologically as members of the Jewish community. For this reason, the idea of Jewish religion was largely irrelevant to eastern European Jews. By the nineteenth century, however, eastern European Jews were engaged in a dialogue with their western counterparts and rejected in multiple ways the idea that Judaism was a religion. In the twentieth century, a number of Jewish American thinkers also opposed the notion that Judaism was a religion, arguing that this idea was a distortion resulting from the strictures of European Jewish life, which, they maintained, were no longer relevant in the United States.

Second, my use of the phrase Jewish religion in this book is conceptual rather than terminological. I am less concerned, in other words, with whether various Jewish thinkers use the term religion to describe Judaism than with whether their conceptions of Judaism are best explained within the framework of a modern concept of religion. Two interrelated aspects of the modern concept of religion are especially relevant here (and will be elaborated on in the chapters that follow). As mentioned above, one of the main arguments of this book is that the invention of Jewish religion cannot be separated from the emergence of the modern nation-state. The notion that Judaism is a religion suggests that Judaism is something different in kind from the supreme political authority of the sovereign state, and may in fact complement the sovereign state. The modern concept of religion also indicates that religion is one particular dimension of life among other particular and separate dimensions, such as politics, morality, science, or economics. Understood as such, religion may or may not have political, moral, scientific, or economic implications but it is nonetheless to be distinguished from other spheres of human life.

Third, we will see that a number of thinkers discussed in part I of this book reject the term religion as applied to Judaism because of its Protestant associations. Yet we will also see that despite their protestations to the contrary, these thinkers inadvertently portray Judaism as a modern religion in a Protestant sense because their claims about Judaism are predicated on the two aspects of the modern concept of religion described above. So too, we will see that the thinkers explored in part II deny one or both of these two interrelated aspects of the modern concept of religion as they apply to Judaism or Jewishness.

Beyond these three clarifications, as will be clear in the pages that follow, the story told in this book focuses largely on a modern German, pietistic account of religion as articulated by, among others, Immanuel Kant (1724–1804) and Friedrich Schleiermacher (1768–1834). On this account, the primary emphasis is placed on, in Kant's case, rational religion grounded in the autonomous self, or in Schleiermacher's case, the inner experience and pure feeling of the individual self. What is excluded under this model is any notion of religion rooted first and foremost in public life. While neither Kant nor Schleiermacher denies that religion has a social dimension, both subordinate communal forms of religious life to the individual's inner life. This modern notion of religion is in tension not only with the historical practice and self-understanding of Judaism but also with other sorts of Christian and non-Christian self-understanding. The story of how Judaism became a religion may be relevant, then, far beyond the purview of modern Jewish thought, as it is also a tale of one of the most vexed problems of modernity. I turn now to the beginning of the story.

Suggested Readings

Historical Context

Birnbaum, Pierre, and Ira Katznelson, eds. *Paths of Emancipation: Jews, States, and Citizenship*. Princeton, NJ: Princeton University Press, 1995. The essays in this volume highlight the diversity within modern Jewish history, describing the similarities across, but illuminating the differences between, the processes of Jewish emancipation in various European states.

Israel, Jonathan I. *European Jewry in the Age of Mercantilism, 1550–1750*. 3rd ed. Oxford: Littman Library of Jewish Civilization, 1998. Focusing on the history of various Jewries between the fifteenth and eighteenth centuries, Israel argues for the existence of an early modern period distinct from the medieval and postemancipation eras.

Katz, Jacob. *Tradition and Crisis: Jewish Society at the End of the Middle Ages*. Trans. Bernard Dov Cooperman. Syracuse: Syracuse University Press, 2000. Using Poland, Lithuania, Hungary, and Germany between the sixteenth and eighteenth centuries, Katz describes a set of institutions, practices, and attitudes that he takes to be typical of Jewish society during this period. In his afterword, Cooperman in turn provides an overview of scholarly developments during the years following the 1958 appearance of Katz's text.

Ruderman, David B. *Early Modern Jewry: A New Cultural History*. Princeton, NJ: Princeton University Press, 2010. Focusing on Italy, the Netherlands, and central and eastern Europe between the fifteenth and eighteenth centuries, Ruderman argues that the cultural life of early modern Jews was characterized by five developments: accelerated mobility, increased communal cohesion, an explosion of knowledge, a crisis of rabbinic authority, and a blurring of religious identities.

The Jewish Tradition

Fishbane, Michael A. *Judaism: Revelation and Traditions*. San Francisco: Harper and Row, 1987.
Fishbane offers a brief introduction to Jewish history, beliefs, practices, and texts.

Religion

Asad, Talal. *Genealogies of Religion: Discipline and Reasons of Power in Christianity and Islam*. Baltimore: Johns Hopkins University Press, 1993.
According to Asad, modern thinkers influenced by Protestantism break with their predecessors by separating religion from politics and the exercise of power—for example, by taking the term "religion" to refer primarily to individual belief, and defining the word "rituals" as actions that express such belief.
Dubuisson, Daniel. *The Western Construction of Religion: Myths, Knowledge, and Ideology*. Trans. William Sayers. Baltimore: Johns Hopkins University Press, 2003.
Contending that religion is a Western and Christian category that has profoundly shaped our understanding of the world, Dubuisson presents the "history of religions" as a problematic concept and calls for the development of new scholarly models.
Masuzawa, Tomoko. *The Invention of World Religions: or, How European Universalism Was Preserved in the Language of Pluralism*. Chicago: University of Chicago Press, 2005.
Concentrating on the nineteenth century, Masuzawa seeks to reconstruct the process through which the category of world religions has emerged, exploring the ways in which this concept—as well as the scholarly approach it enables—replaced premodern and early modern modes of classifying religions.
Smith, Jonathan Z. "Religion, Religions, Religious." In *Relating Religion: Essays in the Study of Religion*, 179–96. Chicago: University of Chicago Press, 2004.
As the title indicates, Smith explores the histories of terms such as "religion," "religions," and "religious," describing the processes through which these words have come to refer primarily to belief as well as the changing ways in which Western thinkers have identified and classified distinct religions.

Spinoza

Kasher, Asa, and Shlomo Biderman. "Why Was Baruch De Spinoza Excommunicated?" In *Sceptics, Millenarians, and Jews*, ed. David S. Katz and Jonathan I. Israel, 98–141. Leiden: E. J. Brill, 1990.
Kasher and Biderman attempt to reconstruct the circumstances surrounding Spinoza's excommunication, focusing primarily on identifying the views that his contemporaries took to be "abominable heresies."

Nadler, Steven. "Baruch Spinoza and the Naturalization of Judaism." In *The Cambridge Companion to Modern Jewish Philosophy*, ed. Michael L. Morgan and Peter Eli Gordon, 14–34. Cambridge: Cambridge University Press, 2007.

Nadler provides an overview of Spinoza's views on religion and Judaism, explaining the ways in which the seventeenth-century thinker "naturalizes" key elements of Jewish life, ranging from the status of Jewish law to the authorship of the Bible to the nature of God.

Smith, Steven B. *Spinoza, Liberalism, and the Question of Jewish Identity*. New Haven, CT: Yale University Press, 1997.

Spinoza, Smith maintains, seeks to bring Judaism into conformity with liberal politics, discover in Judaism a model for elements of the liberal state, and develop a new rational theology appropriate for individuals participating in such a polity.

PART I

Judaism as Religion

Chapter 1

MODERN JUDAISM AND THE

INVENTION OF JEWISH RELIGION

FOR BOTH BIOGRAPHIC and philosophical reasons, Moses Mendelssohn is rightfully considered the founder of modern Jewish thought. While Mendelssohn lived before individual Jews had political rights, he articulates a vision of how Jews and Judaism could complement the modern nation-state. Mendelssohn gives voice to the claim that I will be exploring throughout this book: that Judaism is a religion. In fact, he invents the modern idea that Judaism is a religion. Yet his argument is fraught with the fundamental tension that would and still does define much of modern Jewish thought: religion is a modern German Protestant category that Judaism does not quite fit into. I will look at the development of this category in greater detail later in this chapter, but for now one can understand this Protestant notion simply as the view that religion denotes a sphere of life separate and distinct from all others, and that this sphere is largely private and not public, voluntary and not compulsory. Although Judaism as it has historically been practiced conflicts with this idea of religion for a number of reasons, which I will discuss, the most basic one is that Judaism and Jewish life have been largely, though not entirely, public in nature.

In characterizing Judaism as a religion, Mendelssohn is aware of and actually emphasizes the implicit problems that follow from trying to define it thus in a German Protestant vein. Indeed, far from simply assimilating Judaism into an alien category, Mendelssohn's attempt to define Judaism within the modern Protestant category of religion brings with it not-so-subtle criticisms of this very category. More particularly, and somewhat paradoxically, Mendelssohn makes his argument not by denying Judaism's public character but by stressing it. In this chapter, I will explore the creative tensions that arise from Mendelssohn's claim that Judaism is a religion. These tensions are relevant far beyond the historical significance of Mendelssohn, for they contain the beginnings of many streams of modern Jewish thinking that followed him, including those strands that criticize his vision but remain within the framework of trying to understand Judaism as a religion and those that attempt to reject this framework.

Mendelssohn, Friend of Gotthold Ephraim Lessing

If one visits the Grosse Hamburger Strasse cemetery today in the former East Berlin, one will see a reerected headstone marking Mendelssohn's grave—the only gravestone standing, since the Nazis destroyed the rest of the cemetery's headstones. Across from the cemetery is Berlin's Jewish high school, founded in 1862, whose building was used by the Nazis as a deportation center for Jews. Mendelssohn's image is engraved in stone on the building, with the inscription "Moses Mendelssohn, Philosopher and Friend of Lessing." This phrase captures what is clearly still taken to be Mendelssohn's legacy—that he was a friend of the great Enlightenment philosopher Lessing (1729–81). On the face of it, it is strange that Mendelssohn's life should be memorialized by who his friend was, perhaps leading one to conclude that Mendelssohn's significance derives only from what must be Lessing's monumental greatness. Yet both in its own time as well as today, Mendelssohn's friendship with Lessing tells us less about the importance of Lessing than it does about the unlikely fact that Lessing, an enlightened Christian philosopher, was actually friends with a Jew. Appreciating the perceived novelty of this improbable friendship allows us a window into not only the complex historical and political situation of early modern Jews but also the philosophical and political quagmire in which Mendelssohn would eventually find himself.

In the eighteenth century, many European philosophers began to highlight notions of reason, science, human progress, and universalism, which often called into question traditional beliefs and customs. This intellectual and cultural movement is frequently referred to as the "Age of Enlightenment." To start to appreciate the cultural, political, and philosophical significance of Mendelssohn, it is necessary to recognize the way in which an abstract conception of "the Jew" was crucial for many Enlightenment philosophers, even, or perhaps especially, when they did not know any actual Jews. The Jew was the test case for the possibility of mass enlightenment; if even the Jew could be enlightened, then enlightenment was a potentiality for everyone.

Nowhere is this sentiment expressed more clearly than in Lessing's play *The Jews*, which tells the story of a Jewish traveler who saves a baron from an unknown robber, who turns out to be the baron's own servant. The baron is unaware that the hero of the play is a Jew, and the Jewish traveler only reveals this fact when the baron offers him his daughter's hand in marriage as a reward for his bravery. The Jewish traveler confesses that he cannot accept this generous offer because he is a Jew, and Jews and Christians are forbidden to marry. The play ends with the baron declaring to the Jewish traveler, "Oh, how commendable the

Jews would be, if they were all like you!" and the traveler responding, "And how worthy of love the Christians would be, if they all possessed your qualities."[1]

In an otherwise-positive review of the play, the Protestant theologian Johann David Michaelis, who I will return to soon, argued that while Lessing had expressed a nice sentiment, it was highly unlikely that such a Jew existed. It was in this context that Mendelssohn was introduced to Lessing by a mutual acquaintance, producing a friendship that symbolized the possibility of universal enlightenment and culminating in Lessing's famous play *Nathan the Wise*. Both Jews and Christians were astonished by Mendelssohn, not just because of his great intellect (in 1763 he won first prize in a philosophy essay contest where the second place went to Kant), but also because he was able to thrive at once within Jewish and German Enlightenment circles.

Mendelssohn was born in Dessau. He received a traditional Jewish education and was a promising Talmudic scholar. In 1743, at age fourteen, he went to Berlin to continue his studies. With the help of other Jews interested in Enlightenment ideas, Mendelssohn was able to teach himself German, Latin, Greek, English, and French as well as mathematics, logic, and philosophy. He quickly became part of the Jewish Enlightenment (Haskalah), which was attempting to make reforms in Jewish education in conjunction with some of the German Enlightenment's ideas. Jews and non-Jews alike knew him as the "Socrates of Berlin."[2]

It is essential to underscore, however, that despite his fame, Mendelssohn, like all other Jews, had no civil rights. Two small facts about Mendelssohn illustrate this point. First, as mentioned, at age fourteen he found his way to Berlin. He walked from Dessau to Berlin (apparently it took him five or six days), which at that time still had a medieval wall around the city. Mendelssohn would have had to enter Berlin through the Rosenthaler gate because this was the only gate through which Jews and cattle were allowed to pass. Second, when Mendelssohn received a permanent personal visa to remain in Berlin in 1763, it could not be transferred to his wife and children if he died. So even though Mendelssohn may have been the Socrates of Berlin, his physical existence remained precarious. He could neither walk nor live where he chose. And because the Jewish community was subject to collective punishment for the behavior of individual Jews, Mendelssohn's relation to the non-Jewish world brought with it implications not just for himself and his family but also for the entire Jewish community.

The instability of Mendelssohn's political position reached its height in 1769 when John Caspar Lavater, a Swiss theologian, challenged him to either refute Christianity or convert. Lavater was baffled by Mendelssohn's persona, as were many Christian thinkers sympathetic to Enlightenment philosophy. From their perspective, if Mendelssohn was so smart, as everyone seemed to agree that he was, then why didn't he simply convert to Christianity? For Mendelssohn, Lavater's challenge was double edged because he had to defend the rationality of Judaism and hence Judaism's compatibility with the German Enlightenment without offending his Christian interlocutors. He had to defend Judaism without refuting Christianity. Mendelssohn responded in his now-famous *Jerusalem: Or on Religious Power and Judaism* by making an eloquent plea for the separation between church and state. It was in this context that he claimed that Judaism was a religion—a proposition that would provide the framework for all German Jewish thought to follow. Before turning to the specifics of Mendelssohn's view of Jewish religion, we must consider in a bit more depth its political context: the rise of the modern nation-state, and more specifically the Prussian state, in the late eighteenth century.

ON THE CIVIC IMPROVEMENT OF THE JEWS

A movement away from the feudal and corporate structure of medieval Europe toward a unified Prussian state went hand in hand with the German Enlightenment's argument for a universal, rational ideal. One may have expected sympathy for the Jews and claims for their full integration into such a unified state. But instead the Jewish community was increasingly accused of being a "state within the state" that could not, by definition, be integrated into the Prussian one. As Prussia consolidated into a state, the Jews were especially resented for their moneylending practices. Yet Jews had no other occupational options beyond moneylending and other commercial pursuits. In Mendelssohn's day, Jews were still banned from artisan trades, farming, and landownership as well as military service.

Jews sympathetic to the German Enlightenment, known as the *maskilim*, shared an important assumption with those who opposed granting civil rights to Jews: that the Jews by definition needed improvement. The difference between the Jewish enlighteners and their Christian opponents was that the former believed that the Jews could change for the better, while the latter held that change was not possible for the Jews because their faults were inherent to them and Judaism. Michaelis, a prominent Protestant theologian and scholar who, as mentioned above, claimed that Lessing's literary portrayal of a rational and moral Jew did and could not cohere with reality, clearly belonged to this second camp. In contrast, the maskilim contended that especially with regard to moneylending, if given the opportunity to change—if Jews could legally become artisans or farmers—Jews could and would change for their own betterment along with the betterment of the state. In preparation for what they hoped would be their eventual acceptance into the Prussian state, the maskilim sought to improve themselves both intellectually and culturally. To this end, they revived Hebrew as a literary, though not a spoken, language in order to suggest that Judaism had a classical language worthy of respect (just as German classicists pointed to Greek).

Christian Wilhelm Dohm, a journalist, political writer, and Prussian civil servant, brought great hope to the prospects for Jewish emancipation when in 1781 he published, at Mendelssohn's behest, *On the Civic Improvement of the Jews*, arguing for the extension of civil rights to Jews. Dohm was willing, as others were not, to follow the Enlightenment's philosophy to its logical conclusion and contend that "the Jew is more a man than a Jew."[3] Dohm suggested that the Jewish tendency for "fraud and usury" was a result of their degraded political situation, which began after the Romans destroyed the Second Temple in 70 CE. He pointed out that prior to the Roman conquest of Jerusalem, the Jewish nation was politically autonomous as well as religiously, culturally, and economically dynamic. The loss of Jewish political autonomy brought with it what Dohm called Talmudic "sophistry" and an obsession with ceremonial minutia. As he put it: "Certainly, the unnatural oppression in which the Jews have lived for so many centuries has contributed not just to their moral corruption, but to the degeneration of their religious laws from their original goodness and utility."[4] From this analysis Dohm concluded that if they were given civil rights, Jews could and actually would improve enough to be worthy citizens of the state.

Two underlying premises in Dohm's thinking are especially noteworthy. First, it is important to emphasize that Dohm's argument that the Jews could improve is based on the assumption that Jews and Judaism are by definition profoundly problematic (again, Dohm takes it for granted that Jews engage in fraud and that Judaism as practiced by the Jews of his day is sophistry). Second, while Dohm makes a historical argument about the nature of Jews and Judaism, his claims are premised on an underlying Christian and especially Lutheran assumption that religious law is intrinsically problematic, as reflected in Martin Luther's strong reading of 2 Corinthians 3:6, "The letter kills, but the spirit gives life." As Dohm remarks, "This anxious spirit of ceremonies and minutiae that has crept into the Jewish religion will certainly disappear again as soon as the Jews receive a greater sphere of activity."[5] As I will show below, Mendelssohn adamantly calls this description of Jewish law into question.

The larger context of Dohm's contention is also intimately tied to his particularly Lutheran perspective on the history of Christianity. The ultimate target of criticism in his treatise is medieval Christendom and its early modern aftereffects. According to Dohm, the degraded situation in which Jews and Judaism find themselves results from the merging of religion and politics by Constantine in the fourth century, and by the Holy Roman Empire thereafter. Prior to Constantine's conversion, Dohm asserts, the Roman conquest of Jerusalem was a good thing for the Jews because they became part of the Roman Empire and even served as soldiers at one time. Even more significantly, the Roman conquest of Jerusalem serves for Dohm as a model for modern Prussia's attempt to become a modern empire. Dohm seeks to reestablish a distinction between church and state with the precedence he finds in the Roman Empire, while also using the Roman Empire as the prototype for internally colonizing the Jews for what he maintains will be the economic betterment of Prussia.

Despite his clearly negative portrayals of Jews and Judaism, Dohm's arguments were by far the most sympathetic within the confines of Enlightenment debates about the Jews. Dohm received many negative responses to his proposals, the most influential rejection of which came from Michaelis (on whose historical work Dohm had actually drawn), who contended not only that the Jews could not improve but that in keeping with Dohm's vision of Prussia's colonial expansion, Jews also ought to be deported to "colonies ... where one might send malefactors and degenerates."[6] In an environment in which Michaelis's response was considered reasonable, if not necessarily optimal, it is not surprising that Jews largely welcomed Dohm's treatise. Again, Dohm was willing, as others were not, to recognize that "the Jew is more a man than a Jew."

Mendelssohn was profoundly grateful to Dohm, but also disagreed with him in three fundamental ways, all of which directly lead to his claim that Judaism is a religion. For one, Mendelssohn speaks of the civic admission of the Jews rather than their civic improvement. He also argues that Jews do not need improvement and, he strongly implies, actually have something to teach Christians. Third and most practically, Mendelssohn stresses that Jews should receive civil rights as individuals and not as a corporate entity. This last point goes to the heart of the difference between Mendelssohn and Dohm, and is also the core of Mendelssohn's assertion that Judaism is a religion. As we saw in the introduction to this book, the status of the corporate Jewish community vis-à-vis the individual Jew delineates the difference between premodern Judaism and Jewish modernity. Mendelssohn moves Judaism into the modern world by contending that politically, but not theologically, the individual Jew is separate from the Jewish community. Mendelssohn defines the very category of Jewish religion by separating Judaism from politics. And he does so by defining as apolitical something that had until then been understood at least in part as political: Jewish law. His definition of Jewish religion, as I will explore in greater detail below, revolves around his claim that Jewish law is in no way political. This is because, Mendelssohn argues, religion by definition, and not just the Jewish religion, is not political.

In developing his understanding of Jewish religion, Mendelssohn concurs with Dohm's view that while religion is separate from the state, it is also an important means through which citizens of the state develop civic virtue. As we saw, Dohm suggests that once Jews are better able to develop habits as citizens, their religion will return naturally to its original goodness, which had been corrupted by the rabbis. For this reason Dohm is willing, unlike many of his contemporaries, to concede that Judaism is a religion like Lutheranism, Calvinism, or Catholicism. Writing at a transitional moment between the medieval corporate political structure of premodern Europe and the emergence of the modern nation-state, Dohm sees no contradiction between Judaism's corporate status and civil law. He believes that the Jewish community would and should retain its autonomy in matters of civil law, because Jewish judges understand, in a way that Christian judges could not, the relevant facets of Jewish law. For Dohm, there is no contradiction between civic freedom and religious autonomy. Jewish judges would still hold the power to excommunicate individual Jews, and the relation between the Jewish community and the state would be no different than the relation between a specific city and the state.

A year after Dohm's treatise was published, Mendelssohn responded to him by taking issue not with his conception of religion but rather with his view of Jewish religion. Dohm is wrong, Mendelssohn contends, to consider *any sort* of political power or coercion as part of a religious community. He states that "the purpose [of an ecclesiastical society] is collective edification, participation in the effusion of the heart, through which we acknowledge our gratitude for God's benefactions and our filial truth in His infinite beneficence."[7] Mendelssohn's claim was immediately shocking to his Lutheran interlocutors, for they understood Judaism, at best, in fundamentally political terms. As the German writer August Friedrich Cranz anonymously wrote in response to Mendelssohn: "Armed Church law still remains the firmest groundwork of the Jewish polity, and the master-spring of the whole machinery. Then good Mr. Mendelssohn, how can you profess attachment to the religion of your forefathers, while you are shaking its fabric?"[8]

JUDAISM AS A RELIGION

The relation between the title and subtitle of Mendelssohn's response to Lavater's challenge, *Jerusalem: Or on Religious Power and Judaism*, captures the thrust of his argument that Judaism is a religion. In the first section of the book Mendelssohn alleges that by definition, the state concerns power and coercion, while religion, properly understood, does not. This means that Judaism, or "Jerusalem," is not concerned with power

and therefore does not conflict with the possibility of the Jewish integration into the modern nation-state. In the second section of the book
Mendelssohn asserts that the Jewish religion is not a matter of belief but
rather of behavior. As he puts it, "Judaism knows of no revealed religion
in the sense in which Christians understand this term. The Israelites possess a divine legislation—laws, commandments, ordinances, rules of life,
instruction in the will of God as to how they should conduct themselves
in order to attain temporal and eternal felicity."[9] Hence, Mendelssohn
concludes, because Judaism does not demand belief of any sort, it by definition does not conflict with enlightened reason and in fact only complements it.

Let me further explore Mendelssohn's argument that Judaism concerns
practice and not dogmatic belief. Mendelssohn claims that "Judaism
boasts no exclusive revelation of eternal truths.... The voice which let
itself be heard on Sinai on that great day did not proclaim, 'I am the Eternal, your God, the necessary, independent being, omnipotent and omni-
scient, that recompenses men in a future life according to their deeds.'
This is the universal religion of mankind, not Judaism."[10] In contrast to
the universal religion of humankind, which Mendelssohn equates with
morality, Judaism, he maintains, is a historical, temporal truth that makes
demands only on the Jewish people, and not on society and morality at
large. Mendelssohn defuses Lavater's challenge by contending that Judaism makes no demands for belief on anyone and no demands for action
on non-Jews. Thus, once again, Judaism does not conflict with but instead complements enlightened society.

Mendelssohn's arguments are not wholly apologetic. He offers an important criticism of his Christian critics by implicitly pointing out the
hypocrisy involved in a Christian call for conversion in the name of enlightened reason. As Mendelssohn suggests, a demand for conversion
violates the definition of religion as noncoercive. At the same time, the
requirement of belief in Christian dogma is also problematic from the
perspective of enlightened reason. Is a belief in incarnation, after all, easily squared with the eternal truths of reason? Mendelssohn contends that
as a religion of law, Judaism avoids both of these problems, and in doing
so offers a crucial example of enlightened religion's relation to the enlightened politics that separates church from state.

In *Jerusalem*, Mendelssohn maintains not only that Judaism does not
conflict with reasoned enlightenment but also that the two are consonant
with one another. Again, Mendelssohn argues that properly understood,
Judaism's ceremonial laws are not dogmas that make claims to eternal
truths. The ceremonial laws instead are founded on the historical truth
of God's revelation at Sinai, and these ceremonial laws script a particular way of life for a particular people. The genius of Jewish ceremonial

law, Mendelssohn suggests, is that in its enactment in Jewish life, it self-consciously requires interpretation. "The ceremonial law itself is a kind of living script, rousing the mind and heart, full of meaning, never ceasing to inspire contemplation and to provide the occasion and opportunity for oral instruction."[11] On Mendelssohn's reading, it is because the Jewish ceremonial law requires constant interpretation and reinterpretation (and is in this sense a "living script") that it avoids idolatry, and is also a model for the nations of the world for avoiding it.

Mendelssohn argues that it is actually in the best interests of Christians to recognize the necessity of Judaism's continued survival. As Mendelssohn reminds his Christian interlocutors, "Now Christianity, as you know, is built upon Judaism, and if the latter falls, it must necessarily collapse with it into one heap of ruins." Mendelssohn hopes also to caution his Christian audience against its own biased assumptions about Judaism: "In judging the religious ideas of a nation that is otherwise still unknown, one must ... take care not to regard everything from one's own *parochial* point of view, lest one should call idolatry what, in reality, is perhaps only *script*." In this connection, Mendelssohn directly rejects Dohm's valorization of Rome's victory over Jerusalem, maintaining that rather than Jerusalem requiring Rome, Rome in fact has something to learn from Jerusalem: "In plundering the Temple, the conquerors of Jerusalem found the cherubim on the Ark of the Covenant, and took them for idols of the Jews. They saw everything with the eyes of the barbarians, and from their point of view." The conquerors of Jerusalem, according to Mendelssohn, focused not on how the cherubim were used within the temple but rather on what the cherubim were: "They saw signs not as mere signs, but believed them to be the things themselves. As long as one still used the things themselves or their images and outlines, instead of signs, this error is easily made."[12] Far from representing the pinnacle of Western civilization's past as well as the goal of its future, as it does for Dohm, the Roman conquest of Jerusalem embodies for Mendelssohn the human propensity toward idolatrous thinking. Against his description of the Roman model, Mendelssohn contends that the brilliance of the Jewish ceremonial law consists in the self-conscious recognition of the need for continued interpretation and reinterpretation. Because the law must always be reinterpreted through the generations (and hence through time), the practice of Jewish law in itself avoids idolatry.

Mendelssohn considers the human propensity toward idolatry a permanent part of the human condition. Unlike some of his contemporaries, such as Lessing, Mendelssohn rejects the notion that the human species progresses for the good. As he puts it, "Individual man advances, but mankind continually fluctuates within fixed limits, while maintaining, on the whole, about the same degree of morality in all periods—the same amount of religion and irreligion, of virtue and vice, of felicity and misery."[13] The ceremonial law is therefore of universal significance, argues Mendelssohn, because it offers a model for warding off what remains a fundamental human problem, idolatry, while not conflicting with reasoned enlightenment.

Let me sum up. Mendelssohn defends Judaism in *Jerusalem* by emphasizing the point that he had made previously in his response to Dohm: religion by definition cannot be coerced, because "the right to our convictions is inalienable."[14] While Cranz and others had maintained that Judaism is at best "armed Church law," Mendelssohn avers that Judaism, and the ceremonial law in particular, captures the true spirit of religion, affecting only the mind and heart. In his historical and political context, Mendelssohn of course does not argue, and could not have done so, that Judaism is superior to Christianity. But he does explicitly suggest that Christianity, as the child of Judaism, still has much to learn from Judaism and especially from Jewish law. Mendelssohn declares that Christianity does not supersede Judaism, and that the Jewish religion, far from embodying the dead letter of the living Christian spirit, is especially prepared for a new age in which church and state would be separated not only as an ideal but also in reality.

MENDELSSOHN'S THOUGHT AND THE GERMAN PROTESTANT IDEA OF RELIGION

As perhaps Mendelssohn knew full well, he did not in the end provide a philosophical justification of Judaism and Jewish law but instead presented an argument meant to diffuse Christian and Enlightenment complaints against Judaism. Accordingly, the nuance and subtlety of his assertions notwithstanding, Mendelssohn's definition and description of Judaism are in a fundamental sense at odds with themselves. Mendelssohn claims that Judaism is not a religion like Christianity because Judaism demands action, not belief. But Mendelssohn also defines Jewish law in completely apolitical terms—that is, precisely in contrast to the laws of the state. As he observes: "The religion [Judaism], as religion, knows of no punishment, no other penalty than the one the remorseful sinner voluntarily imposes on himself. It knows of no coercion, uses only the staff [called] gentleness, and affects only mind and heart."[15] So if Jews don't follow Jewish law because of belief, and if Jews don't follow Jewish law because it is in some sense political, why do or should Jews follow the law?

This basic tension in Mendelssohn's thought was not lost on many of his contemporaries. Mendelssohn enjoyed a philosophical friendship with Kant, arguably the single most important philosopher of the modern era and certainly, as we will see in later chapters, the most significant modern philosopher for Jewish thinkers. Mendelssohn sent Kant a copy of *Jerusalem*. Kant praised the work highly, yet he dismissed Mendelssohn's particular defense of Judaism. Mendelssohn had shown, Kant wrote, that "it is necessary that every religion have unrestricted freedom of thought, so that finally even the Church will have to consider how to rid itself of everything that burdens and oppresses man's conscience."[16]

I will return to Kant soon, but first it is important to note that within Jewish circles, Mendelssohn's friend and younger colleague, David Friedländer, drew the same conclusion as Kant: that Mendelssohn's argument about the necessity of Jewish law for Jews was irrelevant to Mendelssohn's larger point about freedom of conscience. Friedländer had worked alongside Mendelssohn and others to establish the Free School in Berlin in 1778. He also became director of the school and the Hebrew publishing house that was established in conjunction with it. Friedländer, however, did not express his own view of Jewish law during Mendelssohn's lifetime but only after Mendelssohn's death in 1786. This suggests that Friedländer recognized the centrality of the law to Mendelssohn's thought yet nevertheless thought it irrelevant to what he took to be the larger significance of Mendelssohn's contention.

The differences between Mendelssohn and Friedländer in part stemmed from their different personal backgrounds. As mentioned, Mendelssohn came to Berlin from a poor family and with a traditional Jewish education. In contrast, Friedländer was born into a wealthy family in Konigsberg, where he received a Jewish and secular education. When he came to Berlin at the age of twenty-one, he married the daughter of Daniel Itzig, the wealthiest Jew in Berlin. Friedländer increasingly identified more with his educated and affluent German contemporaries than he did with the broader Jewish community. As discussed, while Mendelssohn attempted to separate the individual Jew *politically* from the Jewish community, he did not separate the individual Jew *theologically* from the Jewish community. Friedländer, on the other hand, did not recognize Mendelssohn's distinction between the political and theological structure of the Jewish community. Not only did he refuse the ceremonial law any political or religious status but he also rejected any notion of a messianic future in which Jews, scattered throughout the diaspora, would be reunited as one people. In this vein, Friedländer held that Prussian Jews were to be distinguished from all other Jews: "The great mass of the Jews is characterized by a babbling away of their prayers, conscientious observance of religious ceremonies, and other outward piety, just like the riffraff of other religious groups."[17]

Like Dohm, and unlike Mendelssohn, Friedländer believed that both Jews and Judaism needed major improvements. Unlike Dohm, and like

Mendelssohn, Friedländer maintained that Jews ought to receive rights as individuals and not as a corporate community. And like Dohm, Friedländer linked what he regarded as the degraded status of the Jews with the economic restrictions placed on them. In keeping with this vision, Friedländer proposed in a memorandum to the Prussian authorities in 1787 that Jews no longer be restricted to economic enterprises, and that other opportunities for livelihood such as farming and crafts be opened to them. The memorandum also requested the abolishment of the Jewish community's collective financial responsibility. Friedländer's requests were not granted.

Increasingly frustrated, he decided to convert to Christianity, with the provision that he would not accept any Christian dogma. In 1799, Friedländer published an anonymous letter to Wilhelm Abraham Teller, a Protestant defender of rational religion, in which he laid out his rejection of Mendelssohn's defense of the ceremonial law as well as his own refusal to accept Christian dogma. While Friedländer made his differences with Mendelssohn clear, he nonetheless stressed that Moses, and not Jesus, was the founder of rational religion, going so far as to argue for an affinity between his own views and Moses's original intentions. In this context Friedländer proposed that Jews be granted entry into the Protestant church in accord with this understanding of rational religion. Interestingly, Teller accepted Friedländer's condition about dogma. Yet he insisted that Friedländer acknowledge that Christ's rejection of the law marked the complete overcoming of Judaism for the sake of a more moral, rational, and spiritual religion. Friedländer rejected this provision and decided to remain a Jew. Despite the fact that the large majority of Jews rejected Friedländer's views, his near conversion created an anti-Jewish storm in which Jews and Judaism were again cast as unsavory, and the Jewish people were seen as a foreign element on Prussian soil.

It is precisely in this context that we can appreciate a central component of the invention of the modern Protestant concept of religion by turning again to Kant and then, in the next section, to the father of liberal Protestant theology, Schleiermacher. Above I noted Kant's dismissal of Judaism in his response to Mendelssohn's *Jerusalem*. In *Religion within the Limits of Reason Alone*, published in 1793, Kant not only ignores Mendelssohn's arguments about Judaism but also claims that Judaism is not properly speaking a religion at all because it is only a "collection of mere statutory laws." Kant concedes that Judaism could "always remain, an antiquity, in the historical account of faith," but that a historical account of faith is not to be confused with rational religion.[18]

While Kant claims that his view of rational religion, by definition, is universal, it is profoundly indebted to his Lutheran background and his particularly Lutheran context in two main ways. First, Kant's rejection of Judaism is premised on a distinction between a dead letter and a living spirit—the very distinction that Mendelssohn hopes to overcome in his characterization of Jewish law as a living script. Second, Kant, as Teller would after him, refuses to accept the idea that Christianity is the child of Judaism. Instead, like Teller, Kant can only see Christianity, and therefore rational religion, as having completely overcome or superseded Judaism. In this same vein, much of the negative reaction to Friedländer's letter turned on the perception that Friedländer was attempting to "Judaize" Christianity. Here one can appreciate in clear terms that the modern concept of religion was and is not a neutral category. Rather, for Kant only Protestantism was the historical vehicle for pure rational faith. The universalism claimed by Kant and liberal Protestants generally had a difficult time accommodating Judaism.

RELIGION AND THE MODERN STATE

No single thinker did more to define the modern concept of religion than Schleiermacher, the founder of liberal Protestant theology. Schleiermacher is best known for *On Religion: Speeches to Its Cultured Despisers*, published in 1799.[19] In keeping with the title, the book attempts to defend a conception of religion to those who consider Christianity an outdated relic of the past. Schleiermacher agrees with the cultured despisers of religion that it is wrong to mix religion and politics, but he also argues that religion in that sense is not true religion. Instead, Schleiermacher alleges that the essence of religion constitutes a unique and separate dimension of experience—by definition, separate from all other spheres of life, such as politics, philosophy, morality, and science—and is characterized by what Schleiermacher calls intuition and feeling: "religion's essence is neither thinking nor acting, but intuition and feeling." Religion is thus impermeable to criticisms from other realms of human life and experience: "religion maintains its own sphere and its own character only by completely removing itself from the sphere and character of speculation as well as from that of praxis."[20] In the fourth speech in *On Religion*, Schleiermacher notes that religion must ultimately express itself publicly. Yet he defends what he labels religion's essence by privatizing it. For him, religion is not bound to anything other than intuition and feeling.

Affirming that there is a plurality of religions, Schleiermacher nonetheless presents a religious hierarchy, with monotheism as the highest form, followed by polytheism and finally animism. Schleiermacher also insists that Christianity is a higher form of religion than Judaism. While his conception of religion is predicated on a rejection of Kant, he shares with Kant the notion that Christianity does not in any meaningful sense derive from Judaism, which is at best an artifact of the past. In Schleiermacher's words, Judaism is a "dead religion, and those who at present still bear its colors are actually sitting and mourning beside the undecaying mummy and weeping over its demise and its sad legacy."[21]

Schleiermacher goes further than Kant in divorcing Christianity from Judaism. Only two days after *On Religion* was published, Schleiermacher began a response to Friedländer's letter to Teller. For Schleiermacher, Friedländer's proposal for conversion is a blatant affront to Christianity and reflects what he calls the "disease" of "Judaizing Christianity."[22] Schleiermacher distinguishes between his distaste for Judaism and his many close friendships with Jews. He concludes his argument against Judaism by recommending the emancipation of the Jews, and offers this idea on both religious and political grounds. Schleiermacher believes that Friedländer's proposal stems from a profound hatred of Christianity. Offended by Friedländer, and hoping to avoid further insult to Christianity by Jews attempting to convert for political reasons, Schleiermacher asserts that Jews should be granted full political rights.

Schleiermacher, though, attaches conditions to the granting of political rights to Jews that are crucial for this chapter's discussion. In order to become citizens, Scheiermacher states, Jews need to repudiate their hope for a messianic future in which Jews would be reunited as one people, and they also need to submit to Prussian law, which would relegate Jewish law to a secondary, ceremonial status at best. In other words, political rights for Jews means Judaism must become a religion in Schleiermacher's sense, assigned to its own distinct sphere of private feeling. Significantly, Schleiermacher proposes that the state control the process of transforming Jews into citizens as well as Judaism into a religion in order to protect Christians and Christianity from the likes of Friedländer.

It is apparent here how the modern concepts of religion and the sovereign state were born together. While it may first appear that the notion of religion as a distinct and private sphere of experience is a fundamentally apolitical idea, it is actually predicated on a conception of state sovereignty. In Schleiermacher's approach to the Jews and Judaism, it is the state's power that determines the apolitical role of religion. Far from ensuring a neutral, "secular" space for political life, the modern concept of religion protects, as Schleiermacher hoped it would, a particularly Protestant concept of religion that places overriding value on, in Kant's case, rational religion rooted in the autonomous self, or in Schleiermacher's case, the pure feeling of the individual self in relation to the wholeness of God or nature. What is excluded in this model is any notion of religion as rooted first and foremost in public practice. What is required, for both

Kant and Schleiermacher, is the subordination of communal forms of religious life to the inner life of the individual, whether expressed in reason or feeling.

CONCLUSION

By way of ending this chapter, let me explore the tensions in Mendelssohn's thought that stem from his position. Mendelssohn seems to reject the German Protestant definition of religion offered by Schleiermacher, who argues, "Religion's essence is neither thinking nor acting, but intuition and feeling." For Mendelssohn, the revealed legislation of Judaism, as opposed to Schleiermacher's liberal faith, is oriented toward both thinking and acting. Again, in Mendelssohn's words, "Among all the prescriptions and ordinances of the Mosaic law, there is not a single one which says: You shall believe or not believe. They all say: You shall do or not do.... The ceremonial law itself is a kind of living script, rousing the mind and heart, full of meaning, never ceasing to inspire contemplation and to provide the occasion and opportunity for oral instruction."[23] Yet along with this rejection of the boundaries placed on the concept of religion by Protestants during the Enlightenment, Mendelssohn also removes any conflict between Judaism and universal truth (what he calls the universal religion of humankind) as well as between Judaism and the state by claiming in both cases that any conflict that would seem to arise is the result of a category error (or put more colloquially, an error of mixing apples with oranges). Judaism is distinct from and not a threat to universal truth, just as Judaism—and indeed Jewish law—is distinct from and not a threat to state law. From a formal perspective, then, if not from the perspective of content, Mendelssohn's definition of Judaism *does* very much fit with Scheiermacher's liberal Protestant definition.

Mendelssohn wants to have it both ways: Judaism is a religion of law requiring action and stimulating contemplation. But when it comes to questions of universal action—that is, state law—and when it comes to universal contemplation—that is, the eternal truths of philosophy— Judaism remains separate and dispensable, except insofar as Judaism calls for obedience to the state's law. To apply Schleiermacher's words to Mendelssohn, we could say that for Mendelssohn, "Jewish law maintains its own sphere and its own character only by completely removing itself from the sphere and character of universal speculation as well as from that of universal praxis."

It is important to yet again underscore that the motivation for Mendelssohn's argument is both obvious and honorable. He is compelled to defend Judaism or risk being forced to convert to Christianity, all without offending his enlightened Christian audience. Nevertheless, the tension between Mendelssohn's claim that Jewish law demands contemplation and action, and that it is in essence dispensable to the pursuit of universal truth and morality, bears itself out also in the subsequent fate of Mendelssohn's philosophy. On the one hand, Mendelssohn provides a traditional conception of the Jewish obligation to obey Jewish law: "He who is not born into the law need not bind himself to the law; but he who is born into the law must live according to the law; and die according to the law."[24] On the other hand, Mendelssohn offers no philosophical or theological justification for why Jews should obey the law, and by virtue of his own definitions, he *cannot* supply any philosophical or theological justification for Jews to follow the law, because he argues that Jewish law is a temporal, historical truth whose legitimacy rests on neither the universally accessible dimensions of philosophical truth nor the dogmas of particular theological belief.

When the liberal society that Mendelssohn had hoped for was, at least to some extent, finally actualized, the question of why Jews should remain Jews would be one that Jews continually asked of themselves. And while modern Jewish thinkers would continue to differ about Judaism's relation to politics and philosophical reason, the thinkers discussed in the first half of this book would all follow Mendelssohn in claiming that Judaism remains intellectually compelling to modern Jews, and concurrently that Jews and Judaism make a unique contribution to modern people and society by remaining at once a part of modern society yet apart from it.

Suggested Readings

Historical Context

Birnbaum, Pierre, and Ira Katznelson. "Emancipation and the Liberal Offer." In *Paths of Emancipation: Jews, States, and Citizenship*, ed. Pierre Birnbaum and Ira Katznelson, 3–36. Princeton, NJ: Princeton University Press, 1995.
Jewish emancipation, the authors argue, should be viewed as neither a "unitary process" occurring across Europe nor a "discrete series of single country experiences" but rather a "family of instances" exhibiting both similarities and differences.

Breuer, Mordechai, and Michael Graetz. *German-Jewish History in Modern Times, Volume 1: Tradition and Enlightenment*. Trans. William Templer. Ed. Michael A. Meyer with Michael Brenner. New York: Columbia University Press, 1996.
In addition to offering an introduction to German Jewish life during the Middle Ages, the essays in this volume provide a comprehensive overview of German Jewish history between 1600 and 1781.

Hertzberg, Arthur. *The French Enlightenment and the Jews: The Origins of Modern Anti-Semitism*. New York: Columbia University Press, 1968.

Focusing on the writings of individuals ranging from religious figures to prominent philosophers, Hertzberg contends that the anti-Jewish sentiment associated with the Enlightenment and French Revolution anticipated as well as paved the way for modern anti-Semitism.

Hess, Jonathan M. *Germans, Jews, and the Claims of Modernity.* New Haven, CT: Yale University Press, 2002.

Hess links debates surrounding Jewish emancipation to Enlightenment conversations about the nature of universalism, outlines the tensions and anti-Jewish views generated by these conversations, and highlights the role of German Jews in revealing such tensions and hostility—all as part of challenging emerging conceptions of universalism and imagining alternative models for modernity.

Katz, Jacob. *Out of the Ghetto: The Social Background of Jewish Emancipation, 1770–1870.* Cambridge, MA: Harvard University Press, 1973.

Katz emphasizes the similarities across and connections between the experiences of Jews in diverse areas, claiming that the events that took place in central and western Europe "became a pattern later followed by Jewry in other parts of the world."

Meyer, Michael A. *The Origins of the Modern Jew: Jewish Identity and European Culture in Germany, 1749–1824.* Detroit: Wayne State University Press, 1967.

Through a series of case studies, Meyer explores attempts to conceptualize the nature of Jewishness among late eighteenth- and early nineteenth-century German Jews. The first four chapters focus on Mendelssohn, Friedländer, and various individuals belonging to the generation of Mendelssohn's children.

Mosse, Werner E. "From '*Schutzjuden*' to '*Deutsche Staatsbürger Jüdischen Glaubens*': The Long and Bumpy Road of Jewish Emancipation in Germany." In *Paths of Emancipation: Jews, States, and Citizenship*, ed. Pierre Birnbaum and Ira Katznelson, 59–93. Princeton, NJ: Princeton University Press, 1995.

Mosse seeks to trace the history of Jewish emancipation in Germany, describing the condition of German Jewry in the late eighteenth century, the process of emancipation between 1781 and 1870, and subsequent developments in the late nineteenth century.

Kant

Despland, Michel. *Kant on History and Religion.* Montreal: McGill–Queen's University Press, 1973.

Ascribing to Kant a belief in the enduring importance of religious institutions and traditions, this monograph claims that his work should be read as initiating a shift central to modern religious thought—namely, a shift away from a focus on God and metaphysics, and toward a focus on human religious life.

Munk, Reinier. "Mendelssohn and Kant on Judaism." *Jewish Studies Quarterly* 13, no. 3 (2006): 215–22.

Munk looks at the relationship between Kant's critique of Judaism and Mendelssohn's arguments in *Jerusalem*.

Wood, Allen W. "Rational Theology, Moral Faith, and Religion." In *The Cambridge Companion to Kant*, ed. Paul Guyer, 394–416. Cambridge: Cambridge University Press, 1992.
> Exploring the role of religion in Kant's writings, Wood outlines Kant's attack on classical proofs of the existence of God, "moral" arguments for God's existence and human immortality, views on the relationship between religion and politics, and posture toward "historical" traditions such as Christianity.

Mendelssohn

Altmann, Alexander. *Moses Mendelssohn: A Biographical Study*. Tuscaloosa: University of Alabama Press, 1973.
> Altmann's biography offers a comprehensive account of Mendelssohn's life and thought.

Arkush, Allan. *Moses Mendelssohn and the Enlightenment*. Albany: State University of New York Press, 1994.
> Identifying Enlightenment liberal politics and attacks on revealed religion as threats to Mendelssohn's commitment to the Jewish tradition, this study suggests that Mendelssohn may have been aware of his failure to adequately address these issues, and that his primary goal may have been to fashion a new version of Judaism appropriate to the modern era.

Breuer, Edward. *The Limits of Enlightenment: Jews, Germans, and the Eighteenth-Century Study of Scripture*. Cambridge, MA: Harvard University Press, 1996.
> Through the lens of Mendelssohn's writings on the Bible, this monograph maintains that he embraced some European cultural ideals, but resisted two challenges posed by his Christian contemporaries: attacks on the version of the biblical text traditionally taken by Jews to be authoritative, and attacks on the modes of scriptural exegesis employed by classical rabbinic sources.

Eisen, Arnold. "Divine Legislation as 'Ceremonial Script': Mendelssohn on the Commandments." *AJS Review* 15, no. 2 (1990): 239–67.
> Eisen argues that while Mendelssohn's treatment of divine legislation suffers from serious flaws, *Jerusalem*'s assertions are in many ways well suited to a world in which Jewish affiliation is a matter of individual choice, and they exhibit affinities with the claims advanced by various contemporary theorists of religion.

Gottlieb, Michah. "Mendelssohn's Metaphysical Defense of Religious Pluralism." *Journal of Religion* 86, no. 2 (2006): 205–25.
> This essay reconstructs and assesses Mendelssohn's defense of religious pluralism, contending that his position is grounded in his views on the nature of language and that he understood religious diversity as a means of combating idolatry.

Sorkin, David. *Moses Mendelssohn and the Religious Enlightenment*. Berkeley: University of California Press, 1996.
> Sorkin identifies similarities linking *Jerusalem*'s author to representatives of the religious Enlightenment—a group of eighteenth-century Christian figures who drew on Enlightenment thought to strengthen religious faith—and suggests that Mendelssohn demonstrates crucial affinities with

the "Andalusian tradition" of medieval Jewish thought—with a constellation of commitments that Sorkin associates with medieval Jewish figures such as Judah Halevi.

Schleiermacher

Crouter, Richard. *Friedrich Schleiermacher: Between Enlightenment and Romanticism.* Cambridge: Cambridge University Press, 2005.
  Chapter 2 highlights a series of similarities between *On Religion* and Mendelssohn's *Jerusalem*, including a common focus on issues of politics, and a shared concern with universalism and particularism. Chapter 5 discusses Schleiermacher's response to Friedländer's offer to convert to Christianity, examining the historical and conceptual factors that shaped the Protestant theologian's position.

———. Introduction to *On Religion: Speeches to Its Cultured Despisers*, by Friedrich Schleiermacher, 1–73. Trans. Richard Crouter. Cambridge: Cambridge University Press, 1988.
  Linking *On Religion* to historical factors such Enlightenment Protestantism, Kantian philosophy, and the development of romanticism, Crouter identifies and analyzes various questions arising from Schleiermacher's views—more specifically, questions involving the cognitive status, historical manifestation, and political significance of religion.

Dole, Andrew C. *Schleiermacher on Religion and the Natural Order.* New York: Oxford University Press, 2010.
  Criticizing the accuracy and assessing the impact of what is described as the received view of Schleiermacher's thought, Dole argues that the Protestant theologian not only linked religion to feeling but also understood religion in social terms.

Klemm, David E. "Culture, Arts, and Religion." In *The Cambridge Companion to Friedrich Schleiermacher*, ed. Jacqueline Mariña, 251–68. Cambridge: Cambridge University Press, 2005.
  Looking primarily at *On Religion*, Klemm outlines Schleiermacher's account of religion as an "intuition" or "feeling" distinct from knowledge and action, and studies the connection between this position and Schleiermacher's views on the nature of culture.

Chapter 2

RELIGION AS HISTORY: RELIGIOUS REFORM AND THE INVENTION OF MODERN ORTHODOXY

IN MARCH 1812, the status of Jews in Prussia changed. Jews were declared citizens of the Prussian state and were permitted to hold academic positions, although not governmental ones. Special taxes and occupational restrictions for Jews were abolished. This change in status came not from Dohm's, Mendelssohn's, or Friedländer's efforts but instead stemmed from the humiliating defeat of Prussia by Napoléon I in 1806. The edict of 1812 reflected the French notion of equality, and emancipated the peasantry along with the Jews while also establishing a modern bureaucracy in Prussia. This positive turn of events would soon become negative for Prussian Jews, because despite their actions and protestations to the contrary, they would be associated with the French and characterized once again as foreigners. Yet in the immediate aftermath of the decree, the liberal society that Mendelssohn had outlined was at least to some extent actualized. The question now was: What value is there to Judaism in an age in which Jews don't have to be defined as Jews, at least from the perspective of the modern nation-state?

The eminent historian of the Jews, Jacob Katz, notes that after emancipation, German Jews and German Jewish culture could have taken three possible roads in answering this question. First, Jews could have simply left Judaism behind and joined the German cultural tradition. Second, Jews could have used German culture to refigure Judaism and Jewish culture in light of the modern era. And third, in Katz's words, "Jewish novelists could have depicted contemporary Jewish society as they experienced it, or the Jewish past as they had learned it, and spun their tales around Jewish characters. Jewish poets could have derived their inspiration from the long succession of Jewish poetical tradition, giving it a new lease on life through a new linguistic garb."[1] Significantly, Katz explains, with a few notable exceptions, such as the German Jewish poet and author Berthold Auerbach (1812–82), German Jews and German Jewish culture largely permitted the first two options and only minimally the third. (As we will see in the second half of this book, eastern European Jewry mainly followed this last route.) A sizable number of German Jews did abandon Judaism for German culture, and as we will see in this chapter, a good many Jews used German culture to refigure Judaism. But for the most part, German culture, and the German Jews who embraced it, did not allow for the possibility of Judaism or Jewishness being part of a larger German culture. As Katz puts it, "Jews had been emancipated; Jewishness was not."[2]

Judaism and Jewishness were excluded from German culture for several reasons, including but not limited to the German notion of *Bildung* (character formation), which by definition elevated to exclusive heights German culture, and the Protestant backdrop of German culture, which denied Christianity's relation to Judaism—an idea that I began to explore in the last chapter. Yet for the purposes of telling the story of how Judaism became a religion, it is helpful again to focus on the twin modern concepts of religion and the sovereign nation-state. As with the French model of nationality, to which the Prussian edict of 1812 was indebted, citizenship meant the subordination of any communal identity to the state and the relegation of religion to the sphere of private sentiment. In Comte de Clermont-Tonnerre's well-known words to the French assembly in 1789, "One must refuse everything to the Jews as a nation but one must give them everything as individuals; they must become citizens."[3] While German Jewish thinkers would quickly disagree with one another about Judaism's relation to historical progress and philosophical reason as well as about the modern status of Jewish law, they would all follow Mendelssohn in suggesting, sometimes despite their protestations to the contrary, that Judaism is a religion that in no way conflicts with the sovereignty of the modern nation-state.

This chapter considers how the framework of religion both characterizes and was criticized by the three modern Jewish movements that developed in Germany, and today still flourish in the United States and to a lesser degree the state of Israel: Reform Judaism, Orthodox Judaism, and positive-historical Judaism, now known as Conservative Judaism (Reconstructionist Judaism is a particularly American development and is discussed in chapter 9). Orthodox Judaism identifies itself as the movement that recognizes the eternal, unchanging nature of Jewish law, while Reform Judaism rejects Jewish law in favor of the universal, ethical contribution that Judaism makes to culture at large. A middle position of sorts, Conservative Judaism, claims to honor the authority of Jewish law while acknowledging the necessity for historical change. As we will see, despite their differences, each movement in its own way adapts Judaism to the modern world, and all three share the claim that theirs is the true, original Judaism: the orthodox movement because Judaism is defined as law, the reform movement because Judaism is defined as ethics, and the conservative movement because Judaism is defined by the dynamic tension between tradition and change.

The differences between these movements stem from nineteenth-century debates about whether Judaism has changed throughout history, and how answering this question might be a precedent for ascertaining Judaism's relation to the modern world. Nineteenth-century German Jewish historians sowed the seeds of Reform and Conservative Judaism today. In what follows, I will explore the development of the modern historical study of Judaism (what was known in its German context as *Wissenschaft des Judentums*) and the Jewish historians who attempted to bring Judaism into the modern world by writing its history. What is today called Orthodox Judaism also has its roots in nineteenth-century Germany, where it defined itself by rejecting the idea that history had something to teach modern Jews about the eternal truth of Judaism and Jewish law. While orthodoxy has historically defined itself against liberal Judaism and its relegation of Judaism to a modern religion, we will see below that modern orthodoxy is actually predicated not on a rejection but rather an intensification of Mendelssohn's premise that Judaism is a religion that in no way conflicts with the sovereignty of the modern nation-state. It is in this sense that as the title of this chapter suggests, Orthodox Judaism, like Jewish religion more generally, is a modern invention.

On the Uses of History

The study of history complemented the Enlightenment's dedication to a new ideal of universal reason and humanity. For the emerging field of modern historiography, studying the prejudices of the past was a way to overcome that past, and move into a new human era marked by scientific, political, and indeed historical progress. Not incidentally, the study of history was understood as an objective science (Wissenschaft). But the purpose of historical study remained, and remains, ambiguous. On the one hand, the study of history, if understood as a path toward human progress, leads to an overcoming or burial of the past. On the other hand, the motivation for studying the past is often the desire to learn from it in order to draw lessons for the present. We have already seen both of these tendencies in my brief discussion of Dohm's *On the Civic Improvement of the Jews*. Dohm studies the Roman conquest of Jerusalem to both provide a new vision for the Prussian empire and overcome what he regards as the deeply problematic remnants of the Holy Roman Empire. While the goal of modern historiography is objectivity, attempts to delineate the contours of the past are almost always written with an eye toward the present.

At the same time, while modern historiography is the study of change over time, the goal of much of eighteenth- and nineteenth-century historiography was to come to the unchanging essence of a phenomenon that either unfolded in time or was distorted by what were contingent historical circumstances. This predilection is already evident in my short exploration of Mendelssohn, Dohm, and Friedländer. All three figures, despite their significant differences with one another, contend that the course of history has negatively distorted Judaism's intrinsically positive essence. While Mendelssohn finds this essence in the living script of the ceremonial law that demands continual reinterpretation, Dohm and Friedländer discover Judaism's essence in Moses's initial revelation.

Both of these tendencies—to look at the past with an eye toward the present, and to posit an ahistorical essence in the midst of an argument about historical change—were particularly vexing in the nineteenth century when Jewish historians started to write Jewish history within the bounds of modern historical methods. As we saw in chapter 1, Protestant theologians not only claimed that Christianity had superseded Judaism but also that properly speaking, Judaism had no history save for its supersession. For Schleiermacher, as noted earlier, the notion that Christianity is historically indebted to Judaism is both inaccurate and deeply offensive. Indeed, Schleiermacher maintains that such a view did not stem from historical facts but only from what he claims is the Jewish hatred of Christianity.

Within internal Jewish debates in the nineteenth century, the idea that Judaism has an essence remained (and today remains) ambiguous and contested. If Judaism has no essence from a scientific-historical point of view, then there is no such thing as Judaism. Rather, there are many Judaisms, all of which, from a historical perspective, are equally valid or invalid. But if Judaism does have an essence, then that essence should provide some clue about how Judaism ought to be reformed in light of new historical circumstances—the advent of the modern nation-state and citizenship for Jews. As we will begin to see in the next section, arguments about the relevance of Jewish history for appreciating the role of Jewish religion in the modern world were in the nineteenth century always simultaneously answers to the external question of Judaism's relation to Christianity as well as the internal question of what sorts of reforms Judaism needed in the modern world.

Before turning to specific claims about reform, it is helpful to return to Mendelssohn briefly. It bears repeating that Mendelssohn rejects the notion of historical progress: "Individual man advances, but mankind continually fluctuates within fixed limits, while maintaining, on the whole, about the same degree of morality in all periods—the same amount of religion and irreligion, of virtue and vice, of felicity and misery."[4] We also saw in chapter 1 that according to Mendelssohn, the ceremonial law allows for and in fact demands different interpretations throughout history, but does not change in terms of the action required. In this way, Mendelssohn attempts to account for both continuity and change within the Jewish tradition. The actions demanded by the law constitute Judaism's unchanging core, while the interpretation of the law marks the tradition's change over time. Understood as such, Mendelssohn avoids having to deal with potential tensions between the way in which Judaism had changed throughout history and the tradition's self-understanding.

At the end of the eighteenth century, Mendelssohn still largely equates the history of Judaism with the Jewish tradition. But by the beginning of the nineteenth century, as the scientific study of Judaism (Wissenschaft des Judentums) was emerging, it was no longer possible simply to affirm this equation. Just as the nation-state had emancipated the individual Jew from the corporate Jewish community, the historian of the Jews sought to free the study of Jewish history from the authority and self-understanding of Jewish tradition. As we will see, however, rather than secularize Judaism, the academic, historical study of Judaism actually helped to crystallize Judaism's new standing as a religion.

ABRAHAM GEIGER AND THE REFORM MOVEMENT

Arguments for reform are always fundamentally conservative, because the goal of reform is to preserve a tradition by reforming (and not rejecting) it. Especially in the case of German Judaism, the alternative to reform was the abandonment of Judaism altogether. As the historical record shows, the reform movement did much to preserve Judaism—a situation that the Prussian authorities recognized and worked to discourage. The reformers did not claim to be revolutionaries. On the contrary, their assertion was that reform and change were not anomalous to the Jewish tradition but instead constitutive of it. Far from abandoning the tradition, the reformers maintained, reform was in reality saving it from those who were burying Judaism by failing to recognize in the tradition an intrinsic vibrancy that allowed for continual change.

Geiger (1810–74), the intellectual founder of the reform movement, equates what he claims is Judaism's world-historical essence with its role as a religion. For Geiger, Judaism's essence is its "universal-religious element."[5] Not only is Judaism a religion, Geiger contends, but it is also the religious genius that ushered the monotheistic worldview into human history. Geiger's equation of Judaism with original monotheism has a twofold implication. First, from an internal Jewish perspective, now that the external shackles of historical accident have been removed, Judaism needs to be reformed in keeping with its essential nature. Second, from an external point of view, the non-Jewish world, and especially the

Protestant one that Geiger and German Jewry inhabit, needs to recognize Judaism's contribution to world history and Western civilization. Far from being a dead relic of the past, Judaism, Geiger argues, is the living spirit from which Protestantism derives. For Geiger, recognition of Judaism's distinctly religious character holds the key to reforming Judaism in keeping with modernity, and also replaces the mistaken conception that modernity is intrinsically antithetical to Judaism with a proper recognition of modernity's inherently Jewish character.

Stressing that the history of Judaism can only be a history of its "spiritual achievements" because "it is precisely to its independence from political status that Judaism owes its survival," Geiger links his religious and nonpolitical conception of Judaism with a commitment to the German national cause: "The Germans were able to give birth to the greatest discoveries ... to the free spirit of the Reformation and to the glory of a literature of world-wide import. It is our wish that the new united *Reich*, led by its imperial dynasty, may be able to record similar achievements."[6] Geiger's notion of Judaism's spiritual achievements goes hand in hand with his attempt to rid the Judaism of his day of any concept of Jewish collective politics or messianic hope. Geiger rightly recognizes that from the perspectives of Judaism and Jewish history, only the existence of a synagogue state could undermine the sovereignty of the German Reich. His claims about Judaism's spiritual achievement bear directly on his affirmation of the possibility of Jewish integration into the German nation-state—which he understands as the privatization of Jewish religious faith within a neutral political order—for Jews and Germans alike.

Geiger divides Jewish history into four periods: revelation, tradition, legalism, and liberation. Revelation is "an era of free, creative formation from within" that extends to the close of the biblical era. Tradition marks the period from the completion of the Bible to the completion of the Babylonian Talmud. Legalism is "characterized by the toilsome preoccupation with the heritage as it then stood" and lasts, Geiger argues, until the middle of the eighteenth century. Finally, liberation begins just as legalism ends. This is Geiger's own era, in which "the bond with the past has not been severed," and "what is being attempted is solely to revitalize Judaism and to cause the stream of history to flow forth once again."[7]

As is clear from his depiction of the transition from the third and longest period of Jewish history, what he calls legalism ("the toilsome preoccupation with the heritage"), to his own period, liberation, Geiger hopes to reform first and foremost what he takes to be contemporary Judaism's fixation on Jewish law. Understood historically, Geiger maintains Jewish law has always changed as its historical circumstances have changed. Based on Greek and Aramaic translations of the Bible, Geiger's *The Original Text and Translations of the Bible in Their Dependence on the Inner*

Development of Judaism, published in 1857, attempts to show that the interpretations of biblical passages changed over time, and then illustrate from these changes the earlier and later layers of accepted religious interpretation of Jewish law. Geiger concludes that freeing contemporary Jews from what to many of his coreligionists appear to be the unchanging authority of Jewish law is not only consistent with but also most appropriate to Judaism's historical development. Unlike many of his Lutheran contemporaries, however, Geiger does not believe that religious law is inherently problematic. Rather, he claims that the law has outlived its usefulness now that in the era of liberation, Jews are no longer forced to separate themselves from their larger society.

Geiger's stance was, and often still is today, depicted as an abandonment of Judaism for the sake of German culture and Protestantism. But Geiger is in reality an audacious critic of the Protestantism of his time. Not only does he continually underscore Christianity's debt to Judaism but he also alleges that what he and his rationalist Protestant contemporaries see as problematic aspects of Christianity—such as asceticism, and the literal belief in the incarnation and resurrection of Christ—derive from elements foreign to Judaism. Christianity therefore, in Geiger's eyes, is at best an imitation of the moral elements of Judaism and at worst a complete distortion of Judaism: "What could be added to the saying of Hillel: 'The Merciful inclineth the scale toward mercy?' If Jesus' utterances concerning the purely moral relations of men to each other are indeed faithfully reported, they ... present nothing new."[8] The implication is that Protestants need Jews to remind them of their moral devotion to the one true God and help them move away from the mythical elements of the Christian tradition.

Geiger presents historical arguments not only about Jewish and Christian origins but also about Islam's origins. His prize-winning dissertation at the University of Marburg, "What Did Muhammad Borrow from Judaism?" tries to demonstrate the simple historical fact that Islam, at least in part, derives from Judaism.[9] This argument has the effect of showing the again rather obvious fact (denied by Geiger's Christian colleagues) that Christianity also, or Jesus more particularly, borrows quite a lot from Judaism. In his dissertation Geiger looks to medieval Spain as a golden age in which Jews and Judaism flourished because of its Islamic environment. By highlighting the affinity between Jewish and Islamic thought, Geiger hopes to underscore the confluence between Judaism and rational culture, and hence Judaism's anticipation of modernity.

Why does Geiger make such brazen claims about Judaism's superiority to Christianity in the context of trying to gain acceptance for Jews and Judaism in German society? We can only answer this question by appreciating the importance of the study of history and the role of the university in the formation of modern German identity. Geiger internalizes the values of Wissenschaft and hopes to show his Protestant interlocutors on their own terms that Judaism is worthy of study. He believes that if people dedicated to the universal ideals of reason and truth are properly educated they will acknowledge the role of Judaism in world history. By implication, Geiger's Protestant contemporaries will accept present-day Jews as part of German society. It is helpful here to return to Katz's analysis discussed above. Geiger's highly aggressive reading of the history of Christianity's debt to Judaism only makes sense in the context of his implicit attempt to defend Judaism's continued right to exist. It bears repeating that this right was not a given. To modify Katz's words slightly, "Jews had been emancipated; Judaism had not."

In order to emancipate Judaism from the shackles of German Protestant historiography, Geiger's science of Judaism aims to show that "Judaism is a grand phenomenon in history." Noting that "the Greeks had neither pattern nor teacher in art or science, they were teacher and master to themselves, they speedily attained such perfection in art as makes them instructors of mankind almost for all time," Geiger asks and answers in the affirmative:

> Is not the Jewish people, likewise, endowed with such a genius, a Religious Genius? Is it not, likewise, an aboriginal power that illuminated its eyes so that they could see deeper into the higher life of the spirit, could feel more deeply and recognize more vividly the close relation between the spirit of man and the Supreme Spirit, that they could more distinctly and clearly behold the real nature of the Moral in man, and then present to the world the result of that inborn knowledge.[10]

The task of the modern Jew, Geiger maintains, is to confess the truth of the one and only God for the sake of all humanity—a confession simultaneously theological and ethical. Let us recall here Isaiah 42:1–7: "Behold My servant, whom I uphold; Mine elect, in whom My soul delights; Have put My spirit upon him, He shall go forth to the nations.... For a light unto the nations; To open the blind eyes, To bring out the prisoners from the dungeon, And them that sit in darkness out of the prison-house." While Christians identify the servant referred to in Isaiah 42 as Jesus, Jewish reformers stress the servant's particularly Jewish character, underscoring what they regard as a Jewish mission to the nations.

While critical of how contemporary historical scholarship depicts Judaism, Geiger is deeply committed to and hopeful about a working German Jewish symbiosis. Geiger follows Mendelssohn in defining Jewish religion in completely apolitical terms in contrast to the laws of the state. Like Mendelssohn, Geiger both embraces and criticizes a modern Protestant conception of religion. By critiquing this concept of religion on historical terms, he thinks that his Protestant interlocutors will rationally come to recognize Judaism's role in world history and its rightful place in modern culture. But equally as important, Geiger embraces a Protestant notion of religion by strongly affirming the state sovereignty that relegates Judaism to a private, confessional status. Where Geiger differs from Mendelssohn is in separating the history of Judaism from the Jewish tradition's self-understanding. While Mendelssohn tries to defend the enduring value of Jewish law on the basis of changing interpretations of that law, Geiger rejects Jewish law in the modern world for the exact same reason. For him, the science of Judaism shows that Jewish law has indeed always been reinterpreted throughout history, and he concludes that the reinterpretation of Jewish law in light of its modern historical circumstances—citizenship for Jews—ought to lead *on Jewish terms* to the relinquishing of Jewish law.

AGAINST HISTORY: SAMSON RAPHAEL HIRSCH AND THE INVENTION OF ORTHODOXY

The traditionalists who responded to Geiger and the reformers laid the foundations for what today is called Jewish orthodoxy. Hirsch (1808–88), the foremost intellectual proponent of what is now labeled Orthodox Judaism, denies exactly what Geiger affirms: that Judaism and Jewish law in particular are subject to historical change, and that Judaism is a religion. As Hirsch puts it in his response to the reformers: "It is only because 'religion' does not mean to you the word of God, because in your heart you deny Divine Revelation, because you believe not in Revelation given to man but in Revelation from man, that you can give man the right to lay down conditions to religion."[11]

Hirsch contends that the reformers and especially Geiger have attempted to transform divine revelation, an eternal, metaphysical fact, into a religion created by humans that can be changed according to human whim and desire. He responds to Geiger's claim that Judaism has changed throughout history with a simple but firm declaration that Judaism and Jewish law have not changed historically. At "all times and in every situation," Judaism and Jewish law are "an untouchable sanctuary which must not be subjected to human judgment nor subordinated to human considerations."[12] For Hirsch, the reformers' transformation of Judaism into a religion is equally wrongheaded because it replaces what he regards as the totality of Jewish life with a small sliver of experience. He eloquently observes that

> Judaism is not a religion, the synagogue is not a church, and the Rabbi is not a priest. Judaism is not a mere adjunct to life: it comprises all of life. To be a Jew is not a mere part, it is the sum total of our task in life. To be a Jew in the synagogue and the kitchen, in the field and the warehouse, in the office and the pulpit, as father and mother, as servant and master, as man and as citizen, with one's thought, in word and in deed, in enjoyment and privation, with the needle and the graving-tool, with the pen and the chisel—that is what it means to be a Jew. An entire life supported by the Divine idea and lived and brought to fulfillment according to divine will.[13]

Somewhat ironically, however, Hirsch's claim for the enduring authority of Jewish law is predicated on a deepening of Mendelssohn's and then Geiger's basic premise: that Judaism, and in particular Jewish law, is by definition not political. Drawing on the very modern concepts that have usurped traditional Jewish identity and authority, Hirsch agrees with Mendelssohn in arguing that Jewish religion is not coercive but instead concerns only the heart and mind. As we saw in chapter 1, in making this assertion Mendelssohn recognizes that the Jewish community historically had used coercion, but he also contends that this coercion betrays the true meaning of both Judaism and religion more broadly defined. This argument in fact is part and parcel of Mendelssohn's effort to reform the traditional Jewish community. In an attempt to maintain the traditional community, Hirsch goes further than Mendelssohn, suggesting that coercion had never existed within the Jewish community, and that the traditional community existed only by virtue of "those loyal to the divine law and the obligation to belong and to support the local congregation."[14] It is this "unity of religious outlook" within the Jewish community and not the political life of the community that in Hirsch's view links Jewish communal life throughout the ages.[15] Hirsch also reiterates Geiger's claim that Judaism concerns spiritual and not political matters in his affirmation of Orthodox Judaism's relation to civil society: "It is precisely the purely spiritual nature of Israel's nationhood that makes it possible for Jews everywhere to tie themselves fully to the various states in which they live."[16]

We have seen that Hirsch shares a great deal with Geiger and Mendelssohn, especially when it comes to affirming the notion and reality of a modern, sovereign state that by definition limits the political power of the corporate Jewish community. What, then, are we to make of Hirsch's rejection of the notion that Judaism is a religion? Despite his protestations to the contrary, Hirsch does seem to understand Judaism as a religion. Just as Hirsch denies that coercive measures were ever part of Jewish law by claiming that the traditional congregation was founded on individual consent, so too he emphasizes that membership in the Jewish congregation is predicated on voluntary belief. Highlighting what he takes to be the supreme importance of voluntary belief, Hirsch even distinguishes between being Jewish and "the genuine Jew" who belongs to the true Jewish congregation whose "timeless principles … will move and guide the genuine Jew, without compulsion … in every fiber of his heart and every stirring of his will."[17]

Hirsch in fact established the modern phenomenon of Jewish sectarianism by highlighting the necessity of *correct belief*. Based on his conception of the genuine Jew and the true Jewish congregation made up of such individuals, he petitioned for a Prussian bill, eventually passed in 1876, that allowed Orthodox Jews to establish a separate community by seceding from the Jewish community recognized by the state. To defend his separatist stance toward non-Orthodox Jews, Hirsch transforms what had been simultaneously a Jewish political and theological concept—heresy—into a purely theological category by separating heresy from the heretic. The heresy that most concerns Hirsch is not one related to the practice of Judaism but rather to Jewish belief, and specifically the *belief* that "the law, both written and oral, was closed with Moses at Sinai."[18] This belief becomes, with Hirsch, the religious dogma that still defines modern orthodoxy. Jewish historians who seek to analyze Jewish law as a historical phenomenon to understand how the law has changed over time specifically reject this dogma, though.

In a manner reminiscent of Saint Augustine's distinction between hating the sin but loving the sinner, Hirsch continually returns in his arguments against reform to a distinction between "heresy and skepticism" (*minut ve-apikorsut*) and "heretics and skeptics" (*minim ve-apikorsim*), acknowledging that he is "deliberately using terms to describe the system [minut ve-apikorsut] rather than individuals [minim ve-apikorsim] who adhere to it."[19] This is because "nowadays we no longer have minim and apikorsim as defined in our legal codes … [but] present-day fellow Jews who subscribe to minut and apikorsut in practice." As if to bring home the point that voluntary belief, as opposed to political identity, defines what he calls the genuine Jew, Hirsch justifies his distinction between heresy and heretics by implying that the relation between Orthodox Jews and non-Orthodox Jews is not any different than the relation between Jews and non-Jews: "Even the most stringently observant Jew is free to maintain contacts and friendly relations with individuals adhering to the most diverse assortment of religious persuasions—Christians, Moslems, heathens."[20]

By consciously creating and affirming Jewish sectarianism, Hirsch makes Judaism more like the Christianity of his time, which in connection with the advent of the modern nation-state was relegating itself to private, confessional status. This is a surprising conclusion, to be sure, simply because orthodoxy presents itself as orthodox—that is, as continuity and not rupture. Yet the historical irony is that Hirsch's orthodoxy is not only modern but rather in a certain sense the most modern of modern Judaisms in molding itself as a religion on the German Protestant model. Hirsch's true Jewish congregation tolerates, although it does not condone, other types of Judaism as well as other religions. Indeed, by embracing the sovereign nation-state Hirsch leaves room for secular politics and also for a kind of religious pluralism, despite his disdain for Jews who are not orthodox.

HISTORY AND POLITICS: THE POSITIVE-HISTORICAL SCHOOL AND ITS AFTERMATHS

Heinrich Graetz (1817–91) began his career as Hirsch's student, dedicated to continuing the fight against reform, and Geiger in particular. Born in the province of Posen where Jews still were not emancipated, Graetz was profoundly affected by reading Hirsch's publications and most sympathetic to Hirsch's stated objection to the notion that Judaism could be narrowed down into a sphere of life called religion. Like Hirsch, Graetz affirms the totality of Judaism and Jewish existence, which includes all aspects of private and public life. Unlike Hirsch, Graetz believes that the only way to take on the reformers is on their own terms. Graetz embraces modern historical scholarship to show that even on his own terms, Geiger's vision of Judaism is narrow and incomplete, especially when it comes to his rejection of Jewish law's contemporary relevance. Like Hirsch, Graetz believes that Jewish law is the lifeline of Judaism without which Jews and Judaism have no future. But rather than seeing Graetz as a kindred spirit, Hirsch believed that by giving credence to historical scholarship, Graetz was only hastening Judaism's death.

Graetz's criticism of the reform movement coheres with an internal critique that began in 1845 when Zacharias Frankel (1801–75) walked out of a conference of reform rabbis in Frankfurt over the issue of the Hebrew language's role in Jewish liturgy. The reformers wanted to eliminate Hebrew from the liturgy, and Frankel believed that they had gone too far, not only in matters of language and liturgy, but also in discarding the Talmud, the Jewish Sabbath, and any conception of a messianic hope. While supportive of reforming Judaism, and also of the centrality and necessity of historical scholarship for the future of Judaism, Frankel contended that the reformers had simply been too quick to capitulate to German cultural pressures.

This internal criticism of the reform movement was in part a response to the political aftermath of Jewish emancipation. Whereas the early nineteenth century was a time of great optimism for Jews in Prussia, by midcentury the emancipation of the Jews had come under attack. In 1841, Prussia's new king, Frederick William IV, exclaimed that the Jews were "contradictory to the national type," and proposed that individual citizenship for Jews be revoked and Jews returned to the status of a national minority. The king's attack on Jewish emancipation came from the "Right" of the political spectrum, but Jewish emancipation was attacked from the "Left" as well. In 1843, Bruno Bauer (to whom Karl Marx responded in his famous "On the Jewish Question") argued that Jews had not proven themselves worthy of emancipation, and could only become so if they gave up the Jewish religion. Frankel and his followers seriously questioned whether Jews and Judaism would ever be accepted by German society, and asserted that reverence for the Jewish past required more loyalty to the strictures of the past than the reform movement had recognized.

The internal criticism of reform was not just a political response but also an intellectual rejoinder to the reformers. For Frankel and others, the reformers viewed Jewish history as wholly passive—that is, as the result of external circumstance beyond the control of the Jewish people. Geiger's view of Jewish law fits this passive model. Positing that Judaism's essence is its "religious-universal element," he perceives what he calls the long era of Jewish legalism as the result of external political circumstances that had forced Jews and the Jewish community into isolation. In contrast to this passive take on Jewish history, Frankel and the positive-historical school see Judaism as an active force in its own history. While agreeing with the reformers that Jewish law had certainly changed over time, the positive-historical school understands Jewish law as the product of active, creative Jewish activity that can and should be altered in the modern age but in no way discarded.

Graetz's first publication, an 1844 review of Geiger's study of the development of Mishnaic Hebrew, reflects the sensibility of the positive-historical school that he helped to establish. He argues that the prophets were not the last Jews who spoke Hebrew, and therefore that Mishnaic Hebrew is not an artificial construction of the rabbinic period, as Geiger suggests. Far from reflecting dry, bookish concerns, the details of Geiger and Graetz's highly technical philological debate bear directly on the question of how contemporary Jews should live their lives. Should the Talmud and rabbinic law be relegated to the past? If one concludes that they are accidents of Jewish history because they do not reflect the true essence of Judaism, then the answer, following Geiger, is yes. But if one concludes that the Talmud and rabbinic law are part of Judaism's creative historical production, then the answer, following Graetz and the positive-historical school, is no. In Graetz's words, "There is nothing more absurd and unhistorical than to assert that a force which penetrated as deeply as did the Talmudic system is the product of an error, of twisted exegesis, of hierarchical ambition, in short, of a historical accident!"[21]

In arguing for the creative vitality of Jewish history, Graetz argues not only against Geiger but also against Georg Wilhelm Friedrich Hegel (1770–1831), who in his philosophy of history declares Judaism a religion of transcendence arrested at the adolescent stage of historical development. Hegel contends that Judaism posits an absolute dichotomy between humanity and God that is then overcome by Christianity's notion of the unity of the human and the divine in Christ's incarnation. Noting that Hegel treats "Judaism with crude prejudice," Graetz seeks to show that Hegel's conception is wrong—and results from a particularly Christian view: "The Christian conception of history, as is well-known, fully denies to Judaism any history, in the higher sense of the word, since the loss of its national independence, an event which coincided with another of great importance for the Christian world.... [A]ll the more urgent is the demand on us to vindicate the right of Jewish history, to present its tenacious and indestructible character."[22]

But while rejecting Hegel's conclusions about Judaism, Graetz understands the science of Judaism in Hegelian terms as producing the Jewish people's "rational consciousness of its life and conditions."[23] Moreover, Graetz adopts Hegel's idealist conception of history as the unfolding of ideas, or what Hegel calls "spirit" through time; in Hegel's succinct formulation: "Just as the germ of the plant carries within itself the entire nature of the tree, even the taste and shape of its fruit, so the first traces of Spirit virtually contain all history."[24] Against both Geiger and Hegel, Graetz maintains that the germ of Judaism is something "infinitely richer, infinitely deeper" than the idea of monotheism. Judaism's essence consists of the interplay between the idea of a transcendent God and the political reality into which this idea is always rendered concurrently. According to Graetz, this constant dialectical relationship between theology and politics means that "Judaism is not a religion of the individual but of the community. That actually means that Judaism, in the strict sense of the word, is not even a religion—if one understands thereby the relationship of man to his creator and his hopes for his earthly existence—but rather a constitution for a body politic."[25]

Before exploring this contention, we must first consider Graetz's view of the structure and course of Jewish history. Against both Geiger and Hegel, he insists that the destruction of the Second Temple in 70 CE did not end Jewish nationhood. Graetz divides Jewish history into four periods, just as Geiger does, but their respective periodizations are different, with great consequence. Graetz's first period begins with the Bible and ends with the destruction of the First Temple in 586 BCE; the second period spans the second commonwealth and concludes with the destruction of the Second Temple in 70 CE; the third period includes the long medieval period through the end of the eighteenth century; and finally the fourth period starts with Mendelssohn and ushers in the science of Judaism that begins to bring Judaism's idea of itself to self-consciousness. The details of Graetz's history of these four periods are less important for our purposes than is its general structure. The key point for Graetz is that Judaism and Jewish history are always simultaneously characterized by religious and political factors. The course of Jewish history is the dialectical play between Judaism's religious and political dimensions, with a greater emphasis on Judaism's religious factor during some periods and on its political factor during others as the spirit of Judaism unfolds over time.

Against Geiger and the reformers, Graetz refuses to detach Judaism and contemporary Jews from a hope for a messianic future. Although the fourth period of Jewish history has begun, Graetz stresses that Judaism's existence as a diaspora religion is not the final end of its history, since the goal of Jewish history is in his view a new unification of Judaism's spiritual and political dimensions. To illustrate this point, Graetz offers an analogy:

> Once a son has been educated and matured by his father's guidance and teaching, the father himself sends the boy away from the hearth and ships him out into the world to gather experience and to test his paternal teaching in the thousand conflicts of life. But the father has no intention of letting his beloved boy perish in a distant land. With the strength and independence that comes through bitter experience, the son will return to his house and inherit his father's estate.[26]

As this suggests, no matter how well integrated Jews and Judaism might be or become in the German nation-state, the final end of Jewish history is the ultimate unification of the spiritual and political dimensions of Judaism.

We can now return to Graetz's claim that "Judaism is not a religion of the individual but of the community." While his commitment to the scientific study of history and indeed to Hegel is part and parcel of his allegiance to German culture and the German state, Graetz will not go as far as Geiger or even Hirsch in denying a political dimension to Judaism. Granting Judaism a political dimension means, as Graetz indicates, that Judaism does not quite fit the category of religion.

Graetz was hailed and has continued to be hailed as one of the most important historians of the Jews as well as a crucial ancestor of Conservative Judaism. His eleven-volume *History of the Jews* has been translated into many languages and remains widely read. Yet perhaps most tellingly in the context of the story of the invention of the idea of Jewish religion, after Graetz published his final volume, Heinrich von Treitschke, a German nationalist historian who published an anti-Jewish tirade against Germany's Jews, publicly attacked him. Treitschke did not hide his personal disdain for Graetz's work in particular, reporting that he "could scarcely find words to express his disgust."[27] In substance, Treitschke's emotional reaction to Graetz was not unlike Schleiermacher's response to Friedländer. The only motivation for Graetz's history, argued Treitschke, was a hatred of Christianity and German culture. Treitschke declared that Jews were foreigners who had invaded German soil and polluted German culture. But whereas in the late eighteenth century Schleiermacher believed that the solution to what he perceived as the Jewish hatred of Christianity was the granting of full political rights to Jews, at the end of the nineteenth century Treitschke rejected the idea of the liberal state that the edict of 1812 emancipating the Jews had ushered in.

Leaving aside the blatant anti-Jewish intent and overtones of his response to Graetz, it is perhaps not difficult to understand why from his German nationalist perspective Treitschke was offended by Graetz's history. After all, the implication of Graetz's analysis was that Christianity and German cultural achievements originated in the sources of Judaism. If Hegel's philosophy of history had shown that human self-consciousness (what Hegel calls "absolute spirit") culminated in the modern German nation-state, Graetz had countered that Judaism had by definition already achieved the unity of human self-consciousness that Germany was just on the cusp of grasping. We saw above that Geiger also shared this strategy with Graetz, arguing that Germans ought to acknowledge the original contribution of Jews and Judaism to Western civilization, and thus grant them respect in their own right. Where Geiger differed from Graetz was in stipulating that "the new united Reich, led by its imperial dynasty," was the only kind of political association worthy of Jewish loyalty. By refusing to relinquish in theory, though not in practice, the political dimension of Judaism, Graetz had refused, at least from the perspective of a German nationalist, any glory to Germany.

Tellingly, Graetz did not find many defenders in the Jewish community. In fact, the most prominent German Jew at the time, Hermann Cohen (1842–1918), who had been Graetz's student, publicly attacked Graetz's claim that Judaism was a constitution for a body politic. I will discuss Cohen's conception of Jewish religion in the next chapter. Here, I need but note again that the concepts of religion and the modern sovereign state

were born together. As long as Judaism stayed in its place as a private confessional religion and did not challenge the German nation-state, Judaism
could continue to exist quietly and Jews could be full citizens of the state.

We have seen in this chapter how each of the three denominations of
modern Judaism—Reform, Orthodox, and positive-historical Judaism,
known today as Conservative Judaism—grapple with the question of
whether Judaism is a religion. While Geiger unabashedly criticizes the
content of the German Protestant conception of religion, he nonetheless affirms the form of this Protestant notion in arguing that Judaism is
not just a religion but also the religion par excellence. We have seen that
Hirsch blatantly rejects the idea that Judaism is a religion, but still implicitly supports and strengthens this notion by emphasizing the voluntary
and individual nature of the genuine Jew's commitment to the true Jewish
congregation. Only Graetz announces the explicitly political dimension
of Jewish history and continued Jewish existence, denying that Judaism
could be narrowed down to a purely religious spirit. Yet it was Graetz's
contention that was deemed most unacceptable both to Germans and his
fellow Jews.

In stressing the simultaneous religious and national dimensions of Judaism, Graetz drew inspiration from Nahman Krochmal (1785–1840),
an eastern European Jew whose book, *The Guide for the Perplexed of
Our Time*, was edited by Leopold Zunz (1784–1886) and published in
1851. The book's title is a direct reference to Moses Maimonides (1135–
1204), arguably the most important Jewish thinker to emerge from the
medieval period, and his work *The Guide of the Perplexed*, arguably the
most significant Jewish text to arise from the medieval period (and some
would maintain from any period of Jewish history and thought). The
perplexed for whom Maimonides writes is the Jew worried about the potential conflict between Judaism and Aristotle's philosophy. In contrast,
the perplexed for whom Krochmal writes is the Jew confused about the
potential tension between Judaism and modernity (and modern historiography more specifically). Krochmal's title implies that while the times
have changed (hence the "of our time" in the title), continuity exists between the Jewish past and present—that is, between Maimonides and
Krochmal. This continuity, however, also involves the organic evolution
of Judaism through history. As Graetz would try to do later, Krochmal
seeks to show that Judaism does indeed have a history and especially
that rabbinic Judaism is not a distortion but instead an extension of the
religion of the Hebrew Bible.

Graetz draws on at least three of Krochmal's main themes: that Judaism unfolds in history, an argument that Krochmal, like Graetz, makes in dialogue with Hegel; that Judaism is the most universal of religions not despite its particularity but rather because of it; and that in contrast to all other nations, the Jewish nation alone has been able to endure throughout history because the spirit of the nation has, from its origins, dissolved the ultimately false dichotomies between particularity and universality, transcendence and immanence, and religion and politics. Yet Krochmal, unlike Graetz, made his assertions in Hebrew as well as in the eastern European context (discussed in part II of this book) in which Jews did not have civil rights. His writings, therefore, were only relevant to those who were interested in reading about his ideas (the perplexed of his time) and were not a source of political controversy. The situation was different with Graetz.

On the one hand, the German and German Jewish reactions to Graetz tell us something important about the history of German Judaism, and as will be clearer in the second part of this book, the Jewish experience in western Europe more broadly. To return to Katz's crucial point, emancipation meant that Jews were free as individuals, but that Jewishness and even a full embrace of Judaism could not be freely expressed within German culture. The notions of being German and citizenship in the modern state excluded the possibility of other types of collective belonging. That Judaism was a religion meant that Judaism was a religion of the individual, because religion was defined as private. (Once again, even Hirsch, or perhaps especially Hirsch, internalized this framework.) But on the other hand, as we will see in the next chapter, the notion that Judaism is a religion is one that Jewish thinkers would continue to struggle with yet ultimately affirm in multiple historical, political, and geographic contexts as well as within seemingly contradictory ideological frameworks.

Suggested Readings

Geiger

Heschel, Susannah. *Abraham Geiger and the Jewish Jesus*. Chicago: University of Chicago Press, 1998.
   Heschel argues that by describing ancient Judaism as a liberal phenomenon and Jesus as a Jewish figure, Geiger meant to justify his project of Jewish reform and pose a serious challenge to German Protestants —to suggest that Christians seeking the faith of Jesus would find it in Judaism rather than Christianity, and that Judaism thus possesses world-historical significance as the source of authentic religion.
Koltun-Fromm, Ken. *Abraham Geiger's Liberal Judaism: Personal Meaning and Religious Authority*. Bloomington: Indiana University Press, 2006.

Koltun-Fromm argues that Geiger frequently appeals to "personal meaning" and its authority to ground a commitment to Jewish texts and practices, and that Geiger's views on these issues continue to be relevant for "postmodern" Jews.

Petuchowski, Jakob J., ed. *New Perspectives on Abraham Geiger*. Cincinnati: Hebrew Union College Press, 1975.

The essays in this volume explore various aspects of Geiger's thought and career, including his conception of Judaism, historical scholarship, and activity as a religious reformer.

Graetz

Liberles, Robert. "Steeped in the Past: Heinrich Graetz's Views of the Jewish Future." In *Text and Context: Essays in Modern Jewish History and Historiography in Honor of Ismar Schorsch*, ed. Eli Lederhendler and Jack Wertheimer, 27–43. New York: Jewish Theological Seminary of America, 2005.

Seeking to reconstruct Graetz's conception of the Jewish future, Liberles argues that the historian took Wissenschaft to play a key role in the rejuvenation of Jewish life, was cautiously supportive of early Zionist projects, and harbored deep reservations about the future of Jewish life in Germany.

Schorsch, Ismar. "Ideology and History in the Age of Emancipation." In *The Structure of Jewish History and Other Essays*, by Heinrich Graetz, trans and ed. Schorsch, 1–62. New York: Jewish Theological Seminary of America, 1975.

This essay devotes special attention to Graetz's attacks on Reform Judaism, the nationalistic elements in his writings, and the ways in which he gradually came to adopt elements of the views he sought to undermine.

Hirsch

Lesser, Harry. "Samson Raphael Hirsch." In *History of Jewish Philosophy*, ed. Daniel H. Frank and Oliver Leaman, 721–31. New York: Routledge, 1997.

Lesser provides an overview of Hirsch's views on philosophy and Judaism, exploring the ways in which Hirsch appropriated various aspects of Kant's thought but rejected other elements of Kantian philosophy.

Liberles, Robert. *Religious Conflict in Social Context: The Resurgence of Orthodox Judaism in Frankfurt am Main, 1838–1877*. Westport, CT: Greenwood Press, 1985.

Focusing on the history of the Frankfurt Jewish community, Liberles attempts to show that the spread of reform in Germany was not as total as is sometimes thought, and that Hirsch's primary historical significance was as a communal leader rather than as a religious philosopher.

Krochmal

Harris, Jay M. *Nachman Krochmal: Guiding the Perplexed of the Modern Age*. New York: New York University Press, 1991.

Harris presents Krochmal's diverse writings as a unified corpus that responds to Protestant attacks on the Jewish tradition—as an attempt to utilize, for the defense of Judaism, the philosophical and historical resources central to modern Protestant thought.

Historical Context

Brenner, Michael, Stefi Jersch-Wenzel, and Michael A. Meyer. *German-Jewish History in Modern Times, Volume 2: Emancipation and Acculturation, 1780–1871*, ed. Michael A. Meyer with Michael Brenner. New York: Columbia University Press, 1997.

The essays in this volume provide a comprehensive overview of German Jewish history between 1780 and 1871.

Ellenson, David. *After Emancipation: Jewish Religious Responses to Modernity.* Cincinnati: Hebrew Union College Press, 2004.

Ellenson explores diverse ways in which Jewish religious leaders, in the wake of emancipation, have reshaped inherited traditions in light of modern society and culture. Parts II and III focus on the emergence of reform and orthodoxy during the nineteenth and early twentieth centuries.

Meyer, Michael A. *The Origins of the Modern Jew: Jewish Identity and European Culture in Germany, 1749–1824.* Detroit: Wayne State University Press, 1967.

Through a series of case studies, Meyer examines attempts to conceptualize the nature of Jewishness among late eighteenth- and early nineteenth-century German Jews. Chapters 5 and 6 focus on early efforts to reform education and worship, and the emergence of the Wissenschaft des Judentums.

———. *Response to Modernity: A History of the Reform Movement in Judaism.* New York: Oxford University Press, 1988.

Meyer offers a comprehensive history of Jewish religious reform between the eighteenth and twentieth centuries.

Schorsch, Ismar. *From Text to Context: The Turn to History in Modern Judaism.* Hanover, NH: University Press of New England, 1994.

In this collection of essays, Schorsch looks at the development and importance of historical consciousness in modern Jewish life.

Sorkin, David. *The Transformation of German-Jewry, 1780–1840.* New York: Oxford University Press, 1987.

Exploring the emergence and impact of a "new ideal of man," Sorkin argues that German Jewish intellectuals sought to both acquire political rights and produce a new type of Jewish individual and community.

Yerushalmi, Yosef Hayim. *Zakhor: Jewish History and Jewish Memory.* Foreword Harold Bloom. Seattle: University of Washington Press, 1996.

Contrasting traditional ways of understanding history with the practice of "modern Jewish historiography," Yerushalmi suggests that the latter stands in tension with both classical Jewish belief and Jewish communal memory.

Chapter 3

RELIGION AS REASON AND THE SEPARATION
OF RELIGION FROM POLITICS

IN THE LAST CHAPTER, I discussed the emergence of modern Jewish historians and their role in the creation of Jewish religion. I now turn to modern Jewish philosophers who define themselves as fundamentally opposed to history as such, but who, like the figures explored in chapter 2, also affirm the modern idea that Judaism is a religion, whether explicitly or implicitly. Within different geographic locations, and historical and political contexts—Hermann Cohen in early twentieth-century Germany, Joseph Soloveitchik (1903–93) in the late twentieth-century United States, and Yeshayahu Leibowitz (1903–94) in late twentieth-century Israel—the thinkers considered in this chapter maintain that Judaism is defined not by history but rather by rational adherence to Jewish law. Like Krochmal, discussed in chapter 2's conclusion, Cohen, Soloveitchik, and Leibowitz all claim continuity with Maimonides's thought (though their interpretations of Maimonides all differ from each other's as well as from Krochmal's). In linking each of their philosophies to Maimonides, these modern Jewish philosophers reject Kant's derogatory assertions about Judaism and Jewish law, mentioned briefly in chapter 1. Cohen, Soloveitchik, and Leibowitz, in so doing, criticize Protestant conceptions of religion. Nevertheless, we will see that each still adheres to a Protestant concept of religion in defining Jewish religion as primarily a private and not a public matter when it comes to modern political life.

The resemblances between Cohen's, Soloveitchik's, and Leibowitz's positions are remarkable, because of both the different historical and political contexts in which they write and their significantly varied ideological commitments. In the last chapter, I explored the perhaps surprising kinship between Hirsch's orthodox thought and what is generally considered to be Mendelssohn's liberal thought. In this chapter, I will investigate the revealing similarity between Cohen's explicitly liberal thought and Soloveitchik's and Leibowitz's self-proclaimed orthodox thought. We will see that this structural similarity is far more considerable than what might be taken as the substantial differences among their political contexts and philosophical positions.

COHEN AND RELIGION'S SHARE IN REASON

If Mendelssohn symbolizes a quest for a German Jewish cultural symbiosis, Cohen exemplifies a quest for a philosophical symbiosis. Like Mendelssohn, Cohen received a traditional Jewish education, but he was increasingly attracted to the study of philosophy. Cohen initially studied with Graetz at the Breslau Theological Seminary (a forerunner of the Jewish Theological Seminary of America), but left to pursue a career in philosophy. Remarkably for a Jew who remained openly Jewish, Cohen became a professor of philosophy at Marburg and was the founder of a highly influential philosophical school known as Marburg neo-Kantianism. While Cohen had always remained tied to the Jewish community, like Mendelssohn before him he was compelled to become a public spokesperson for and defender of Judaism. Cohen's moment came when Treitschke published an anti-Jewish pamphlet in 1880, in large part, as noted briefly in chapter 2, as a response to Graetz's *History of the Jews.* Cohen replied to Treitschke in 1880 with "Ein Bekenntnis zur Judenfrage" (A Confession on the Jewish Question). Cohen soon became one of the most influential Jewish intellectuals in Germany as well as a spokesperson for liberal Judaism.

Despite Graetz's significant influence on his mature thought about Judaism, Cohen criticizes his conception of Judaism, alleging that it is particularistic and not true to the universal, ethical nature of Judaism, which is not a body politic but instead a religion in keeping with German Protestantism. Cohen also rejects the most basic tenet of Graetz's thought—that history determines Judaism's meaning and structure—and offers instead a philosophical articulation of Judaism's literary sources. Cohen argues that membership in the Jewish community is predicated on a specific religious outlook, which he calls "the inwardness of personal faith."[1] While Cohen is not interested in creating a new sectarian movement, as Hirsch was, Cohen nonetheless implicitly endorses a version of what Hirsch calls the genuine Jew. For Cohen, the genuine Jew is one who adheres to the idea of "pure monotheism," discussed below. Taking Hirsch's depoliticization of the Jewish community one step further, Cohen's position suggests that a non-Jew loyal to the idea of pure monotheism may be a genuine Jew, and a Jew whose ideas do not conform to the notion of pure monotheism may not have such a status.

If Cohen's thought resembles Hirsch's, it is because Cohen, like Hirsch, is Mendelssohn's heir. Cohen differs from Mendelssohn, however, in two important respects, the first philosophical and the second political, with both reflecting the different historical moments in which they each write. Mendelssohn's argument about Judaism as a religion of law is meant to show Judaism's fundamental rationality in comparison to Christianity as a religion of dogma. But as we saw in chapter 1, Kant concludes from Mendelssohn's contention not that Judaism is a religion of reason but rather that it represents a dry legalism that has no ethical content when compared to Christianity. Kant claims that only an enlightened Christianity is true religion or, as the title of his book would have it, "religion within the limits of reason alone." Given his own philosophical commitment to Kant, Cohen thus has to make his argument about Judaism's intrinsic rationality within the context of Kant's critique of Judaism.

Cohen's second difference with Mendelssohn relates to his understanding of Judaism's relationship to politics. Writing in the eighteenth century, Mendelssohn's main political problem is to show the confluence between Judaism and the possibility of a liberal politics. Writing at the end of the nineteenth century and the beginning of the twentieth, Cohen has the added question of how to respond to the advent of the Jewish nationalist movement, Zionism, which is examined in detail in part II of this book. Mendelssohn writes in part to convince Jews that they have reason to hope for the possibility of a new political order in which they would be full and equal citizens of the modern nation-state. Cohen writes at a time when the reality of the modern nation-state has been realized, but its promises to dispel anti-Semitic prejudice have not come to fruition. Mendelssohn's commitment to the political and philosophical ideals of the German Enlightenment brings with it the belief that anti-Semitism would recede as rationality came to replace prejudice. Such a view is no longer possible for Cohen, as anti-Semitism had only increased with the establishment of the German nation-state in 1871. This was evident in, among other things, Treitschke's nationalist tirade.

Cohen's response to both the post-Kantian philosophical challenge and the Zionist political challenge is captured in his assertion that Judaism best represents a religion of reason, because the sources of Judaism, meaning the Jewish textual tradition, express the purest form of monotheism. In this sense, Cohen gives philosophical articulation to Geiger's reformist history, although as we will see shortly, this philosophical argument requires, for Cohen, a defense of Jewish law and a rejection of Geiger's historicism. Cohen's definition of monotheism is straightforward. Monotheism means not simply that there is only one God but also that God is incomparable to any other being. In making this claim, Cohen draws on Maimonides and what is known as "negative theology." This is the idea that because God is so different from human beings, and because human beings can only talk about God in human language, we can only describe God by what God is not. In Cohen's terms, monotheism means that God is unique, and as such, there is an insurmountable difference between the human being and God. The literary sources of Judaism are, for Cohen, the first to present this truth to humanity.

Whereas Mendelssohn is content to show that Judaism does not contradict reason, Cohen goes further, claiming that Judaism and reason are in an important sense synonymous. Cohen develops a highly complex logic in his *Logic of Pure Cognition* (Cohen's corollary to Kant's *Critique of Pure Reason*) that is modeled on calculus and attempts to describe the conditions that make science possible. In his *Logic*, Cohen suggests that pure monotheism's (i.e., Judaism's) idea of the unique God's creation of the world makes the concept of science possible. As Cohen puts it in his posthumous and most explicitly Jewish work, *Religion of Reason out of the Sources of Judaism* (Cohen's corollary to Kant's *Religion within the Limits of Reason Alone*), "If the unique God were not the creator, being and becoming would be the same; nature itself would be God. This, however, would mean: God is not. For nature is the becoming that needs being as its foundation."[2] For the purposes of this chapter, I will leave aside the technicalities of Cohen's claims about nature and science to focus on how his formulation of pure monotheism is at once an argument against Kant's derogatory description of Judaism and a rejection of Zionism. Let me turn first to Cohen's response to Kant's view of Jewish law and then to Cohen's refusal of Jewish nationalism.

Cohen maintains that Kant's parochialism leads to his misinterpretation of Mendelssohn: "[Kant's] view is only possible if one considers it self-evident and beyond doubt that the Jewish laws can be experienced as a heavy yoke."[3] Kant's negative view of law, according to Cohen, has no philosophical basis but rather a prejudiced theological one that "originate[s] in the polemic, in which Paul criticized the Mosaic teaching, which he called and characterized law."[4] Cohen is correct that following most Protestant readings since Luther, Kant reads Paul as implicitly criticizing Jewish law and arguing for grace over law as the only means for salvation. Having shown that Kant has no good philosophical reason and only an unfounded theological assumption to define law as intrinsically coercive, Cohen suggests that Kant should have recognized on his own terms that far from being antithetical to ethics, law is the basis of it. So too, far from being, in Kant's words, "an antiquity, in the historical account of faith," Judaism, Cohen asserts, as a religion of law, is the paradigm of a religion of reason.

Once again we see a pattern noted in the last two chapters: while explicitly criticizing a Protestant conception of religion, Cohen's notion of Judaism nonetheless can be understood only within a Protestant category of religion. Like Mendelssohn, Cohen holds that Jewish law is in no way political but only religious. As Mendelssohn did, Cohen contends that

Judaism is not a nation within a nation but instead a community that is bound together by laws that only Jews are obliged to follow. Cohen insists that the Jewish religion exists not just for the sake of Jews but also for all of humanity; in its particularity, the observance of Jewish law by Jews preserves pure monotheism for all peoples. Cohen makes an argument for Jewish difference, or what he calls "Jewish isolation," in the context of his claim about the significance of Jewish law. Cohen writes:

> The law makes possible that isolation which seems indispensable to the care for, and continuation of, what is, at once, one's own and eternal. Isolation in the world of culture! ... Monotheism is at stake; ... With monotheism, the world of culture is at stake.... Therefore, isolation is indispensable to Judaism, for its concept as well as for its cultural work.

Reiterating Mendelssohn's argument, Cohen continues that even in its isolation, the law is not negative but rather "a positive force that stimulates, inspires, fortifies, and deepens religious ideas and beliefs."[5]

We can now consider Cohen's philosophical response to Zionism. Whereas Zionism claims to seek the normalization of the Jewish people, Cohen maintains that Zionism destroys the world-historical mission of the Jewish people, which is to model pure monotheism for the nations of the world. If the Jewish people were a nation among nations, they would lose their uniqueness; indeed, as Zionists would agree, the Jewish people would then not be isolated among the nations but instead would exist among the nations as a nation of its own. Political Zionism, discussed in part II of this book, developed in response to the persistence of anti-Semitism, and its supporters, such as Theodor Herzl (1860–1904), contended that the modern Jewish experience shows that the nations of the world will not allow Jews to assimilate. Cohen recognizes this Zionist premise and the historical reality of anti-Semitism, and accounts for both in his view of a Jewish mission to the nations. He in fact suggests that the reality of anti-Semitism and the history of Jewish suffering is not something to be overcome; rather, they are the price that is paid for the truth of pure monotheism. With reference to Isaiah 53, Cohen contends that "as Israel suffers, according to the prophet, for the pagan worshipers, so Israel to this very day suffers vicariously for the faults and wrongs which still hinder the realization of monotheism."[6]

Cohen's conception of the vicarious suffering intrinsic to Jewish monotheism parallels his account of what he calls religion's share in reason. Once again, Cohen maintains that the meaning of the particularity of the Jewish people, and even that of Jewish suffering, does not end with the Jewish people but instead has universal significance: "Israel's suffering has no tragic connotation, since it has no national particularism as its motivation, and therefore no aesthetic interpretation can give a proper account of it. Suffering is the characteristic feature of religion, and it is the task of monotheism that is symbolically expressed through the suffering of those who profess Jewish monotheism."[7] Cohen suggests that Jewish suffering should not be relieved through a political solution, as Zionists propose. Rather, Cohen proposes that innocent, vicarious suffering for the sins of others is a universal model of ethics and religion toward which all of humanity ought to aspire.

Ethics and Atonement

Cohen's analysis of the Jewish Day of Atonement, Yom Kippur, brings together his conceptions of the world-historical mission of the Jewish people and what he calls "the inwardness of personal faith." The inwardness of personal faith, for Cohen, does not refer to any particular dogmatic belief but rather to the individual's internalization of ethical responsibility. In keeping with rabbinic tradition, Cohen emphasizes that an individual's confession of sin on the Day of Atonement can only be made in a communal context. As if to stress this point, the Day of Atonement's liturgy is in the plural—for example, "we have sinned, we have lied." An individual thus takes responsibility for the sins of the whole community regardless of whether the person has committed a particular sin (such as cheating, for instance). An individual only truly becomes an individual, what Cohen labels a "unique I," after internalizing such responsibility. For this reason, Cohen suggests that the individual Jew's confession in a communal context that takes place on the Day of Atonement is "the symbol for the redemption of mankind."[8]

As the individual Jew does for the Jewish community on Yom Kippur, Cohen claims, Israel suffers representatively for all humankind:

> Monotheism had to become self-conscious in those who profess it. Therefore, just as one acknowledges the punishment meted out by an earthly judge, so those who professed monotheism had to recognize and acknowledge suffering as God's providence, ordained for the purpose of their self-sanctification, their education to the maturity of the I in its correlation with God. Israel's suffering symbolically expresses the reconciliation of man with God. Israel's suffering is its "long day," as the German vernacular calls the Day of Atonement.... The Day of Atonement is the symbol for the redemption of mankind.[9]

Just as the individual Jew takes responsibility for the sins of the whole Jewish community, so too the Jewish community as a whole takes responsibility for the sins of those who "still hinder the realization of monotheism." In both cases, suffering is for the purpose of "self-sanctification," which Cohen equates with the "maturity of the I." We can now better understand what Cohen means by the inwardness of personal faith. This inwardness is neither a feeling nor a particular set of dogmas; it is the self-conscious internalization of responsibility not only for oneself but also for the sins of others.

But who exactly still hinders the realization of monotheism? In answering this question, we can appreciate the simultaneously apologetic and subversive nature of Cohen's conception of Judaism. On the one hand, Cohen stresses Judaism's affinity with Protestantism, arguing that Protestantism is precisely a religion *of the individual*: "This is the real sense of the new faith: an emphasis on the personal, and therefore immediate sense of subjective responsibility of the religious conscience. This conscience does not take refuge in the protection and power of the Church."[10] Rejecting Graetz's claim that "Judaism, in the strict sense of the word, is not even a religion—if one understands thereby the relationship of man to his creator and his hopes for his earthly existence—but rather a constitution for a body politic," Cohen declares that "with reference to the scientific concept of religion I am unable to discover any distinction between Jewish monotheism and Protestant Christianity."[11] Yet on the other hand, Cohen—as Mendelssohn, Geiger, and indeed Graetz had before him—explicitly claims that this likeness is not due to Judaism's modeling itself on Protestantism but rather to Protestantism's borrowing from Judaism: "For Luther, faith developed out of the Psalms. For the subsequent period, it was grounded even more deeply in the prophets."[12]

Cohen's reading of Isaiah 53 perhaps best underscores the profoundly subversive aspect of his work. The Christian tradition of course understands the suffering servant described in Isaiah 53 as Jesus. Cohen rereads Isaiah with Jewish eyes, claiming that the servant is the Jewish people. Cohen's reading suggests that at best, the Christian reading of Isaiah 53 is an imitation of Judaism. Who, then, does Cohen think hinders the realization of monotheism? Christians. Cohen makes it clear that he thinks Protestantism is a profound advance in the history of Christianity, but also suggests that Protestants themselves still hinder the realization of monotheism. Protestants can only clear away their own obstruction by understanding their reliance on Jews and Judaism. Until they are able to do so, the Jewish people will suffer vicariously for the sins of Protestants.

In an important sense, there is no reason why Cohen's reading of Isaiah 53 should be controversial. The book of Isaiah is part of the Hebrew Bible (what Christians call the Old Testament), and many strands of the premodern Jewish tradition had read Isaiah 53 just as Cohen does. At the same time, it is just a historical fact that what we call Christianity today developed in tandem with second-century Judaism. For these reasons, the claim that Isaiah 53 has an original, Jewish context should not be contentious. But here again the German Protestant context in which Cohen writes is key. Different as they are from one another, neither Schleiermacher, nor Kant, nor for that matter, Treitschke can stomach the idea that Christianity originated from within internal Jewish debates. For both Schleiermacher and Treitschke, the mere suggestion of Christianity's Jewish roots is an insult to both Christianity and Germany. Cohen's reading of Isaiah 53 means to subvert the Christian reading of the text. And as suggested by his affirmation of the notion that the Jewish people suffer vicariously for the faults of others, Cohen is prepared to suffer the consequences, and he obviously realizes that the response to this reading of Isaiah might be an anti-Semitic backlash. Indeed, on the basis of his own philosophy, Cohen is compelled to speak the truth of pure monotheism, no matter what follows, for this is the Jewish people's historical role.

We will see in chapter 5 that Cohen's moral valuation of Jewish suffering has two important late twentieth-century manifestations in French Jewish philosophy and religious Zionism. I turn now to Soloveitchik's orthodox philosophy, which echoes in significant ways Cohen's liberal thought. In particular, I will explore the striking affinities between their conceptions of the rationality of Jewish law as well as their stress on the making of the true individual through atonement. These resemblances are no accident, for Soloveitchik was a student of Cohen's philosophy and fused Cohen's thought with his own eastern European intellectual heritage.

Soloveitchik and the Lonely Man of Faith

Soloveitchik was born in Pruzhan, Poland, the heir to a great rabbinic lineage. His great-grandfather Joseph Baer (1820–92) was the cohead of the Volozhin Yeshivah, which was the prototype of the great Talmudic academies of the nineteenth and twentieth centuries; his grandfather Hayim (1853–1918) developed a highly analytic method of Talmud study (discussed in chapter 6). In 1925, after studying with his father and receiving a secular education in Warsaw, Soloveitchik became a student at the University of Berlin, where he completed a doctoral dissertation on Cohen's philosophy. He immigrated to the United States in 1932, and quickly became one of the twentieth century's most important intellectual leaders of modern orthodoxy. Soloveitchik shares the basic premise of all the German Jewish thinkers I have explored in this book so far: that Judaism, and especially Jewish law, is not political but instead concerns the intellectual and spiritual dimensions of human experience. Soloveitchik's basic claim is the same as Hirsch's: that Jewish law (*halakhah*) always remains unchanging and authoritative for Jews. In his philosophical writings, Soloveitchik describes a model of the human being that he calls "halakhic man," to whom he contrasts "intellectual man" and "religious man." Halakhic man combines the rationality of intellectual man with the spirituality of religious man.

Soloveitchik follows Cohen in understanding Judaism, and in particular Jewish law, as being harmonious with science and especially mathematics: "Halakhic man resembles somewhat the mathematician who masters infinity only for the sake of creating finitude, delimited by numbers and mathematical measures, and cognizing it."[13] In making this claim, Soloveitchik, like Cohen, draws inspiration from Maimonides. Soloveitchik affirms not only an intellectual affinity between his thought and that of Maimonides but also calls Maimonides his "one friend" in a lonely world.[14]

Soloveitchik is critical of what he sees as the excesses of spirituality in modern Protestant thought: "Religious man begins with this world and ends up in supernal realms; halakhic man starts out in supernal realms and ends up in this world."[15] In this sense, Soloveithchik opposes certain Protestant understandings of religion that follow Schleiermacher's lead in rejecting law in favor of authentic feeling or experience. Halakhah, for Soloveitchik, is an attempt "to translate the qualitative features of religious subjectivity ... into firm and well-established quantities ... through the medium of objective, quantitative measurements."[16] Yet as Cohen explicitly did before him, Soloveitchik nevertheless implicitly affirms a Protestant idea that religion is private and individual. As he puts it, "Judaism ... is grounded in its awareness of and esteem for the individual."[17]

Nowhere is Soloveitchik's emphasis on the individual as apparent as in his essay "The Lonely Man of Faith," initially written for a popular audience. In this work, Soloveitchik considers the different portrayals of Adam in the first two chapters of Genesis. Like halakhic man, the lonely man of faith combines two seemingly irreconcilable perspectives on the world. According to Soloveitchik, the Adam described in the first chapter of Genesis is a technological genius who wants to imitate God the creator. The Adam portrayed in the second chapter, in contrast, is a man of wonder who wants to understand God. These two Adams parallel Soloveitchik's accounts of intellectual and religious man. Yet whereas in his book *Halakhic Man*, Soloveitchik is more critical of religious man than he is of intellectual man, in *The Lonely Man of Faith* he is more critical of the technological Adam who wants to master the world at the cost of his spiritual core. In both books, however, Soloveitchik stresses the dual nature of the human being, expressed respectively by the different Adams of the first two chapters of Genesis as well as intellectual and religious man. This dual nature, which by definition cannot be reconciled, is at the heart of Soloveitchik's account of the irreducibly singular and indeed lonely individual human being.

We can appreciate Soloveitchik's conception of the individual human being by focusing on two further correspondences between his thought and Cohen's: the rejection of historicism, and the centrality of repentance. Soloveitchik's analysis of the tension between the two creation stories in Genesis is an implicit rejection of a historical-critical approach to the Bible that views tensions in the biblical text as evidence of the Bible's human authorship. For biblical critics, the Bible is a compilation of the works of multiple authors. In this case, the first chapter of Genesis is authored by P (the priestly source), and the second chapter is authored by J (the Yahwist source). Among the evidence for two different sources for these two stories are the different names used for God in each chapter ("Elohim" is used in the first one, and "Yahweh" in the second) and the different order of creation in each chapter (in Genesis 1, the order is plants, sea creatures and birds, animals, and man and woman created together; in Genesis 2, the order is Adam, plants, animals, and Eve out of Adam's rib). We need not concern ourselves with the details of the claims and implications of biblical criticism here but rather must only note that Soloveitchik acknowledges the intrinsic tensions between the two stories and in fact stresses the differences between the two, especially as they relate to the nature of the creation of the human being. As such, Soloveitchik's analysis refuses the claims of historical approaches to the Bible and affirms instead what he regards as the Bible's timeless truth, which in the case of Genesis concerns the dual nature of the human being.

The Bible's view of the creation of the human being is intimately tied to the Bible's perspective on the relation between man and woman. In the first story in Genesis, man and woman are created together. In the second story, woman is created from man's rib. Many modern commentators, Jewish and Christian, have been uncomfortable with the second story because it seems to imply that man is superior to woman. In contrast, Soloveitchik accents what he calls Adam's "sacrificial gesture" in creating Eve.[18] Just as Cohen contends that to be a genuine individual is to sacrifice for the sake of others, so too Soloveitchik claims that this second Adam is a true individual because he literally sacrifices a part of himself—his rib—for the sake of Eve. While he argues that the Adam of the first Genesis story is innately social—he is created together with a partner—Soloveitchik maintains that it is the Adam of the second story who, because of his self-sacrifice, is capable of creating a "community of commitments."[19] Soloveitchik suggests that a true community is one in which individuals sacrifice themselves for one another. Like Cohen before him, Soloveitchik maintains that self-sacrifice does not mean the negation of an individual's identity but rather the creation of the individual's irreducible uniqueness.

Soloveitchik also echoes Cohen in characterizing the act of repentance as the path toward authentic individuality. In Soloveitchik's words, by repenting, the human being "cancels the law of identity and continuity which prevails in the 'I' awareness by engaging in the wondrous, creative act of repentance.... When he finds himself in a situation of sin, he takes advantage of his creative capacity, returns to God, and becomes a creator and self-fashioner. Man, through repentance, creates himself, his own 'I.'" Again reiterating the structure of Cohen's thought, Soloveitchik makes an analogy between the individual Jew's act of atonement in relation to the Jewish community and the Jewish community's act of atonement in relation to the world:

> The Jewish people see their own fate as bound up with the fate of existence as a whole.... Physical reality and spiritual-historical existence—both have suffered greatly on account of the dominion of the abyss, of chaos and the void, and their fates parallel one another.... The Jewish people bring a sacrifice to atone, as it were, for the Holy One, blessed be He, for not having completed the work of creation. The Creator of the world diminished the image and stature of creation in order to leave something for man, the work of His hands, to do, in order to adorn man with the crown of creator and maker.[20]

Just as the Adam of the second story sacrifices a part of himself in order to further God's work of creation—that is, in order to create Eve—so too the Jewish people sacrifice and atone because God's creation is not yet complete. As does Cohen, Soloveitchik understands atonement as suffering. And like Cohen, Soloveitchik views suffering as intrinsic to the betterment of the human being. Yet Soloveitchik, in a departure from Cohen's thought, does not identify suffering with an ethical mission but rather with a theological vision of the human being's relationship to God:

> Suffering comes to elevate man, to purify his spirit and sanctify him, to cleanse his thoughts of the dregs of superficiality and vulgarity; to refine his soul and broaden his horizons. A general principle: suffering—its purpose is to correct the flaw in man's personality.... Suffering appears in the world to contribute something to man, to make atonement for him.... Suffering obliges man to return in full repentance to God.[21]

Given the profound structural similarities between Cohen's and Soloveitchik's philosophies, what might account for this difference in how they view the role of suffering? The difference between Cohen's liberal worldview and Soloveitchik's orthodox one might become apparent here.

Cohen, as did Geiger before him, emphasizes ethics in place of theology, whereas Soloveitchik is more straightforwardly theological. There is certainly some truth to this explanation, yet given the deep resemblances between Soloveitchik's and Cohen's thoughts, and especially their almost identical analyses of the creation of true individuality through repentance, this version is not sufficient. Attention to the different historical and political contexts in which Cohen and Soloveitchik write may provide a more ample explanation. Two points are important here. First, Cohen writes before the Nazi genocide of European Jewry. To many Jews after the Holocaust, Cohen's claim that the Jewish people suffer innocently for the sins of others is deeply problematic because it suggests that Jews ought to make themselves passive victims to history's violence. Writing after the Holocaust, Soloveitchik retains Cohen's notion that self-sacrifice is central to Jewish religiosity, but he make no claims about a specific Jewish mission to suffer for the sake of the nations of the world.

Second, Cohen writes in a context in which he continually feels obliged to justify Judaism in explicitly Protestant terms. We encountered above his attempt to reread Isaiah 53 in an effort to remind Protestants of their Jewish origins as well as his statement "with reference to the scientific concept of religion I am unable to discover any distinction between Jewish monotheism and Protestant Christianity."[22] In contrast, Soloveitchik writes in an American context in which he does not find it necessary to proclaim Judaism's identity with Christianity. Soloveitchik actually denies this identification, insisting instead that with regard to matters of religion or theology, Judaism and Christianity cannot—by definition—come to mutually agreeable commonalities. He rejects the idea of interreligious dialogue because he believes that such dialogue violates the untranslatable, or lonely, character of Judaism and Jewishness that bear a formal similarity to the lonely man of faith who cannot communicate his acute sense of loneliness and individuality. As Soloveitchik puts it:

> Our approach to the relationship with the outside world has always been an ambivalent character, intrinsically antithetic, bordering at times on the paradoxical.... In a word, we belong to the human society and, at the same time, we feel as strangers and outsiders. We are rooted in the here and now of reality as inhabitants of our globe, and yet we experience a sense of homelessness and loneliness as if we belonged somewhere else. We are both realists and dreamers, prudent and practical on the one hand, and visionaries and idealists on the other. We are indeed involved in the cultural endeavor and yet we are committed to another dimension of experience.[23]

As suggested by the last line of this quotation, Soloveitchik does not deny that Jews are part of U.S. society. Rather, he insists that with regard to political and ethical matters, Jews are fully committed to U.S. society. But

when it comes to theology or religion, there are no grounds for commonality, and Judaism remains separate from both politics and ethics.

While Soloveitchik in no way affirms (and if anything, only rejects)
Cohen's equation of Judaism with Protestantism, it is still important to
notice how his view of Judaism conforms in both structure and spirit to
Cohen's Protestant conception of Judaism. Judaism, for Soloveitchik, is a
religion for it represents "a dimension of experience" wholly different in
kind from all other dimensions of human experience. Despite his historical, cultural, and political distance from Cohen's Germany, Soloveitchik,
in the United States, continues Cohen's project of delineating the Jewish
religion of reason. For both Cohen and Soloveitchik, the Jewish religion
is rooted in the rational and apolitical observance of Jewish law that
speaks to the timeless existential task of the human being: to become an
authentic and mature individual through the lonely tasks of self-sacrifice
and repentance.

Leibowitz: Jewish Religion and the Jewish State

Let me now turn to Leibowitz, perhaps the twentieth century's most
iconoclastic Jewish thinker and also an Orthodox Jew. Leibowitz was
born in Riga in 1903. Before immigrating to Palestine in 1934, he studied chemistry and philosophy in Berlin, and then medicine in Basel. For
almost sixty years, until his death in 1994, Leibowitz taught courses in
biochemistry, the history of science, and philosophy at the Hebrew University of Jerusalem. Although he continually affirmed his Zionist commitment, Leibowitz became a harsh critic of the way in which Judaism
was used as a political tool in the Israeli state. His criticism intensified in
1967 after Israel gained control of the Gaza Strip and the West Bank as
a result of the Six-Day War. Although, as we will see in chapter 5, some
Zionists ascribed religious significance to what they perceived as Israel's
miraculous victory in 1967, Leibowitz viewed this military triumph as
an unmitigated disaster for the Jewish state for two reasons. For one, he
warned that dominating another people would bring ruin to the Jewish
people. He also passionately rejected the ascription of religious importance to any military victory. Leibowitz extended his condemnation of
the occupation of the Gaza Strip and the West Bank into an argument
about the absolute separation between church and state, or between religion and politics. Warning that Israel could become a "fascist state,"
Leibowitz cautioned about the grave consequences of the blending of
religion and politics for the future of the state of Israel.[24] But beyond
the politics of the modern nation-state, Leibowitz's concern was that the
idolatrous consecration of the land of Israel corrupts and could destroy

the Jewish religion. In this vein, he famously regarded religious pilgrimages to the Western Wall as akin to a "religious disco."[25]

Leibowitz's claims are predicated on the modern idea that I have been exploring in this book: that Judaism is a religion, defined as wholly separate from the modern nation-state. Notably, Leibowitz makes his arguments on the basis of what he contends are commitments to Zionism and Jewish orthodoxy. His allegiance to Zionism consists simply in his view that given the tragic history of persecution and mass murder of the Jewish people, Jews need a state of their own for the practical purpose of self-protection. In Leibowitz's words, "Zionism is the expression of our being fed up with being ruled by *Goyim* [non-Jews or the nations of the world]."[26] Leibowitz's view conforms to the position of political Zionists who contend, as the label suggests, that Zionism is a *political* solution for the Jews.

On the basis of his political conception of Zionism, Leibowitz emphasizes that "Zionism has no connection to Judaism in its essential religious sense of the obligation to observe Torah and Mitzvoth." Especially in an age where Jews are exercising political sovereignty, Leibowitz stresses that Jews in Israel and elsewhere must return to Judaism's essential religious nature:

> We must distinguish between the historical exilic existence of the Jewish people and its present existence as possessing political autonomy. Previously, the individual conscious of his Jewish identity could not live his life as a Jew except through complete immersion in the Jewish collective—the religious community.... Our generation has created a framework for Jewish existence which is not religious, which is not conducted by religious institutions, is not committed to religious values, and has no religious meaning. We must examine afresh the significance of religion for a Jewish person and for the Jewish people and its state.... [O]nly he who does not regard religion as a collective national-political manifestation, but views it as setting personal goals and values, is capable of surmounting the crisis.... [I]f in the exilic history of the Jewish people the collective aspect of the Jewish religion was emphasized, it is our obligation today to emphasize its personal aspect.[27]

Leibowitz self-consciously acknowledges the changes that modernity has brought to Jews and Judaism, but he nonetheless insists that Jewish law remains the same throughout time.

His modern orthodoxy, like Hirsch's and Soloveitchik's, rejects the notion that historical investigation can bring us to an understanding of the essential and unchanging character of Jewish law. In Leibowitz's words, "The abiding and constant element in Jewish history, the Halakhah, is essentially ahistoric.... To consider history as the foundation of faith is to deplete religion of all religious significance."[28] Like Cohen and Soloveitchik, Leibowitz claims a deep affinity with Maimonides in defining what Judaism and Jewish law are. He characterizes Maimonides as the "greatest authority of Judaism" and models his own faith on Maimonides's example of "divine worship with one's person."[29]

As both a Zionist and an Orthodox Jew, Leibowitz is extremely disdainful of the kind of liberal German Judaism to which Cohen gives voice. Leibowitz, in fact, describes liberal Judaism as a "historical distortion of Judaism" that "empties Judaism of its religious content and reduces it to ethical humanism."[30] He especially rejects the idea, put forward by both Cohen and Geiger, that there is a Jewish mission to be "a light unto the nations." Instead, Leibowitz contends that a Jew's duty is not to humanity as a whole or even to other Jews but rather, *and only*, to God through observance of God's laws. "The individual who has attained perfection wishes to be alone with God.... The purpose of the Torah is not social improvement, and the ultimate ground for the Mitzvoth [commandments] is not concern for man's needs in his social existence."[31]

Despite Leibowitz's distancing of himself from liberal Judaism, especially of the German Jewish variety, it is important to recognize that his very conceptions of Judaism and Jewish law are remarkably consistent with liberal German Jewish thought, whose main innovation, as we have seen in the last two chapters, is to try to fit Judaism into a Protestant category of religion. More particularly, Leibowitz's account of the individual Jew's religiosity is structurally identical to Cohen's (and Soloveitchik's) conception of the creation of the unique individual through the act of repentance. Like Cohen, Leibowitz uses the liturgy of Yom Kippur to illustrate what he takes to be the essence of Jewish religiosity: "The Day of Atonement—over the past two thousand years a definitive expression of Jewish religiosity, the legitimacy of which has never been questioned—has the Ne'ilah prayer as its climax.... The essential concern of Ne'ilah, its unique content, is the sin and repentance of each individual.... Ne'ilah is the expression par excellence of individualistic religiosity."[32] Just as Cohen and Soloveitchik do, Leibowitz claims that repentance does not negate but instead is the enactment of true individuality.

Given his marked affinity with Cohen's and Soloveitchik's accounts of what he labels "individualistic religiosity," it is all the more notable that Leibowitz, the only actual scientist among the three, departs from both Cohen and Soloveitchik in divorcing Jewish religion from modern science. As Leibowitz observes, "Man's consciousness of standing before God has nothing to do with his knowledge of the world."[33] In contrast, as we have seen in this chapter, both Cohen and Soloveitchik affirm an intimate relation between the Jewish religion and science. Again, as Cohen puts it, "If the unique God were not the creator, being and becoming would be the same; nature itself would be God. This, however, would mean: God is not. For nature is the becoming that needs being as its foundation." And in Soloveitchik's words, "Halakhic man resembles somewhat the mathematician who masters infinity only for the sake of creating finitude, delimited by numbers and mathematical measures, and cognizing it."

What accounts for the difference between Leibowitz, on the one hand, and Cohen and Soloveitchik, on the other? Leibowitz answers this question, making it clear that he is not rejecting a premodern Jewish embrace of the interrelatedness of science and religion, such as is found in Maimonides's philosophy, but only the modern relation between science and religion. According to Leibowitz, the modern divorce between religion and science stems from the modern conception of scientific knowledge as objective information about the world, not concerned with what Leibowitz calls "meaning." In response to Cohen's and Soloveitchik's affirmations of the mutuality of science and Judaism, Leibowitz would perhaps reply that Cohen and Soloveitchik are operating within a premodern conception of what science is—that science can speak to issues of both fact and value.

The proper scope and meaning of modern science is of course beyond the purview of this book. Within the story of how Judaism became a religion, however, Leibowitz's insistence on an absolute split between modern science and Judaism is nonetheless quite instructive. For all of Leibowitz's efforts to defend what he regards as the timeless truth of Judaism, his notion of Judaism as a religion is not only distinctly modern but in an important respect also more Protestant than either Soloveitchik's or Cohen's conceptions. Leibowitz, in even stronger terms than Mendelssohn, insists that the Jewish religion is wholly separate from the speculation of scientific truth as well as the practices of citizenship demanded by the modern nation-state. In contrast, Cohen, with Soloveitchik following him, declares that the Jewish religion is quite relevant and conducive to modern science, while wholly separate from modern political practices. So we must ask again: Why does Leibowitz argue as he does when even he acknowledges that his view of the absolute separation between the Jewish religion and science is a break with previous Jewish views, and especially with that of Maimonides, who is Leibowitz's (as well as Cohen's and Soloveitchik's) intellectual hero? Put another way, given Leibowitz's orthodox commitment to the unchanging character of Judaism, would it not have made more sense for him simply to say that modern science has a flawed understanding of human knowledge if it claims that objective knowledge is the only kind of truth there is? In a crucial sense, this is exactly what Cohen and Soloveitchik claim: that Judaism, as they understand it, coheres with scientific or mathematical knowledge, and not to appreciate this unity is to be wrong both from a Jewish *and* scientific perspective.

The most plausible way to explain Leibowitz's insistence on an absolute dichotomy between the Jewish religion and modern science is to look to his profound commitment to preserving the very category of religion, which he defines as a completely distinct sphere of life existing in conjunction with other distinct spheres of life. Let me quote Leibowitz one last time: "What has been said in this context about religious faith holds equally for other spheres of human thought; history, psychology, or sociology, for example, have meaningful actions as their subject and are therefore not amenable to the methods of inquiry of modern natural science. Religion differs from them all in its direct normative significance. It obliges man to worship God."[34] Like Schleiermacher, Leibowitz is dedicated to safeguarding the sphere of religion from all other spheres of human life. And like Schleiermacher, Leibowitz seems to believe that this is the only strategy that, in the midst of modernity's challenges, can save religion.

We have seen that Leibowitz is a staunch defender of the unchanging nature of the Jewish religion as well as an opponent of what he depicts as historical distortions of Judaism, which he associates first and foremost with liberal Judaism. Yet we have also seen that Leibowitz makes his case for orthodoxy on the shoulders of Mendelssohn, who invents the Jewish religion by insisting on an absolute difference between "the relation between man and nature, and the relation between creature and Creator."[35] Almost three hundred years after Mendelssohn writes in Prussia in the hope of a new liberal order, Leibowitz writes in the state of Israel in the hope of maintaining the modern liberal political arrangements that Mendelssohn had envisioned. Leibowitz's view of the relation between religion and politics is even more liberal than Mendelssohn's. After all, while arguing for the separation between religion and politics, Mendelssohn allows that religion can influence the state in nonpolitical ways. As Mendelssohn notes, "The only aid religion can render to the state consists in teaching and consoling; that is, in imparting to the citizens, through its divine doctrines, such convictions as are conducive to the public weal, and in uplifting with its otherworldly consolations the poor wretch who has been condemned to death as a sacrifice for the common good."[36] Leibowitz, as we have seen, goes further than Mendelssohn in denying that there is any relation whatsoever between the Jewish religion and being a citizen of a modern nation-state.

Conclusion

We have seen in this chapter that Mendelssohn's invention of the idea that Judaism is a religion travels not only through time but through space as well. In the German Jewish context, Cohen gives philosophical voice to the concept of Jewish religion in order to defend a diaspora existence to his Jewish contemporaries who may be attracted to Zionism, to in turn defend what he argues is the Jewish essence of Protestantism, and perhaps most basic of all, the promises of the modern liberal state at a time when both Jews and non-Jews have reason to doubt these promises. While Cohen is self-consciously a proponent of liberal Judaism, his philosophical articulation of the Jewish religion as creating the true individual becomes the basis of Soloveitchik's self-consciously orthodox thought. Writing in the United States, Soloveitchik draws on Cohen's analysis of atonement as the unique vehicle that creates Jewish individuality. For Soloveitchik, the image of the lonely but authentically true individual also comes to describe the relationship between the Jewish community and its surroundings. As the lonely people of faith, the Jewish people and Jewish religion can live comfortably as part of the U.S. democratic order, but will also always remain apart from their neighbors. Finally, Leibowitz, perhaps unwittingly, draws on the same liberal Jewish assumptions he elsewhere strongly criticizes: the notion that Judaism is about the individual's religious life, and that Judaism and the modern nation-state concern two wholly different states of affairs, which should always remain separate. As we have seen, Leibowitz makes these claims in the Israeli context in order to warn against what he regards as the idolatrous—and spiritually and politically dangerous—conflation of the Jewish religion and Jewish state.

On perhaps the most fundamental level, Cohen, Soloveitchik, and Leibowitz share a presupposition that, as we will see in the rest of this book, has been called into question by many different modern Jewish thinkers. This presupposition is that the modern nation-state is good for the Jews and good for Judaism. For Cohen, the modern nation-state is good for the Jews and Judaism because both adhere in their own way to rationality as well as ethics. For Soloveitchik, the modern nation-state and the United States in particular are good for the Jews because U.S. democracy allows the lonely people of faith to exist without outside interference. Finally, for Leibowitz the modern nation-state, in the form of the state of Israel, is good in that it allows the Jewish people to protect themselves while also permitting Judaism to exist as a religion apart from politics. For all three thinkers, the modern nation-state makes room for the Jewish religion, just as Mendelssohn had hoped it would.

Suggested Readings

Background

For the history of German Jewry after 1870, see suggested readings for chapter 4. For the history of U.S. Jewry, see suggested readings for chapter 9. For the history of Zionism, see suggested readings for chapter 8.

Cohen

Gibbs, Robert, ed. *Hermann Cohen's Ethics*. Leiden: Brill, 2006.
> Exploring Cohen's writings on ethics, religion, and Judaism, the essays in this collection examine his philosophical system and relationship to various premodern and modern figures.

Munk, Reinier, ed. *Hermann Cohen's Critical Idealism*. Dordrecht: Springer, 2005.
> The essays in this collection focus on Cohen's historical context, philosophical system, and writings on religion and Judaism.

Myers, David N. "Hermann Cohen and the Quest for Protestant Judaism." *Leo Baeck Institute Year Book* 46 (2001): 195–214.
> Myers suggests that along with his Protestant contemporaries, Cohen shares a diverse array of ethical, theological, and political commitments, but that Cohen breaks with these Christian thinkers by insisting on the Jewish provenance of ideas central to Western culture.

Poma, Andrea. *The Critical Philosophy of Hermann Cohen*. Trans. John Denton. Albany: State University of New York Press, 1997.
> Poma outlines Cohen's reinterpretation of Kant, reconstructs Cohen's system of philosophy, and argues that Cohen's late writings on religion and Judaism are continuous with this system—that these works address issues generated by, and provide a crucial complement for, Cohen's logic, ethics, and aesthetics.

Schwarzschild, Steven S. "The Title of Hermann Cohen's 'Religion of Reason out of the Sources of Judaism.'" In *Religion of Reason out of the Sources of Judaism*, by Hermann Cohen, trans. Simon Kaplan, 7–20. 2nd ed. Atlanta: Scholars Press, 1995.
> This essay provides an introduction to the structure of Cohen's argument in *Religion of Reason out of the Sources of Judaism*, with special attention to his particular brand of neo-Kantianism.

Seeskin, Kenneth. "How to Read *Religion of Reason*." In *Religion of Reason out of the Sources of Judaism*, by Hermann Cohen, trans. Simon Kaplan, 21–42. 2nd ed. Atlanta: Scholars Press, 1995.
> This essay offers an introduction to the background, claims, and reception of Cohen's *Religion of Reason out of the Sources of Judaism*.

Leibowitz

For the relationship between Leibowitz and Emmanuel Levinas, see suggested readings for chapter 5.

Goldman, Eliezer. Introduction to *Judaism, Human Values, and the Jewish State*, by Yeshayahu Leibowitz, vii–xxxiv. Ed. Eliezer Goldman. Trans. Eliezer

Goldman, Yoram Navon, Zvi Jacobson, Gershon Levi, and Raphael Levy. Cambridge, MA: Harvard University Press, 1992.

Goldman provides an introduction to Leibowitz's biography and thought, focusing on issues such as his epistemological premises, conception of Judaism, and views on religion and politics.

Hellinger, Moshe. "A Clearly Democratic Religious-Zionist Philosophy: The Early Thought of Yeshayahu Leibowitz." *Journal of Jewish Thought and Philosophy* 16, no. 2 (2008): 253–82.

Acknowledging that Leibowitz is known for his insistence on a strict separation between religion and politics, this essay argues that his early writings adopt a different posture and advance a form of religious Zionism. Exploring the process through which Leibowitz came to abandon these early views, Hellinger presents this conceptual transformation as a shift from the "democratic" to the "liberal."

Mendes-Flohr, Paul. "Maimonides in the Crucible of Zionism: Reflections on Yeshayahu Leibowitz's Negative Theology." In *Maimonides and His Heritage*, ed. Idit Dobbs-Weinstein, Lenn E. Goodman, and James Allen Grady, 181–92. Albany: State University of New York Press, 2009.

Noting the existence of various affinities linking Leibowitz to the Protestant theologian Karl Barth, Mendes-Flohr contends that Leibowitz's separation between religion and politics shapes his approach to Maimonides's work, and that Leibowitz ends up endorsing key "humanistic" positions despite attacking humanistic religion and politics.

Sagi, Avi. "Contending with Modernity: Scripture in the Thought of Yeshayahu Leibowitz and Joseph Soloveitchik." *Journal of Religion* 77, no. 3 (1997): 421–41.

Sagi explores the similarities between these thinkers' approaches to the significance of scripture, and maintains that while Soloveitchik and Leibowitz disagree about the precise meaning conveyed by scripture, both seek to defend the Bible's importance against scientific and historical challenges, and do so by distinguishing scientific and historical knowledge from the type of meaning that the Bible yields.

Soloveitchik

Hartman, David. *A Living Covenant: The Innovative Spirit in Traditional Judaism*. New York: Free Press, 1985.

Hartman argues that Soloveitchik's work should be read as an attempt to bring together two competing tendencies in biblical and rabbinic thought: a posture that emphasizes themes such as humanity's intellectual adequacy and mutuality with God, and one that demands silence and resignation from human beings before the divine will.

Kaplan, Lawrence J. "Hermann Cohen and Rabbi Joseph Soloveitchik on Repentance." *Journal of Jewish Thought and Philosophy* 13, no. 1 (2004): 213–58.

Kaplan highlights the striking affinity between these thinkers' views and tries to explain a key point of disagreement—the fact that Soloveitchik, unlike Cohen, endorses the classical rabbinic claim that repentance grounded in love transforms past misdeeds into meritorious actions.

Munk, Reinier. *The Rationale of Halakhic Man: Joseph B. Soloveitchik's Conception of Jewish Thought*. Amsterdam: J. C. Gieben, 1996.

Exploring his dissertation on Cohen and writings from the 1940s, Munk seeks to reconstruct Soloveitchik's understanding of the type of thought and way of life generated by Jewish law.

Ravitzky, Aviezer. "Rabbi J. B. Soloveitchik on Human Knowledge: Between Maimonidean and Neo-Kantian Philosophy." *Modern Judaism* 6, no. 2 (1986): 157–88.

Outlining two central elements of Soloveitchik's work—his replacement of Maimonides's emphasis on knowledge of the cosmos with a stress on knowledge of Jewish law, and his insistence on treating halakhah as an autonomous, self-sufficient cognitive system—Ravitzky looks at the basis for these moves in Maimonidean and neo-Kantian philosophy as well as the tensions that emerge from the arguments that Soloveitchik advances.

Chapter 4

RELIGION AS EXPERIENCE:

THE GERMAN JEWISH RENAISSANCE

IN THE LAST THREE CHAPTERS I explored a trajectory of modern Jewish thought, beginning with Mendelssohn and peaking with Cohen, that posits a confluence between Judaism and rationality. As we have seen, this argument goes hand in hand with an affirmation of modern liberal politics in which Jews and Judaism would exist as a minority that would contribute to the majority culture. I turn now to disillusionment with these sorts of assertions in German Jewish thought in the early twentieth century.

Tellingly perhaps, the Jewish intellectuals who were disillusioned with claims for philosophical rationality and political liberalism were of the generation that had benefited from the social and political strides for which thinkers like Mendelssohn and Cohen had worked. Yet in rejecting their parents' and grandparents' aspiration for a German Jewish cultural and philosophical symbiosis, young, disaffected Jews brought about a renaissance of Jewish life in Germany between the two world wars. Among these German or German-speaking intellectuals were Gershom Scholem (1897–1982), the founder of the modern study of Jewish mysticism; the writer Franz Kafka (1883–1924); Leo Strauss (1899–1973), who became one of the most important political philosophers in the United States and to whom I will turn in chapter 8; and Martin Buber (1878–1965) and Franz Rosenzweig (1886–1929), who I will discuss in this chapter.

Emphasizing what they regard as the authenticity of lived Jewish experience as opposed to what they consider the deadening effects of modern rationalism, Buber and Rosenzweig reject what they deem overly apologetic arguments for a confluence between Judaism and modernity. Experience, and not rationality, they contend, is the basis of a Jewish life. As we will see below, Buber and Rosenzweig characterize what each maintains is the content of Jewish experience differently; while Buber underscores the centrality of the experience of dialogue between two people to the exclusion of Jewish law and ritual, Rosenzweig stresses the necessity of law and ritual. Despite this crucial difference, Buber and Rosenzweig both claim that the lived experience of Judaism, as they each describe it, offers something to humanity at large: the return to an authentically human existence that modernity has eclipsed.

Yet we will see in this chapter that despite their shared rejection of the liberal, rationalist tradition of German Jewish thought that came before them, both Buber and Rosenzweig support a central assumption that I have been examining in this book: that Judaism is something distinct in kind from politics, which both thinkers define only in terms of the modern nation-state. We will see that while they each rebuff the modern term "religion" as applied to Judaism, Buber and Rosenzweig nonetheless inadvertently affirm the modern idea that Judaism is a religion.

THE EASTERN EUROPEAN JEW

Before turning to Buber and Rosenzweig in some detail, I must note an important underlying theme in earlier German Jewish arguments about the inherent rationality of Judaism. These arguments almost always brought with them derogatory images of eastern European Jews and Judaism as the counterexample against which German Jews defined themselves. The German Jewish thinkers I have considered in the last three chapters—including Mendelssohn, Geiger, Graetz, Cohen, and Hirsch—were all dedicated to a German notion of Bildung, which involved a commitment to self-improvement, rationality, and refinement. For Germans and German Jews alike, eastern European Jews represented the coarseness and vulgarity that was the opposite of German culture.

Debates about synagogue worship were one venue for arguments about the rationality of Judaism. In 1818, Eliezer Liebermann, an advocate of Jewish reform, implored Jews to adopt what he alleged was the proper decorum for synagogue worship. Detailing and advocating for changes to synagogue services to better reflect the religious service at the reform temple in Hamburg, Liebermann wrote:

> They utter their prayers in an intelligible and lucid manner. They have chosen for an advocate between them and their Father in heaven an upright man, a rabbi eminent in Torah and wisdom and an accomplished orator.... All join together with him to praise and glorify in a pleasant and becoming fashion, verse by verse and word by word. No one speaks nor are any words exchanged: the irreverent voices of frivolous conversation are not heard.[1]

Liebermann's description of what he claimed was proper synagogue etiquette not only conformed to a Protestant service but also implicitly found its counterexample in traditional Jewish forms of worship as practiced by eastern European Jews who were not yet "enlightened." Following Liebermann's order of description in the above quotation, we can deduce his assumptions about a traditional Jewish service. Congregants mumble their prayers at their own pace, and do not attempt to do so in unison. A rabbi does not deliver a sermon on a generally edifying topic; this is a modern phenomenon, modeled on a Protestant cleric offering a homily. A traditional Jewish service is perhaps better understood as a cacophony rather than a harmony—meaning that each voice prays at its own pace, and no attempt is made for unison. Finally, in a traditional Jewish service congregants often do tend to talk among themselves, even when they perhaps should not. Liebermann's portrayal of a decorous synagogue service did not just express a positive model of a synagogue service to which Jews ought to aspire but rejected the inverse of this model as well, which he implicitly ascribed to a traditional, eastern European Jewish service.

Negative portraits of eastern European Jews by German Jews consisted of more than different views of proper manners. In accord with the German conception of Bildung, social virtues, such as manners, were seen as intimately tied to intellectual virtue. Eastern European Jews were deemed both uncouth and uneducated. The intellectual traditions of eastern European Jews were depicted as either irrational or hyperrational. For instance, while Geiger described Hasidism—an eastern European mystical and spiritual movement that began in the eighteenth century (discussed in greater detail in chapter 6)—as "ignorance and laziness of thought," Friedländer characterized it as "an incomprehensible mixture of cabalistic, mystical and neo-platonic ideas."[2] Referring more specifically to the eastern European approach to the Talmud, Graetz claimed that Polish Jews had a love of "twisting, distorting, ingenious quibbling, and a foregone antipathy to what did not lie within their field of vision."[3]

Mendelssohn and Cohen were far more sympathetic to the plight of eastern European Jews than were many of their contemporaries. But their defense of their eastern coreligionists boiled down to their insistence that eastern European Jews could actually be civilized if they were properly educated by German Jews.[4] The first step, according to Mendelssohn, was for Jews to stop speaking Yiddish and instead learn to speak German properly. Linking what he considered bad habits of speech to bad behavior, Mendelssohn worried that "this jargon [Yiddish] has contributed not a little to the immorality of the common man; and I expect a very good effect from the increasing use of the pure German idiom."[5] In order to help Jews learn German, Mendelssohn set out to translate the Bible into German. But the German of Mendelssohn's Bible translation was written with Hebrew characters so that Jews who did not know German could read it. Mendelssohn's translation effort was thus an attempt at reeducation. Also with reeducation in mind, in 1784, Mendelssohn's students founded the first modern Hebrew journal, *Hame'asef*.

Why were German Jews so worried about being associated with eastern European Jews? To begin with, the geographic proximity of Poland to Germany, and Berlin especially, was a cause for anxiety among German Jews. As we saw in Mendelssohn's case, Berlin was literally the gateway for Jews who were migrating from eastern to western Europe. In 1772, Prussia acquired Poland's western provinces, and in 1783 and 1785, Prussia also took Posen (Graetz's birthplace). German Jews were nervous that for all their hard work at improving themselves and acquiring German culture, they would nonetheless be associated with their unrefined brethren. German Jews also depicted their eastern European brethren in negative terms because they sought to deemphasize any national aspect of the Jewish religion. Portraying eastern European Jews negatively suggested that German Jews had more in common with their fellow German citizens than with other Jews. As we have seen in the last three chapters, the attempt to rid Judaism of any notion of collective politics was at the core of the invention of Jewish religion.

Two implicit assumptions inform the negative depiction of eastern European Jews by German Jews. First, the assumption was that European culture was the only form of culture. Second, in keeping with this first premise, the assumption was that Jews did not have a culture of their own that could or should be preserved. To repeat Katz's words, cited in chapter 2, "Jews had been emancipated; Jewishness was not."

It was against this mind-set that German-speaking Jews of the early twentieth century rebelled. In stark contrast to previous German Jewish thinkers, Scholem, Kafka, Buber, and Rosenzweig all believed that it was German Jewry that could learn from eastern European Jewry, and not the other way around. The rejection of the notions of rationality and political progress by Scholem, Kafka, Buber, and Rosenzweig went hand in hand with their shared affirmation of what they regarded as the authentic lived experience of eastern European Jews, who did not apologize for their Judaism or Jewishness by trying to make them conform to external cultural standards. As Rosenzweig summed it up: "From Mendelssohn on, our entire people has subjected itself to the torture of this embarrassing questioning; the Jewishness of every individual has squirmed on the needle point of a 'why.'"[6] Kafka's interest in Yiddish theater, Scholem's concern with Jewish mysticism, Rosenzweig's focus on what he saw as the organic character of Jewish communal life, and Buber's stress on Hasidism were all efforts to overcome the so-called success of the German Jewish paradigm that had left these intellectuals cultured and educated by German standards, but Jewishly ignorant and existentially lost. Let me turn now to Buber and Rosenzweig.

Away from Ideas and Back to Experience

Buber and Rosenzweig reject the question "Why be Jewish?" by emphasizing what each regards as the lived experience of Judaism. The problem, as Buber and Rosenzweig see it, is that Jews in general and German Jews in particular have lost access to a living Judaism. Rosenzweig's own biography was a case in point. He grew up in an assimilated but proud Jewish family. Having immersed himself first in medicine, then in history, and then in philosophy and theology, Rosenzweig wrote a major treatise on Hegel's philosophy of the state and was subsequently offered an academic position. Rosenzweig, however, became increasingly dissatisfied with philosophy and academia, and began to consider theological questions. Significantly, Judaism was not a live option for Rosenzweig. Like a good number of his contemporaries, he decided to convert to Christianity, although he chose to do so as a Jew, which meant that he had to first learn about Judaism. Rosenzweig immersed himself in the study of Judaism, and after what he described as a profound experience on Yom Kippur in 1913, he chose to remain a Jew.[7] During World War I, Rosenzweig served as a soldier for Germany, and in 1918, he found himself in German-occupied Poland. Encountering eastern European Jews for the first time, he was taken by what he saw as the vitality of their Jewish lives in comparison with the paucity of his own German Jewish experience. In 1921, Rosenzweig published his magnum opus, *The Star of Redemption*, which asked and attempted to answer the question of whether the experience of God's revelation is possible in the modern world. I will return to Rosenzweig's *Star* after considering Buber's thought briefly.

Unlike Rosenzweig (and Scholem and Kafka), Buber received a solid Jewish education in his youth. Buber's mother abandoned him and his father when Buber was a child, and Buber was subsequently brought up in the home of his paternal grandfather, Solomon Buber (1827–1906), who was a well-known midrash scholar. But despite his upbringing, Buber grew increasingly alienated from any form of living Judaism, and like so many of his contemporaries, became intellectually steeped in non-Jewish studies (which in Buber's case even included a deep interest in and knowledge of Chinese religion and poetry). Yet also like so many of his contemporaries, Buber became increasingly disillusioned with the promises of German culture and politics. As a university student, he initially became interested in not Judaism but rather Zionism, which he characterized as "the restoration of the connection, the renewed taking root in community."[8] It was from this desire for connection that Buber began studying Hebrew again, which eventually led to his translations of Hasidic tales.[9] Buber confessed that prior to his disillusionment with the promises of German culture and politics, he "regarded Hasidism not essentially otherwise than Graetz does: I looked down on it from the heights of a rational man." Yet when he was finally able to read the Hasidic stories in their original Hebrew, Buber experienced a profound conversion: "It was then that, overpowered in an instant, I experienced the Hasidic soul. The primally Jewish opened to me, flowering to newly conscious expression in the darkness of exile.... Judaism as religiousness, as 'piety,' as Hasidut, opened to me there. The image out of my childhood, the memory of the zaddik (righteous man) and his community, rose upward and illuminated me."[10]

What exactly did Buber's experience of the Hasidic soul consist of? As Buber describes it in a book aptly titled *Hasidism and Modern Man*:

> The Baal Shem [the founder of Hasidism in the eighteenth century] teaches that no encounter with a being or a thing in the course of our life lacks a hidden significance.... If we neglect this spiritual substance sent across our path, if we think only in terms of momentary purposes, without developing a genuine relationship to the beings and things in whose life we ought to take part, as they in ours, then we shall ourselves be debarred from true, fulfilled existence.[11]

Modern Jews and indeed modern people, argues Buber, have debarred themselves from "true, fulfilled existence" with their emphasis on rationality over and against lived experience. Hasidism is important for modern people (and not just modern Jews) because it accesses a level of reality that has been forgotten but can still be retrieved.

Buber's most famous philosophical articulation of this position is found in his now-classic book of 1922, *I and Thou*, in which he presents himself in the role of a physician engaged in curing the "sickness of our age."[12] Humanity is sick, Buber claims, because people have lost access to a fundamental dimension of human existence, or what he calls our "ontological orientation," which he describes in this text as the "I-Thou" relationship and later as dialogue. Simply put, Buber contrasts two modes of experiencing the world: the "I-It" relation and the I-Thou relations. The I-It relation is an instrumental one in which a person treats another as an object to be used. I-It relations are of course necessary, for example, in the realm of science, where we manipulate the world for our own benefit. But while he acknowledges that human life always exists within the realm of I-It relations, Buber maintains that I-Thou relations express the truest dimension of reality. An I-Thou relationship exists for its own sake. Equally as important, the I and the Thou of the I-Thou relation exist only in relation to each other, which means that they define each other. In an I-Thou relationship, therefore, it is not possible to separate the I from the Thou in any absolute sense.

Implicit in Buber's affirmation of the I-Thou relationship is a criticism of both rabbinic Judaism and modern liberal politics, which both define themselves in terms of the rule of law. For Buber, law by definition expresses an I-It relationship, because everyone is the same under the law, which means that each person is an object of the law. Buber maintains that the modern Jewish movements—reform, conservative (termed positive-historical in Germany), and orthodox—are far more alike than they are different. Each movement understands Judaism in I-It terms: ethics for the reform movement, history for the positive-historical movement, and law for the orthodox movement. For Buber, Hasidism uniquely manifests the I-Thou relation and provides the necessary corrective to other forms of Judaism. Hasidism, though, is not for Buber an aberration in the history of Judaism. Rather, Buber claims, the Hasidic focus on true, fulfilled existence recaptures the Bible's original message to humanity.

Buber makes this point perhaps most clearly by way of his interpretation of the Ten Commandments. While many people might think that the Ten Commandments epitomize law, Buber disagrees:

> The Ten Commandments are not part of an impersonal codex governing an association of men. They are uttered by an *I* and addressed to a *Thou*. They begin with the *I* and every one of them addresses the *Thou* in person. An *I* "commands" and a *Thou*—every *Thou* who hears this *Thou*—"is commanded." ... The word does not enforce its own hearing. Whoever does not wish to respond to the Thou addressed to him can apparently go about his business unimpeded. The He who speaks the word has power, ... [but] He has renounced this power of His sufficiently to let every individual actually decide for himself whether he wants to open or close his ears to the voice, and that means whether he wants to choose or reject the I of "I am."[13]

For Buber, God is neither a lawgiver nor an enforcer of law. The Ten Commandments represent, for him, the mark of a personal relationship that each individual has with the divine, in contrast to "an impersonal codex" (or code of law) that by definition treats all individuals the same under the law. In Buber's view, the Ten Commandments do not reflect God's power to enforce these laws but rather the relinquishment of power by God for the sake of human freedom to accept or reject God's presence. Religion properly understood, or what Buber calls "religiosity," is the dynamic relationship between God and the human being in which both partners freely relinquish their autonomous freedom and power in order to relate to one another. According to Buber, Hasidism embodies this shared encounter of God and the human being. The inner experience of relation, for Buber, as opposed to the external constructions of ideas and law, constitutes the human experience of divine revelation.

As with Buber, the focus of Rosenzweig's thought is the shared encounter between God and the human being. In 1921, as mentioned earlier, Rosenzweig published a highly complex philosophical treatise titled *The Star of Redemption*, which asked and tried to answer the question of whether the experience of God's revelation was possible for the modern person. *Star* explores the limitations of some of the dominant trends of German philosophy and in particular German idealism, including Hegel's and Cohen's philosophies. Rosenzweig argues that idealism cannot account for death, language, or art. These limitations, he suggests, open up the possibility, and only the possibility, of divine revelation—an experience that can and does wholly transform the individual human being.

Rosenzweig contends that without God's revelation, human beings can at best understand their lives only in terms of their own limited and ultimately transient viewpoint. He describes revelation as commanding love. Rosenzweig begins his discussion of revelation in the *Star* by quoting the Song of Songs and then commenting:

> Love is strong as death. Strong in the same way as death? But against whom does death display its strength? Against him whom it seizes. And love, of course, seizes both, the lover as well as the beloved, but the beloved otherwise than the lover. It originates in the lover. The beloved is seized, his love is already a response to being seized.[14]

For Rosenzweig, God's love seizes the human being and demands that the human being love God back. Rosenzweig's descriptions of revelation and love contain two objections to an overly rationalist approach to the divine. Rosenzweig begins with the question of death, because the possibility of death calls into question the idea that human thought can grasp all aspects of experience. After all, by definition I cannot know my own death. It is on the basis of this first objection to an overly optimistic picture of the possibilities of human knowledge that Rosenzweig makes his second claim: that revelation, far from being instituted in law or contained in human knowledge, is actually a matter of experience.

Although Rosenzweig is deeply influenced by Cohen's philosophy and even more so by the moral force of Cohen's personality, he nonetheless blatantly and forcefully rejects Cohen's definition of the Jewish religion as one of reason. It should be clear, for instance, that Rosenzweig's claims about death and love are very much arguments against Cohen. Rosenzweig's ambivalence toward Cohen is perhaps best captured in Rosenzweig's continual wordplays, in *Star* and beforehand, on the verbs *erzeugen*, which means "to generate," but also with the older meaning of "to beget"; *bezeugen*, which means "to testify or witness"; and *zeugen*, which means "to procreate." Cohen often uses the term "*erzeugen*" to suggest the generation of concepts on a logical model—that is, one concept generates or produces the next concept. We also saw in the last chapter that for Cohen, the sources of Judaism bear witness (bezeugen) to the truth of pure monotheism. As discussed, for Cohen, a non-Jew who has the right ideas about pure monotheism bears witness to Judaism better than a Jewish person with the wrong ideas. It is this overly intellectualized position that Rosenzweig seeks to reject by emphasizing the experience of being Jewish, and he frequently uses wordplays to differentiate his position from Cohen's. For example, in an essay from 1915, Rosenzweig writes: "The [Jewish] people do not generate their God, rather they receive and witness him."[15] Rosenzweig extends this wordplay in the third part of *Star*, claiming that the existence of Jews, and not the ideas of Judaism, bears witness (bezeugen) to God's revelation: "Bearing witness takes place in bearing [*Das Bezeugen geschieht im Erzeugen*]."[16]

Despite his rejection of Cohen's rationalist premises, however, Rosenzweig follows Cohen in holding that Jews bear witness (by nature of their existence and not by virtue of their philosophically correct ideas) to God's revelation, which is for all of humanity. For Rosenzweig, returning modern Jews to the possibility of authentic Jewish life thus has world-historical implications as well. So too, Buber considers the return to true, fulfilled existence a matter of not just Jewish but also universal significance. For all their criticism of the rationalist tradition of German Jewish thought that preceded them, Buber and Rosenzweig follow modern German Jewish thinkers—including Mendelssohn, Geiger, Hirsch, and Cohen—in proclaiming the modern world's need, and not just the modern Jewish need, for Jewish wisdom.

Translation and Jewish Education

The question for both Buber and Rosenzweig became, how can the modern Jew return to lived Jewish experience? After completing *Star*, Rosenzweig gave up any pretension to academic philosophy, concentrating instead on a number of adult Jewish education projects. In 1920, he founded the Freies Jüdisches Lehrhaus, which focused not on the professional training of rabbis and historians but rather on basic adult education. As Rosenzweig famously put it, "Books are not now the prime need of the day. But what we need more than ever, or at least as much as ever, are human beings—Jewish human beings."[17] The goal of the Lehrhaus was for modern Jews to encounter the Jewish textual tradition in its original languages and thereby give well-educated but nevertheless Jewishly ignorant Jews the tools with which to return to Jewish life. But even as they learned Hebrew, early twentieth-century German Jews, in Rosenzweig's view, continued to exist in an inescapable state of translation even or especially when they returned to Judaism. As he told Scholem, "In a sense we are ourselves guests at our own table, we ourselves, I myself. So long as we speak German (or even if we speak Hebrew, modern Hebrew, the Hebrew of '1921'!) we cannot avoid this detour that again and again leads us the hard way from what is alien back to our own."[18]

Rosenzweig's lifelong work in translation culminated in his joint translation of the Bible into German with Buber; the work began in 1925 and was finished by Buber in Jerusalem in 1961. In the first section of this chapter, I mentioned Mendelssohn's attempt at translating the Bible into German. Recall that one of Mendelssohn's purposes in this translation was to teach German Jews proper German. Mendelssohn's starting point was that many Jews of his time were familiar with the Hebrew of the Bible. Retaining the Hebrew alphabet, Mendelssohn translated Hebrew into German, thereby allowing his modern Jewish readers to learn German. Almost 150 years later, Buber and Rosenzweig translated the Bible into German in order to urge its readers to learn Hebrew. Whereas Mendelssohn's method of translation was aimed at using familiarity with the Bible to make German familiar, Buber and Rosenzweig's method consisted in utilizing familiarity with German to make the Bible unfamiliar.

Here it is helpful to turn briefly to Schleiermacher once again. An expert translator himself, Schleiermacher theorized not only about religion but also about the process and meaning of translation. As he observed, "Either the translator leaves the author in peace, as much as possible, and moves the reader towards him; or he leaves the reader in peace as much as possible, and moves the author towards him."[19] Mendelssohn chose the latter while Buber and Rosenzweig picked the former. In perhaps an intensification of Schleiermacher's description of translation as leaving the author in peace, Buber and Rosenzweig demanded that the strangeness of their translation awaken German readers from their slumber to encounter the Bible's alien and commanding voice. Buber and Rosenzweig's translation of the Bible stood apart from previous German Jewish efforts at translation in their attempt to force the German language to express the concepts and connotations contained in the sounds of the Hebrew original. Drawing on both German philosophical and Jewish traditional resources, they insisted that the Bible was oral poetry, and that a translation must conform to its basic breathing units. Despite the different grammatical structures of Hebrew and German, Buber and Rosenzweig also resolved to reproduce in German the underlying themes signaled by the repetition of words in Hebrew. For Buber and Rosenzweig, the literal acts of translation and reading a translation of the Bible must reorient and indeed disorient the modern person. As Rosenzweig remarked, "If somewhere it [the Bible] has become a familiar, customary possession, it must again and anew, as a foreign and unfamiliar sound, stir up the complacent satedness of its alleged possessor from outside.... The Bible is written for the sake of the reader who has been denied it."[20]

As we have seen, Buber and Rosenzweig focus on the Bible and revelation, and not on the Jewish religion per se. They in fact both reject the category of religion. For Buber, religion refers to institutions and dogma, both of which correspond to the I-It relation. In contrast to religion, Buber affirms religiosity, which constitutes the I-Thou relation. "Religion means preservation; religiosity means renewal," he notes.[21] Where religion ossifies, religiosity continually transforms. This means, for Buber, that while God reveals God's self to the human being, God does not reveal particular laws. As Buber puts it in *I and Thou*, "Man receives and what he receives is not a content, but a presence, a presence as a strength ... the eternal voice sounds and nothing more."[22] Rosenzweig, like Buber, rejects the category of religion: "God plainly did not create religion, but rather the world." Just as Buber does, Rosenzweig views religion as ossification, and sharply contrasts the difference between religion and revelation: "God has to reveal himself; he has to establish his own religion (which is merely anti-religion) against the *religionitis* of man."[23] For both Buber and Rosenzweig, the relationship between the human being and God is fluid and not fixed. The flexibility of this relation is what allows revelation to transform the human being. Buber and Rosenzweig both insist that religion must be rejected so that God's revelation may again live in the lives of human beings.

ZIONISM AND LAW

For all their similarities, differences remain between Buber and Rosenzweig, especially concerning their respective views of Jewish law and Zionism. We will see in the conclusion of this chapter that these differences also have a bearing on how we might evaluate their respective rejections of the category of Jewish religion. Let me begin with the question of the authority of Jewish law. As we saw above, Buber rejects the ultimate authority of Jewish law, maintaining that law by definition befits not I-Thou relations but instead only I-It ones. For Buber, "Man, he alone, speaks," and while God reveals God's self to the human being, Buber asserts that God does not reveal particular laws.[24] Rosenzweig, in contrast to Buber, affirms the continued authority of Jewish law. Why?

Rosenzweig agrees with Buber that the human being must interpret divine command, and that God's law is always mediated through the language shared between the human being and God. But, Rosenzweig insists, the human being speaks only because God has spoken to humanity already. Rosenzweig states the complex relation between the human and the divine in a letter of July 1924 to Buber:

> For me, too, God is not a Law-giver. But he commands. It is only by the manner of his observance that man in his inertia changes the commandments into Law, a legal system with paragraphs, without the realization that "I am the Lord," without "fear and trembling," without the awareness that the man stands under God's commandment. Could this, then, be the difference between us?[25]

He distinguishes between an understanding of law as a set of particular laws (*Gesetz*) and God's commandment (*Gebot*), which obliges the human being to respond to God. Rosenzweig agrees with Buber that law as Gesetz can eclipse the living relationship between the human being and God. Yet against Buber, Rosenzweig avers that the obligation to respond to God's commandment is the central feature of revelation. In contrast, as we saw in his discussion of the Ten Commandments, Buber maintains that God allows "every individual actually [to] decide for himself whether he wants to open or close his ears to the voice, and that means whether he wants to choose or reject the I of 'I am.'"

Buber's and Rosenzweig's different views of divine authority extend to their different attitudes toward Zionism. In chapter 8, I will consider the differences between political and cultural Zionism in some detail, but for the purposes of this chapter, I need but note Buber's belief that the diaspora holds no future for the regeneration of the Jewish people; he therefore supports the Jewish return to Palestine. Rosenzweig, in contrast, sees himself as a diaspora Jew and affirms the exilic character of Jewish existence. The Jew, he writes, "never lose[s] the untrammeled freedom of a wanderer who is more faithful a knight to his country when he roams abroad, craving adventure and yearning for the home (*Heimat*) he has left behind, than when he is at home (*zuhause*)."[26] Rosenzweig rejects Zionism because he considers homelessness an intrinsic part of Jewish life.

Why do Buber and Rosenzweig differ on Zionism? Like all the German Jewish thinkers I have considered, both Buber and Rosenzweig define Judaism as distinct in kind from the politics of the modern nation-state. The difference between their views of Zionism therefore does not hinge on the question of whether or not the true meaning of Jewish existence is realized in a sovereign state. Both reject the political Zionist notion that Jewish life can be fulfilled only within a sovereign Jewish state. Their divergent perspectives on Zionism are perhaps best understood in connection with their respective conceptions of divine authority. Buber, as we have seen, places the human being's choices at the center of his thought;

rather than demanding particular things from people, God allows them to decide for themselves how they ought to live. In this sense, Buber's Zionism coheres with the basic Zionist view that it is time for Jews to take their fate into their own hands. In contrast to Buber, Rosenzweig believes that the Jewish people must always follow God's lead. This means that until the Messiah comes, the Jewish people will remain in exile.

Whereas Buber affirms Zionism because he embraces the active creation of Jewish life, Rosenzweig rejects Zionism because he believes that the Jewish people are not masters of their own destiny. Rosenzweig's view of Jewish passivity finds a corollary in Cohen's thought. Recall Cohen's claim that "as Israel suffers, according to the prophet, for the pagan worshipers, so Israel to this very day suffers vicariously for the faults and wrongs which still hinder the realization of monotheism." Rosenzweig reiterates this theme almost literally: "Israel intercedes with him [God] in behalf of the sinning peoples of the world and he afflicts Israel with disease so that those other peoples may be healed. Both stand before God: Israel, his servant, and the kings of the peoples; ... so inextricably twined that human hands cannot untangle them."[27] Rosenzweig's avowal of Judaism's diasporic nature is rooted in his insistence that Judaism is not a religion but rather the embodiment of God's revelation. Rosenzweig maintains that the Jewish community's homelessness reminds the nations of the world of God's revelation. Yet strikingly, Buber's interest in Zionism also follows from his resistance to the idea of religion. Only the Jewish return to Palestine and the renaissance of Jewish national consciousness can, for Buber, renew Jewish religiosity.

Conclusion

We have seen in this chapter that both Buber and Rosenzweig attempt to reject the tradition of German Jewish thought that precedes them, rebuffing three central tenets: that Judaism is a religion, that it is based in reason, and that it is most conducive to German culture. Buber and Rosenzweig affirm revelation as opposed to religion, elevate experience and not reason, and pay tribute to forms of eastern European Jewish life in contrast to German Judaism. Yet we have also seen theological and political differences in their philosophies. By way of conclusion, let me explore how an appreciation of these differences might contribute to our understanding of how Judaism became a religion.

Despite their shared resistance to the idea that Judaism is a religion, neither Buber nor Rosenzweig in the end successfully overcomes this categorization. Rosenzweig in fact criticizes Buber for not being able to overcome the category of religion, notwithstanding his efforts to the

contrary. Anticipating his later critique of Buber's view of law, Rosenzweig writes to Buber: "In the I-It, you give the I-Thou a cripple for an
antagonist. The fact that this cripple governs the modern world does not
make it less a cripple." Reversing Buber's distinction between religion and
religiosity in which the latter becomes the former by way of the ossification of law, Rosenzweig suggests to Buber that *without law*, revelation
can only be or become religion:

> What is to become of I and Thou if they will have to swallow up the
> entire world and Creator as well? *Religion? I am afraid so—and I
> shudder at the word whenever I hear it.* For my and your sake, there
> has to be something else in this world besides—me and you![28]

In this letter, Rosenzweig seems to have in mind something like Schleiermacher's definition of religion as feeling. He is suggesting that Buber's
disparaging of the I-It world amounts to portioning off one aspect of
human experience, the I-Thou relation, at the expense of everything and
indeed everyone else. This divvying up of human life is exactly what
Schleiermacher attempted to do when he separated what he called religion from other dimensions of human life in order to save religion from
criticism, whether philosophical, moral, or political.

But Buber could similarly charge that Rosenzweig, in spite of his protestations to the contrary, is also unable to overcome the idea that Judaism
is a religion. It is true that perhaps more than any other German Jewish
thinker, Rosenzweig maintains that Judaism pertains not to one dimension of human experience but instead to the whole human being. As he
puts it, "If he [the German Jew] has prepared himself quite simply to have
everything that happens to him, inwardly and outwardly, happen to him
in a Jewish way—his vocation, his nationality, his marriage, and even, if
that has to be, his Juda 'ism'—then he may be certain that with the simple
assumption of that infinite 'pledge' he will become in reality 'wholly Jew'
(*ganz Jude*)."[29] Yet while Rosenzweig rejects his German Jewish predecessors' confining of Judaism to the private realm, he nevertheless remains
unable to consider the ways in which Judaism *as Judaism* or Jews *as
Jews* might have an impact on political life. Rather than asserting that
Jewish wholeness requires a particularly Jewish involvement in politics
(whatever that might mean), Rosenzweig in fact insists far more than his
predecessors had that Judaism qua Judaism is completely separate from
politics. As Rosenzweig explains it to his friend Eugen Rosenstock: "Is
not part of the price that the Synagogue must pay for the blessing ... of
being already in the Father's presence, that she must wear the bandages of
unconsciousness over her eyes?"[30] As Rosenzweig argues at length in part
III of *Star*, the bandages of unconsciousness blind the Jew especially to
politics. Rosenzweig's understanding of Judaism ends up fitting a liberal

Protestant description of religion because he claims that Judaism maintains its own sphere by removing itself from the political life of the world around it. Like Mendelssohn, Rosenzweig finds himself in the position of describing and defending Judaism and particularly Jewish law as, to use Mendelssohn's terms, a living script encompassing and guiding the whole of life for individual Jews along with the Jewish community. Yet also like Mendelssohn, Rosenzweig simultaneously feels compelled to limit Judaism's living script when it comes to modern political life.

German Jewish thought thus ends where it begins: with the tension between affirming the communal, and indeed public, character of Jewish life, law, and experience, while at the same time denying that this public character is in any way in conflict with the public character of the modern nation-state. From Mendelssohn to Rosenzweig, German Jewish thinkers argue that Judaism is not a religion like Protestantism because Judaism is a religion of law. Yet these same thinkers also describe Judaism, often despite themselves, precisely as a religion in a Protestant sense because they also contend that Judaism is a realm of life entirely different in kind from, and therefore entirely compatible with, the modern nation-state. In the next chapter, I turn to modern Jewish thought after the Holocaust in which precisely this compatibility is called into question. Some strands of post-Holocaust Jewish thought, as we will nonetheless see, refigure while still embracing the modern idea that Judaism is a religion.

Suggested Readings

Buber

For the relationship between Buber, Emil Fackenheim, and Levinas, see suggested readings for chapter 5.

Horwitz, Rivka. *Buber's Way to I and Thou: An Historical Analysis and the First Publication of Martin Buber's Lectures "Religion als Gegenwart."* Heidelberg: Lambert Schneider, 1978.

Horwitz explores the origins and development of Buber's *I and Thou*, emphasizing the importance of Rosenzweig's thought to the composition of this text.

Kepnes, Steven. *The Text as Thou: Martin Buber's Dialogical Hermeneutics and Narrative Theology.* Bloomington: Indiana University Press, 1992.

Bringing Buber into conversation with a diverse array of contemporary thinkers, this text suggests that Buber's views on narrative provide "privileged access" to his dialogic philosophy and theology.

Mendes-Flohr, Paul. *From Mysticism to Dialogue: Martin Buber's Transformation of German Social Thought.* Detroit: Wayne State University Press, 1989.

Underscoring the significance of German sociology to the development of Buber's thought, this monograph argues that Buber's early writings are concerned with the decline and rejuvenation of our aesthetic as well as spiritual sensibilities, but that a focus on society and human relations emerges after World War I.

Schlipp, Paul Arthur, and Maurice Freedman, eds. *The Philosophy of Martin Buber*. La Salle, IL: Open Court, 1967.
The essays in this volume explore issues ranging from Buber's philosophy of history to his views on the nature of knowledge.

Silberstein, Laurence J. *Martin Buber's Social and Religious Thought: Alienation and the Quest for Meaning*. New York: New York University Press, 1989.
Looking at issues ranging from Buber's intellectual context to his views on the nature of Judaism, Silberstein suggests that we should read Buber as a social thinker who is concerned with the nature of human community, an "edifying" philosopher who seeks liberation from convention, and a "revisionist" reimagining our understanding of Judaism.

Urban, Martina. *Aesthetics of Renewal: Martin Buber's Early Representation of Hasidism as Kulturkritik*. Chicago: University of Chicago Press, 2008.
Urban argues that Hasidism allowed Buber to articulate a model for the Jewish consciousness envisioned by cultural Zionism, and to develop a cultural critique that involved the creation of a Jewish modernism.

Historical Context

Aschheim, Steven E. *Brothers and Strangers: The East European Jew in German and German Jewish Consciousness, 1800–1923*. Madison: University of Wisconsin Press, 1982.
Aschheim explores German and German Jewish discourse surrounding eastern European Jews, suggesting that conceptions of this group—whether assessed positively or negatively—served to provide images of Jewish authenticity.

Barkai, Avraham, and Paul Mendes-Flohr. *German-Jewish History in Modern Times, Volume 4: Renewal and Destruction, 1918–1945*. Ed. Michael A. Meyer with Michael Brenner. New York: Columbia University Press, 1998.
The essays in this volume provide a comprehensive overview of German Jewish history between 1918 and 1945 as well as an account of the German Jewish diaspora.

Biemann, Asher D. *Inventing New Beginnings: On the Idea of Renaissance in Modern Judaism*. Stanford, CA: Stanford University Press, 2009.
Focusing on "renaissance" among German Jews between 1890 and 1938, Biemann highlights the links between developments among Jewish intellectuals and broader classical and humanistic traditions, proposing that we should think of renaissance as more than a simple return to the past— that it involves the creation of a past that is different from the present and is thus understood as an object to be recovered.

Brenner, Michael. *The Renaissance of Jewish Culture in Weimar Germany*. New Haven, CT: Yale University Press, 1996.
Brenner examines the rise of a distinctive German Jewish culture between 1918 and 1933, arguing that this phenomenon involved neither a complete return to nor radical break from the preexisting patterns of Jewish life. More specifically, he takes the process through which this culture emerged to involve three trends central to German society: a quest for community, the synthesis of knowledge, and a search for authenticity.

Kaplan, Marion. *The Making of the Jewish Middle Class: Women, Family, and Identity in Imperial Germany.* New York: Oxford University Press, 1994.

Kaplan studies the contribution of Jewish women to the emergence of a distinctive German Jewish bourgeoisie, considering the roles of Jewish women in a variety of settings—for example, in the household, community, and university as well as in employment outside the home.

Lowenstein, Steven M., Paul Mendes-Flohr, Peter Pulzer, and Monika Richarz. *German-Jewish History in Modern Times, Volume 3: Integration in Dispute, 1871–1918.* Ed. Michael A. Meyer with Michael Brenner. New York: Columbia University Press, 1997.

The essays in this volume supply a comprehensive overview of German Jewish history between 1871 and 1918.

Mendes-Flohr, Paul. *German Jews: A Dual Identity.* New Haven, CT: Yale University Press, 1999.

Exploring the ways in which German Jewry negotiated its dual affiliation with German culture and the Jewish tradition, Mendes-Flohr suggests that a German Jewish "symbiosis" existed within the minds of many Jews, regardless of whether an actual dialogue occurred between Jewish and non-Jewish Germans.

Mosse, George L. *German Jews beyond Judaism.* Bloomington: Indiana University Press, 1985.

Focusing on the first half of the twentieth century, Mosse analyzes the history and nature of the widely discussed "German Jewish dialogue." Considering factors such as Jewish participation in popular culture and left-wing politics, he seeks to show that this dialogue was initially grounded in ideals central to German humanism, but that cultured Jews found themselves increasingly marginalized even before the rise of Nazism.

Rosenzweig

For the relationship between Rosenzweig, Fackenheim, and Levinas, see suggested readings for chapter 5.

Batnitzky, Leora. *Idolatry and Representation: The Philosophy of Franz Rosenzweig Reconsidered.* Princeton, NJ: Princeton University Press, 2000.

Presenting Rosenzweig as a "hermeneutical" thinker who explores the possibility of religious authority in the modern world, Batnitzky addresses issues such as Rosenzweig's relationship with the German Jewish tradition, affinities with contemporary religious thinkers, and reflections on politics, art, and the category of religion.

Gordon, Peter Eli. "Rosenzweig Redux: The Reception of German-Jewish Thought." *Jewish Social Studies* 8, no. 1 (2001): 1–57.

Gordon provides an overview of the history of scholarship on Rosenzweig, seeking to illuminate the reasons behind the ongoing appeal of this German Jewish thinker.

———. *Rosenzweig and Heidegger: Between Judaism and German Philosophy.* Berkeley: University of California Press, 2003.

Gordon argues that we best understand Rosenzweig when we place him in his German intellectual context, and that Rosenzweig and Martin Heidegger should both be read as belonging to "Weimar philosophical modernism"—to a mode of philosophy that calls for both a return to a primordial truth and a revolutionary break with tradition.

Mendes-Flohr, Paul, ed. *The Philosophy of Franz Rosenzweig*. Hanover, NH: University Press of New England, 1988.

The essays in this volume examine issues ranging from Rosenzweig's philosophical context to his views on the nature of history.

Mosès, Stéphane. *System and Revelation: The Philosophy of Franz Rosenzweig*. Trans. Catherine Tihanyi. Detroit: Wayne State University Press, 1992.

Mosès seeks to provide a detailed commentary on and reconstruct the philosophy that emerges from Rosenzweig's *Star of Redemption*. Looking at an array of issues such as the *Star*'s philosophical origins and scholarly reception, Mosès argues that Rosenzweig's text describes human existence as open to the experience of transcendence.

Chapter 5

JEWISH RELIGION AFTER THE HOLOCAUST

IN THE LAST FOUR CHAPTERS, I have explored different but complementary arguments that Judaism is best defined as a religion. Defining Judaism as a religion, as these chapters have shown, implicitly supports the idea that Judaism in no way interferes with and may even complement the modern nation-state. The notion of religion thereby reinforces the idea of the modern nation-state, and vice versa. While the thinkers that I have considered in these last chapters differ in important ways, they all basically agree that political modernity, which allows Jews to become citizens of the modern nation-state, is good for the Jews as well as for everyone. For this reason, the claim that Judaism is a religion implies a certain faith in the modern nation-state and the modern world.

In the aftermath of the Holocaust, a number of Jewish thinkers reevaluate this faith in the promises of modernity and particularly those of the modern nation-state. After all, the granting of full political rights to Jews in Europe culminated not in new political societies based in reason as well as committed to freedom and equality but instead in the systematic extermination of six million Jews. I will consider in this chapter how the Holocaust may alter arguments about the nature of Judaism and modernity by examining two seemingly unrelated streams of thought: religious Zionism, and late twentieth-century French philosophy. What unites these otherwise-disparate strands of thought is the questioning and rejection of the intrinsic value of modern political institutions.

Despite their profound differences, religious Zionists, such as Emil Fackenheim (1916–2003) and Zvi Yehudah Kook (1891–1982), and a number of French Jewish philosophers, such as Emmanuel Levinas (1906–96), share the claim that Judaism is precisely that which transcends mundane politics in order to bring about the possibility of a redemptive world order that stands beyond the modern nation-state. Notwithstanding this shared premise, however, religious Zionists since Fackenheim and Kook along with Jewish thought inspired by Levinas often arrive at radically opposing political conclusions. For religious Zionists, the land of Israel, the state of Israel, and the Jewish people are literally part of a final redemption. In contrast, for followers of Levinas, the state of Israel and the

Jewish people are universal models or representatives of ethics. This deep divide between schools of thought nevertheless masks a profound similarity. Both of these schools respond to the Nazi genocide and what they claim are the false promises of modernity by rejecting the modern liberal distinction between religion and politics. In turn, both schools of thought attempt to reinsert religion into politics. In exploring the ideas of these thinkers, we will see that after the Holocaust, the contention that Jewish religion does not interfere with the state gives way to the assertion that Jewish religion, and only Jewish religion, can give the state its meaning.

THE CHALLENGE OF POST-HOLOCAUST JEWISH THOUGHT

Before turning to post-Holocaust Jewish thought, let us recall that Jewish disillusionment with modernity's promises began before the Holocaust. As discussed in chapter 4, Buber and Rosenzweig reject what they take to be an overly apologetic affirmation of Jewish emancipation and the promises of modernity. Yet as we saw, by positing an absolute split between Judaism and the modern nation-state, they remain, perhaps despite their intentions to the contrary, within the framework set in motion by Mendelssohn, who invented the idea that Judaism is a religion in order to make room for the emergence of the modern nation-state. In spite of their profound differences from one another, Fackenheim, Kook, and Levinas could each be said to be Buber's and especially Rosenzweig's intellectual heirs in extending disillusionment with modernity to questioning the legitimacy of the modern nation-state itself. Let me begin first with Fackenheim, who, like Levinas, self-consciously describes himself as a disciple of Rosenzweig.

Fackenheim was born in Halle, Germany. He was a student of philosophy and close to finishing his training to become a reform rabbi when, in November 1938, the Nazis staged a ferocious riot against the Jews. Fackenheim was arrested and taken to Sachsenhausen, a concentration camp, and held for several months. After he was finally released on the condition that he leave Germany, he traveled to Sweden, where he was quickly deported to Canada as an enemy alien. Fackenheim was imprisoned for a year and a half in Canada before gaining asylum. Eventually, he became a professor of philosophy at the University of Toronto and subsequently at the Hebrew University of Jerusalem. The philosophical, theological, and political challenges of the Holocaust are the central themes of Fackenheim's prolific work.

According to Fackenheim, the Holocaust is at once incomprehensible and unique. In his words, "The more the psychologist, historian or 'psychohistorian' succeeds in explaining the event[s] or action[s] [of the

Holocaust], the more nakedly he comes to confront its ultimate inexplicability."[1] No matter how much information we may gather about the mechanics of the Holocaust, human reason can neither grasp the depths of Nazi depravity nor the simple fact that as opposed to prior persecution and violence directed toward the Jews, the Nazis tried to extinguish the Jewish people not for what they believed or did but rather simply for who they were. It is human reason's recognition of this incomprehensibility that accounts, in Fackenheim's view, for the Holocaust's uniqueness.

How, then, should a Jew respond to the Holocaust? For Fackenheim, the burden of answering this question is almost unbearable.

> How dare a Jewish parent crush his child's innocence with the knowledge that his uncle or grandfather was denied life because of his Jewishness? And how dare he not burden him with this knowledge? The conflict is inescapable.[2]

Fackenheim maintains that the weight of this challenge is equal for both religious and secular Jews. For the former, the question is, Why did God fail to save the Jewish people? The question for the latter is, How could human beings do this to each other? While Fackenheim does not—and indeed claims by definition that he cannot—provide answers to these questions, he still draws a lesson from the Holocaust's incomprehensibility: "The Voice of Auschwitz commands Jews not to go mad. It commands them to accept their singled out condition, face up to its contradictions, and endure them."[3] After the Holocaust, a Jew can only endure, and in fact is *commanded* to do so, in the face of such evil and despair. Fackenheim formulates his response to the Holocaust in terms of Jewish law. Judaism traditionally has 613 commandments; yet as Fackenheim argues, after the Holocaust there is a 614th commandment: Jews are forbidden to give Hitler a posthumous victory, which means that Jews must resist Hitler by remaining Jews.[4]

For Fackenheim, the commandment to resist Auschwitz's "celebration of degradation and death" extends to the establishment and preservation of the state of Israel: "It is necessary not only to perceive a bond between the two events [the Holocaust and the establishment of Israel] but also to act as to make it unbreakable."[5] As we saw above, according to Fackenheim the Holocaust challenges religious and secular Jews alike. So too, he suggests, when it comes to the Israeli state, it is not possible to separate religious and secular meanings from practical demands. Especially after Israel's victory in the Six-Day War in 1967, in which Israel captured the biblical lands of Judea and Samaria (also known as the West Bank), and reunited the city of Jerusalem, a distinction between the religious and secular realms is untenable. In Fackenheim's words, "The reborn Jerusalem is overcoming the religious-secular split ... with world-historical consequences as yet unknown." All of Israel's military victories, Fackenheim contends, constitute "a will in touch with an absolute dimension ... and even those acting on this may well be astonished by its accomplishments."[6]

With this brief overview of Fackenheim's philosophy, I will now consider how it fits into the story of the invention of the idea of Jewish religion. Fackenheim follows Rosenzweig in defining Judaism as commanding revelation. Yet Fackenheim both intensifies and goes far beyond Rosenzweig's emphases on the paucity of reason and the need to respond to God's uncompromising command. Whereas before the Holocaust Rosenzweig maintains that reason's limits make room for the experience of revelation, which is God's commanding voice, after the Holocaust Fackenheim contends that reason's bankruptcy in light of the Holocaust brings with it the commanding voice of Auschwitz, which demands that secular and religious Jews alike persist in being Jews. As we saw in chapter 4, Rosenzweig's conception of revelation is tied to his rejection of Zionism. For Rosenzweig, God commands, which means that God, and not the human being, is sovereign. Rosenzweig believes that Jewish homelessness constitutes Jewish experience until God decides otherwise. After the Holocaust, Fackenheim reverses Rosenzweig's position on Zionism, holding that the state of Israel "affirms [life] by an act of faith which defies comprehension."[7]

Where does this leave Jewish religion? The central thesis of this book has been that the idea of Jewish religion cannot be understood apart from the idea and historical fact of the modern nation-state, or from the notion that religion and politics comprise, and ought to do so, separate realms of human life. Fackenheim's philosophy refigures this arrangement. For Fackenheim, the Holocaust discredits the false promises of secular modernity, including the notion that Jews can be integrated as full citizens in a modern nation-state as well as any traditional theological explanation of Jewish suffering. But at the same time, the Holocaust's aftermath also demands that secular and religious Jews unite in resisting any future threat to the existence of the Jewish people. The state of Israel is a modern nation-state, but as Fackenheim argues, it only gains its reality and meaning through its theological mission. If in the modern conception, the state makes room for Jewish religion and thereby allows Jewish religion the right to exist, Fackenheim's post-Holocaust thought suggests that Jewish religion grants and indeed commands the state of Israel not only to exist but also to endure.

We have seen that Fackenheim assigns religious meaning to the state of Israel. He even goes so far as to claim that the Jewish people may find salvation in this state. Fackenheim denies that Israel, as a state, has messianic significance, though. Here he sharply distinguishes between what he calls "the experience of salvation" and "the Messianic event." The experience of salvation, writes Fackenheim, is "the sudden removal of a radical threat—a removal so astonishing that the more it is explained the deeper the astonishment becomes."[8] Fackenheim likens the establishment of Israel to the parting of the Red Sea after the Israelites' exodus from Egypt. Both are miraculous, onetime occurrences that alleviate a particular threat—in the case of the Red Sea, the threat of the approaching Egyptian army; in the case of Israel, the threat of not resisting the Holocaust and giving Hitler a posthumous victory. But in contrast to both these events, Fackenheim avers, the messianic event "will remove from humanity as a whole the evils of poverty and injustice, hatred, and war."[9] The state itself, then, cannot be thought of in messianic terms. I now turn to arguments that, contra Fackenheim, the establishment of the state of Israel is a messianic event of world-redemptive proportions.

MESSIANISM AND ZIONISM BEFORE AND AFTER THE HOLOCAUST

Zionism first emerged in the nineteenth century as a secular movement that self-consciously saw itself as a break with the Jewish past (this issue is discussed in detail in chapter 8). At its most basic level, Zionism rejected the notion that Jews should keep waiting for God to bring an end to Jewish suffering and exile from the land of Israel. In response to the continued persecution of Jews in the diaspora, political Zionists called for Jewish political autonomy, which meant that Jews had to establish a state of their own and govern themselves. Prior to the Holocaust, most traditionalist Jews rejected Zionism exactly for this reason: from a traditional Jewish perspective, the Jewish people will be gathered out of exile and will return to the land of Israel in the messianic future, and only God will decide when the Messiah comes.

Still, a small minority of religious Jews did embrace the Zionist movement, not in an effort to hasten the Messiah's coming, but rather as a political response to Jewish persecution and suffering. Rabbi Isaac Reines (1839–1915), who in 1902 founded the religious Zionist party, Mizrahi, clearly stated that he embraced Zionism as a political necessity, but that political Zionism needed to be completely separate from God's redemption of the world. As he put it:

> Anyone who thinks the Zionist idea is somehow associated with future redemption and the coming of the Messiah and who therefore regards it as undermining our holy faith is clearly in error.... The entire point of this idea is merely the improvement of the condition of our wretched brethren.... And if some preachers, while speaking of Zion, also mention redemption and the coming of the Messiah and

thus let the abominable thought enter people's minds that this idea encroaches upon the territory of true redemption, only they themselves are to blame, for it is their own wrong opinion they express.[10]

By completely distinguishing Zionism and God's final redemption of the Jewish people, Reines was able to work pragmatically with secular Zionists, with whom he shared the goal of alleviating Jewish suffering.

If Reines insisted on an absolute distinction between Zionism and the messianic future, which lay only in God's hands, Rabbi Abraham Isaac Kook (1865–1935) sought a total synthesis between politics and theology. Kook was born in Latvia and received a traditional yeshiva education. In 1904, he immigrated to Palestine, and in 1924, the British, who controlled Palestine at the time, appointed him the chief rabbi of Palestine. When Kook arrived in Palestine, tensions were high between what was known as the Old Yishuv, the old settlement of religious Jews, and the New Yishuv, the new settlement of secular Zionists. Members of the Old Yishuv had come to the land of Israel because they sought to live in study and prayer in the holy land of the Jewish people; they did not seek to establish any kind of modern state. For the most part, Jewish communities outside the land of Israel financially supported the Old Yishuv. Members of the New Yishuv, in contrast, had come to settle the land in order to establish, they hoped, a Jewish state. They were antireligious and often socialists. The New Yishuv members did not study Torah or spend their time in prayer but rather sought to cultivate the land and develop new forms of economic productivity. Kook tries to unify the Old and New Yishuvs. For him, joining forces with secular Zionists was in no way a violation of traditional Judaism but rather a religious requirement.

For Kook, Zionism and the possible establishment of a state are concrete steps in the messianic process. Even if secular Zionists do not understand themselves this way, they are, according to Kook, on a messianic mission. Kook also believes that the traditionalists have misunderstood their own tradition. As he writes in 1920, "Nothing in our faith, either in its larger principles or in its details, negates the idea that we can begin to shake off the dust of exile by our own efforts, through natural, historical processes."[11] Thus, according to Kook, the Zionists and traditionalists are each partially right and partially wrong. The Zionists are right about the need to return to the land, but wrong in not understanding the messianic underpinnings of their mission. The traditionalists are right in their devotion to God, but wrong in not understanding that their narrow focus on study and prayer is a result of the Jewish experience of exile. What is needed, then, is a synthesis of Zionism and traditionalism, and this is what Kook attempts to provide, both practically and theoretically.

He views the Jewish relationship to the land of Israel in mystical and metaphysical terms. The ingathering of the Jewish people in the land of Israel will, he believes, usher in the Messiah. In particular, Kook sees the Jewish return to Jerusalem, as described in Zechariah 9:12, as initiating the messianic process. When I turn soon to Kook's son, Zvi Yehudah, we will see that the significance of Jerusalem would become decisive for religious Zionism after the Holocaust. Before doing that, however, I must also note the role of penitence and humiliation in the elder Kook's thought. According to Kook, the Jewish return to the land of Israel is an act of repentance: "Certainly the light of the Messiah, the deliverance of Israel, the rebirth of the people and the restoration of its land, language and literature—all stem from the source of penitence, and all lead out of the depths to the heights of penitence." Quoting Isaiah 25:8, "remove the humiliation of the people of God from all the earth," Kook counsels that part of the messianic process is profound anguish over the humiliations visited on the Jewish people throughout history as the result of their exile.[12] We will see that this emphasis on humiliation and anguish would also become decisive for religious Zionism after the Holocaust.

Kook died in 1935, and therefore did not live to witness the establishment of the state of Israel, or for that matter, the destruction and murder of European Jewry. Although he sees the devastation wrought by World War I, he nevertheless remains an optimist about the future of Judaism as well as of all humanity. Often using the metaphor of light, Kook believes that just as the light of individual Jews will spread to the Jewish nation, so too the light of the Jewish nation will spread to the world: "The light of penitence will be manifested first in Israel, and she will be the channel through which the life-giving force of the yearning for penitence will reach the whole world, to illuminate it and to raise its stature."[13] We have of course already encountered this idea in modern Jewish thought. Let us recall that Geiger claims that the Jewish people's genius (Geiger's phrase) is the moral vision resulting from the idea of pure monotheism. The Jews and Jewish religion are, as noted earlier, "a light unto the nations" (Isaiah 42). Yet for Geiger and the reformers, this description is part and parcel of an argument for defining Judaism as a religion that may complement but in no way interferes with the modern nation-state. This arrangement is not only what Kook rejects but also what he considers a humiliation for which the Jewish people need to repent. In his optimism and universalism, Kook's thought coheres with the modern Jewish thought that I have explored in the last four chapters, yet he turns the liberal understanding of the modern state inside out. He does so by transforming the idea that the state permits religion to exist so long as it does not interfere with the state into the notion that religion permits the state to exist. By way of this inversion, Kook lays the intellectual and theological ground for what would become messianic Zionism in the post-Holocaust Israeli state.

In his lifetime, Kook did not have a large following, and religious Zionism was not a significant political or religious movement. After the elder Kook's death, though, his son continued to disseminate his father's ideas, and following the Six-Day War in 1967, religious Zionism became a major force in Israeli political life. Why? In the weeks preceding the Six-Day War, when Arab armies began to gather on Israel's borders, most Israelis and increasingly many Jews in the United States believed that Israel's very existence was in question. This existential threat was likened to the possibility of a second Holocaust. Contrary to this fear and expectation, however, Israel's dramatic victory in just six days resulted in the reunification of Jerusalem along with the capture of the biblical lands of Judea and Samaria as well as the Gaza Strip (which was not part of biblical Israel). Having this deep fear of destruction followed so closely by a victory viewed as miraculous became a watershed moment for Israelis and many American Jews. Zvi Yehudah understood the reunification of Jersualem and Israel's capture of the biblical lands of Judea and Samaria in light of his father's vision of the beginning of the messianic era. It is in this context that religious Zionism as a mass movement was born.

For the younger Kook, the redemption of the land is intimately tied to the destruction of the Holocaust. We saw above that while the elder Kook emphasized the need for Jewish atonement for the exile, he still remained optimistic about what he regards as progress toward world redemption. The younger Kook's vision, on the other hand, is far more tragic and far less universal than his father's:

> The Jewish people has been brought here, severed from the depths of exile to come to the State of Israel. The blood of the six million represents a substantial excision for the body of the nation.... God's people had clung so determinedly to the impurity of foreign lands that, when the End Time arrived, they had to be cut away, with a great shedding of blood.... This cruel excision ... reveals our real life, the rebirth of the nation and the land, the rebirth of the Torah and all that is holy.... These historical, cosmological, divine facts must be seen as such. Seeing is more than Understanding; it is encounter, encounter with the Master of the Universe.[14]

Kook avoids ascribing blame to the Holocaust's victims. He does not maintain, as some of his ultraorthodox contemporaries do, that the Holocaust is punishment for the sins of assimilated Jewry. Rather, Kook's claim is subtler, suggesting that there is something redemptive about the shedding of blood in the Holocaust because it led to the creation of the Israeli state. What matters for Kook is, in his words, "the body of Israel," which as it did for his father, finds its corollary in the land of Israel. Both the Holocaust and the creation of the state are historical moments in the divine drama. They are, as Kook writes, at once "historical, cosmological, [and] divine facts."

For the younger Kook, the state of Israel is also a profoundly political fact. Let us recall the significance of Jerusalem for the elder Kook. Again, reading Zechariah 9:12, the Jewish return to Jerusalem would, for Kook, initiate the messianic process. For the younger Kook, the reunification of Jerusalem and capture of biblical lands has not only theoretical but also practical political implications. The younger Kook's thought, beginning in 1968, and later his own political leadership, in 1974, led to the establishment of the settler movement, also known as Gush Emunim (block of the faithful), whose self-appointed task is to settle Judea and Samaria.

Much has been written—and no doubt, more will be written—about the relationship between religious Zionism and the internal politics of the Israeli state. For my purposes here, however, I need but focus on the relationship between the state and religion in the religious Zionist worldview. As we saw in the case of the elder Kook, the establishment of the state would be, despite secular Zionists' claim to the contrary, a religious stepping-stone toward the final redemption. The state, then, for Kook the father, has a religious purpose. This is certainly the view of religious Zionists in the aftermath of the Six-Day War and into the early 1970s. But this relationship has become increasingly, if not irrevocably, strained since the late 1970s as the state of Israel agreed to trade land for peace, first in making peace with Egypt in 1977, and then with the Oslo Accords of 1993. In 1995 Yigal Amir, who drew some support from national religious parties, assassinated Israeli prime minister Yitzhak Rabin because of Rabin's support for Oslo. Amir claimed a rabbinic warrant for the murder: according to him, Rabin was actually the murderer because he was putting the security of the people and the land of Israel at risk. Citing Talmudic precedent, Amir described Rabin as a *rodef*, someone pursuing someone else with the intent to murder. According to rabbinic law, a bystander is obliged to kill such a person for the sake of saving the life of an innocent.

In 1995 Amir was, for the most part, regarded as an extremist even by the religious Right, but tensions between the state and religious Zionists have continued to mount in the aftermath of Rabin's assassination and the ultimate failure of the Oslo Accords. For instance, Israel's withdrawal from the Gaza Strip in 2005 was strongly opposed and was preceded by demonstrations of hundreds of thousands of Israelis, many of them religious Zionists. While most of these demonstrations were nonviolent, it is important to remember that for religious Zionists, Gaza never was part of biblical Israel. One enormous question that remains for any possibility of an Israeli-Palestinian peace agreement is what kind of violent struggle might take place should the state of Israel choose to withdraw from lands that constitute part of biblical Israel—that is, from the West Bank, or Judea and Samaria. It was these lands as well as the reunification of Jerusalem that spurred religious Zionism as a significant political movement within the framework of the Israeli state. Yet for religious Zionists, the possibility of trading Judea and Samaria for peace has become a question about the state's legitimacy itself. The elder Kook's claim that the secular state supports religious ends has morphed into the contemporary religious Zionist claim that the secular state is an impediment to religious ends and therefore must be rejected. Put another way, religious Zionists have not given up on the Jewish state; rather, they now question whether the state of Israel is in fact the Jewish state.

French Philosophy and Postliberalism

The gap between the political reality of the Jewish state and its ideal meaning is a feature of not only contemporary religious Zionism but also the philosophy of Levinas, a French phenomenologist. In many ways, Levinas's philosophy could not be more different than Kook's. The younger Kook emphasizes the particularity of the Jewish people and the physical land of Israel almost to the exclusion of any concern with universal values. Levinas, in contrast, claims that the uniqueness, indeed the election, of the Jewish people represents the uniqueness, or election, of each individual person who is defined by the most universal of ethical imperatives: to see each and every other person as an "orphan, widow, or stranger" in need, and to give of oneself to another accordingly. Perhaps even more basically, Kook and Levinas could not have been more different as individual people. Kook, after all, was in large part responsible for the late twentieth-century Jewish religious radicalism that has altered Middle Eastern politics for the foreseeable future. Levinas, on the other hand, was a French professor of philosophy who devoted his days to considering the Western philosophical tradition's relation to ethical responsibility. Yet for all their differences, aspects of Kook's and Levinas's thought are remarkably similar. After the Holocaust, both refigure the liberal understanding of the relation between state and religion. Kook and Levinas both transform the idea that the state justifies religion into the notion that religion justifies the state. I will look first to Levinas's broad philosophical concerns and then to how his arguments play out in relation to the state of Israel.

A Lithuanian Jew by birth, Levinas studied philosophy in Germany and then settled in France. During World War II, he served in the French army, and was captured by the Germans in 1940. Luckily for Levinas, captured Jewish soldiers were at the time held in prisoner-of-war camps along with other French soldiers, whereas later on Jewish soldiers were sent to concentration camps. Levinas lived out the war as a prisoner while his wife and daughter were hidden in a monastery; they all survived this period. After the war, Levinas devoted himself to adult Jewish education and eventually secured a university position teaching philosophy. He dedicated the rest of his life to asking and answering the philosophical question of whether the Holocaust makes ethics meaningless.

Unlike Fackenheim, however, Levinas does not view the Holocaust as unique. Instead, the Holocaust epitomizes the human capacity for evil. Yet Levinas contends that the possibility of murder and violence, and even the possibility of evil, does not refute but rather confirms the fact that human beings are fundamentally ethical creatures. Levinas's understanding of Judaism plays a decisive role in this argument. He contrasts Judaism as ethics with what he views as the amoral and therefore immoral philosophy of his teacher Martin Heidegger (1889–1976), whose sympathy (and work) for the Nazi party is a source of deep anguish for Levinas. Heidegger's philosophical concern is only with the question "What is?" (what Heidegger calls the question of being) and not with what Levinas regards as the more basic question, "What do I owe another person?" (what Levinas labels ethics). Levinas equates his view of ethics with Judaism, which he often calls "Hebrew," as opposed to the Western philosophical tradition culminating with Heidegger that he refers to as "Greek." After the Holocaust, Levinas suggests, philosophy needs Judaism to rescue it and show that we are not wrong to believe that human beings are moral creatures.

The form of this rescue is not a knockdown argument on the basis of reason (Levinas, following Heidegger, rejects this kind of philosophical method) but instead phenomenological descriptions of the nature of human existence. Despite their different conceptions of reason, Levinas comes close to Cohen in contending that the ultimate meaning of human existence, which both claim Judaism uniquely represents, is suffering innocently for the sake of others' sins. As Levinas puts it, "[Every individual uniquely] even bears responsibility for the persecuting by the persecutor."[15] For Levinas, as for Cohen, suffering innocently for others is not a valorization of suffering but instead a consequence of ethical responsibility.

There are more parallels between Levinas's claims and those of the modern Jewish thinkers I have previously explored. Levinas defines his post-Heideggerian, post-Holocaust philosophy by way of the terms "totality" and "infinity." Levinas's notion of totality is similar to Buber's conception of the I-It relationship as well as Soloveitchik's description of the first Adam. Totality, like Buber's I-It and Soloveitchik's first Adam, is defined by mastery and manipulation. Yet Levinas goes further than Buber and Soloveitchik in ascribing to totality a particular moral valence. Levinas equates what he calls totalizing ways of thinking (as epitomized by Heidegger's philosophy) with violence and murder. Despite this moral condemnation of totality, Levinas nonetheless insists that totality is not problematic in and of itself but only if we take it to be the ultimate meaning of human existence. Totality, Levinas maintains, is only made possible by the truer reality of what he refers to as infinity. Infinity is my particular responsibility for "the other," by which Levinas means my responsibility for each and every other person. Whereas Buber suggests that the I-Thou relation is one of mutuality, though, Levinas contends that while I am responsible for the other person, the other person has no responsibility for me.[16]

Let me return to Levinas's relation to Cohen. While I noted above their shared insistence on the ethical meaning of suffering innocently for the sins of others, the divergence between them is just as instructive. The difference between Cohen and Levinas lies in their respective evaluations of the modern nation-state. Cohen is committed to the modern nation-state, and the distinction between religion, on the one hand, and ethics and politics, on the other. The modern rule of law, for Cohen, creates the ethical foundation of politics because the law, by definition, makes everyone equal. In contrast, religion creates free individuality, which as we saw in chapter 3, means for Cohen a spirit of inwardness. In understanding religion in terms of the individual, Cohen adheres, as he proudly acknowledges, to the historical spirit of Protestantism (which as we also saw in chapter 3, Cohen claims is fundamentally Jewish). Religion in Cohen's view is a necessary complement to the universal structure of public law—that is, the state. According to Cohen, ethics and politics are incomplete without religion, but they are nonetheless goods in themselves. Levinas sharpens the dichotomy between ethics and politics, while also defining religion as ethics. Unlike Cohen, Levinas views individuals, not groups, as the only source of goodness and true universality in the world. Levinas's suspicion of public and communal life, along with his insistence that innocent suffering is the best proof we have that we are moral beings, marks his post-Holocaust thought, just as Cohen's faith in the liberal order of politics and the modern nation-state marks his pre-Holocaust thought.

Levinas rejects the philosophical foundations of political liberalism and the modern nation-state by attempting to refigure the trinity of the French Declaration of the Rights of Man: freedom, equality, and fraternity.[17] Levinas redescribes the concept of fraternity, arguing that fraternity is made possible not by equality but rather by a fundamental inequality.

As Levinas observes, "The equality of all is borne by my inequality, the surplus of my duties over my rights."[18] Levinas means by this that our duties are more fundamental than our rights. He views the establishment of the Israeli state as the model for a political order different than rights-based liberalism. Levinas calls the state of Israel "monotheistic politics," which is characterized by duties (what Levinas portrays as ethics) and not rights (what Levinas labels politics). In keeping with his vision of monotheistic politics, he actually denies what political Zionists see as the political significance of Israel—that is, political autonomy for the Jewish people. In Levinas's words: "What genuinely matters about the State of Israel is not that it fulfills an ancient promise, or heralds a new age of material security ... but that it finally offers the opportunity to carry out Judaism's social law."[19] Judaism's social law, for Levinas, is not a set of public precepts; it is the ethical response that I owe another person. This ethical response is the true meaning of Judaism as well as religion generally: "Justice as the *raison d'être* of the State, that is religion. It pre-supposes the high science of justice. The State of Israel will be religious because of the intelligence of its great books which it is not free to forget. It will be religious through the very action that establishes it as a State. It will be religious or it will not be at all."[20]

Especially after 1967, Levinas's use of theological imagery to describe the state of Israel intensifies. Levinas depicts the *theological* meaning of Zionism after the Six-Day War in the following terms:

> The Nazi persecution and, following the exterminations, the extraordinary fulfillment of the Zionist dreams of a State in which to live in peace is to live dangerously, gradually became history. The passion in which it was finished and this bold new beginning, in spite of conflicting signs affecting them, were felt, even yesterday, to be signs of the same notion of being chosen or damned—that is to say, of the same exceptional fate.[21]

Note the parallels to the younger Kook's post-1967 description of Israel's victory. Again, in Kook's words, "This cruel excision [of six million Jews] ... reveals our real life, the rebirth of the nation and the land, the rebirth of the Torah and all that is holy...." In an essay from 1968, Levinas accentuates his emphasis on holy martyrdom: "It is not because the Holy Land takes the form of a State that brings the Reign of the Messiah any closer, but because the men who inhabit it try to resist the temptation of politics; because this State proclaimed in the aftermath of Auschwitz, embraces the teaching of the prophets; because it produces abnegation and self-sacrifice."[22] Note that although Levinas denies any messianic significance to the state qua state, he still suggests that the resistance to the "temptation of politics" *does* bring the reign of the Messiah closer.

Like Kook, Levinas associates the Messiah with self-sacrifice. As Levinas states, abnegation and self-sacrifice are at the heart of his philosophy. Individuals do not just have responsibility for themselves but rather for all others, which means that responsibility is infinite. A political system based on the rule of law cannot bear the infinite responsibility at the heart of Levinas's conception of monotheistic politics. Indeed, for Levinas, our duties, even to our persecutors, are always greater than our rights to self-preservation. Just as the actual state of Israel increasingly does not correspond to what religious Zionists understand as the true Jewish state, so too Levinas makes it clear that the actual Israel, as a modern nation-state, does not correspond to what he calls monotheistic politics. The meaning of the existence of the Israeli state, in Levinas's view, does not concern home and security for the Jewish people but instead the risk that the Jewish people are willing to take in potentially martyring themselves for the sake of all others.

Levinas's concern is philosophical ethics, and the Kooks' concern is theology. We need to acknowledge this highly significant difference, while also recognizing the profound formal similarities between Levinas's philosophy and religious Zionism. After the Holocaust, Levinas and Kook reject the promise of modernity as expressed in the modern nation-state as well as the privatization of religion. Both replace the idea that the modern nation-state can tolerate religion with the notion that only Jewish religion, as a religion of *self-sacrifice*, can justify and give meaning to the modern state.

Conclusion

By way of summation as well as transition to part II, let me consider why Fackenheim, the Kooks, and Levinas belong in the first part of this book (Judaism as religion) as opposed to the second half (detaching Judaism from religion). Here a contrast between Cohen, Soloveitchik, and Leibowitz, on the one hand, and Fackenheim, the Kooks, and Levinas, on the other, is instructive. As I concluded in chapter 3, Cohen, Soloveitchik, and Leibowitz, despite their different ideological commitments as well as historical and political contexts, all affirm the idea that the modern nation-state does and ought to make room for Jewish religion. In contrast, we have seen in this chapter that Fackenheim, the Kooks, and Levinas transform this notion, contending instead that Jewish religion makes room for the modern state. While they do invert the relation between religion and the state, they do not change the terms of the conversation. That is, the Kooks and Levinas still view modern Judaism in terms of the relation between religion, on one side, and the politics of sovereign nation-states, on the other. The thinkers that I will explore in part II are either not part of or explicitly reject the terms of this modern conversation.

Suggested Readings

Background

Braiterman, Zachary. *(God) after Auschwitz: Tradition and Change in Post-Holocaust Jewish Thought*. Princeton, NJ: Princeton University Press, 1998.

> Exploring the development and content of post-Holocaust theology, Braiterman devotes special attention to the emergence of what he calls "antitheodicy"—refusals to justify or explain the relationship between God, suffering, and evil.

Mittleman, Alan L. *The Politics of Torah: The Jewish Political Tradition and the Founding of Agudat Israel*. New York: State University of New York Press, 1996.

> Mittleman looks at the role of Isaac Breurer, Hirsch's grandson, in creating the religious Zionist political party, Agudat Israel, and its conception of a Torah state.

Morgan, Michael L. *Beyond Auschwitz: Post-Holocaust Jewish Thought in America*. New York: Oxford University Press, 2001.

> Analyzing the development of post-Holocaust theology in the United States, Morgan links the novelty and significance of such thought to its reflections on the relationship between history and identity.

Ravitzky, Aviezer. *Messianism, Zionism, and Jewish Religious Radicalism*. Trans. Michael Swirsky and Jonathan Chipman. Chicago: University of Chicago Press, 1996.

> Focusing on religious versions of Zionism and anti-Zionism, Ravitzky examines the theological and ideological roots of various controversies concerning religion, nation, and state.

Scholem, Gershom. *The Messianic Idea in Judaism and Other Essays on Jewish Spirituality*. Foreword Arthur Hertzberg. New York: Schocken Books, 1995.

> While exploring a variety of topics, the essays in this volume devote particular attention to the nature and role of messianism in Jewish history.

Schwartz, Dov. *Faith at the Crossroads: A Theological Profile of Religious Zionism*. Trans. Batya Stein. Leiden: Brill, 2002.

> Schwartz provides an overview of religious Zionism, emphasizing the ways in which this movement has been forced to reimagine key aspects of the Jewish tradition.

Fackenheim

Greenspan, Louis, and Graeme Nicholson, ed. *Fackenheim: German Philosophy and Jewish Thought*. Toronto: University of Toronto Press, 1992.

> The essays in this volume consider what the editors identify as two central bodies of Fackenheim's work: his reflections on the history of German philosophy, and his reflections on Jewish life and thought.

Morgan, Michael L., and Benjamin Pollock, ed. *The Philosopher as Witness: Fackenheim and Responses to the Holocaust.* Albany: State University of New York Press, 2008.

The essays in this volume concentrate on key themes in Fackenheim's thought, examine his relationship with other thinkers, and develop the implications of his views.

Patterson, David. *Emil L. Fackenheim: A Jewish Philosopher's Response to the Holocaust.* Syracuse, NY: Syracuse University Press, 2008.

This text devotes particular attention to issues such as Fackenheim's critique of earlier German and German Jewish thinkers, understanding of the singularity of the Holocaust, and reflections on the state of Israel.

Portnoff, Sharon, James A. Diamond, and Martin D. Yaffe, ed. *Emil L. Fackenheim: Philosopher, Theologian, Jew.* Leiden: Brill, 2008.

The essays in this volume explore the biographical, philosophical, and theological aspects of Fackenheim's thought.

The Kooks

In addition to the treatment of these thinkers by Schwarz and Ravitzky in the works cited above, the following texts provide introductions to the Kooks' thought:

Aran, Gideon. "A Mystic-Messianic Interpretation of Modern Israeli History: The Six-Day War as a Key Event in the Development of the Original Religious Culture of Gush Emunim." *Studies in Contemporary Jewry* 4 (1988): 263–75.

Exploring reactions to the Six-Day War among followers of the younger Kook, this essay outlines the ways in which this conflict was taken to confirm the Kookist emphasis on land and peoplehood over the state, how Kookist thinkers distinguished between the war's political meaning and religious significance, and the ways in which such figures understood developments that clashed with Kookist theological commitments.

Gellman, Ezra, ed. *Essays on the Thought and Philosophy of Rabbi Kook.* Rutherford, NJ: Fairleigh Dickinson University Press, 1991.

The essays in this volume look at the elder Kook's views on issues ranging from the nature of God to the concept of law.

Hoch, Richard L. "Sovereignty, Sanctity, and Salvation: The Theology of Rabbi Tzvi Yehudah Ha-Kohen Kook and the Actions of Gush Emunim." *Shofar* 13, no. 1 (1994): 90–118.

This essay provides an overview of Kook's biography, an account of his views on the nature of redemption, and a comparison of his position with other forms of Zionism.

Kaplan, Lawrence J., and David Shatz, eds. *Rabbi Abraham Isaac Kook and Jewish Spirituality.* New York: New York University Press, 1995.

The essays in this volume focus on Kook's political thought, views on faith and culture, and relationship with the Jewish tradition.

Singer, David. "Rav Kook's Contested Legacy." *Tradition* 30, no. 3 (1996): 6–20.

Singer suggests that while some contemporary thinkers associate the elder Kook primarily with values such as openness and tolerance, other readers place a heavy emphasis on the messianic dimensions of his Zionism. This essay devotes especial attention to the younger Kook's controversial reading of his father, exploring the gradualist, activist, and political elements of the elder's thought.

Levinas

For the relationship between Levinas and Strauss, see suggested readings for chapter 9.

Atterton, Peter, Matthew Calarco, and Maurice Friedman, eds. *Levinas and Buber: Dialogue and Difference*. Pittsburgh: Duquesne University Press, 2004.

In addition to reconstructing a "dialogue" between Levinas and Buber, the essays in this volume study these thinkers' views on topics ranging from ethics to religion.

Caygill, Howard. *Levinas and the Political*. London: Routledge, 2002.

Focusing on issues ranging from Levinas's engagement with the French intellectual tradition to his views on Zionism and the state of Israel, Caygill seeks to reconstruct the development and content of Levinas's understanding of "the political."

Cohen, Richard A. *Elevations: The Height of the Good in Rosenzweig and Levinas*. Chicago: University of Chicago Press, 1994.

Analyzing these thinkers' use of the Western philosophical tradition as well as resources derived from revealed religion, Cohen argues that Rosenzweig and Levinas developed new modes of thinking that place moral obligation to the other above all competing concerns.

Gibbs, Robert. *Correlations in Rosenzweig and Levinas*. Princeton, NJ: Princeton University Press, 1992.

Gibbs contends that Rosenzweig should be classified as a philosopher, Levinas should be treated as a Jewish thinker, and such readings can help us develop a program for the future of Jewish philosophy.

Moyn, Samuel. *Origins of the Other: Emmanuel Levinas between Revelation and Ethics*. Ithaca, NY: Cornell University Press, 2005.

Exploring Levinas's relationship to thinkers such as Heidegger and Rosenzweig, Moyn claims that Levinas appropriates the concept of "the other" from interwar Protestant theology, this concept acquires an ethical dimension only after World War II, and Levinas's conception of Judaism should be seen as his own "invention"—as deeply grounded in his own philosophical commitments, rather than as a return to earlier Jewish tradition.

Newton, Adam Zachary. *The Fence and the Neighbor: Emmanuel Levinas, Yeshayahu Leibowitz, and Israel among the Nations*. Albany: State University of New York Press, 2001.

Describing Levinas as an "ethicist" and Leibowitz as a "halakhist," Newton outlines and compares these thinkers' views on a variety of issues—for example, on the nature of politics, Jewish peoplehood, and the relationship between Judaism and philosophy.

PART II

Detaching Judaism from Religion

Chapter 6

THE IRRELEVANCE OF RELIGION AND
THE EMERGENCE OF THE JEWISH INDIVIDUAL

As MENTIONED IN THE INTRODUCTION, two interrelated aspects of a modern concept of religion are especially relevant to the story of the invention of Jewish religion. First, as we saw in the last five chapters, this story cannot be separated from the emergence of the modern nation-state; if Judaism is a religion, it is something different in kind from the supreme political authority of the sovereign state. Second, the modern concept of religion suggests that religion is one particular sphere of life among other particular and separate spheres, such as politics, morality, science, and economics. We saw that a number of thinkers examined in part I, "Judaism as Religion," rejected the term "religion" as applied to Judaism because of its Protestant associations. But despite their protestations to the contrary, these thinkers nevertheless inadvertently portrayed Judaism as a modern religion in a Protestant sense, because their claims about Judaism are predicated on the two aspects of the modern concept of religion just described. The thinkers discussed in part II of the book, "Detaching Judaism from Religion," deny one or both of these assertions about Judaism or Jewishness.

As we saw in chapter 1, the Haskalah, or Jewish Enlightenment, coupled with its political aftereffects, dismantled the framework of premodern Judaism in which the Jewish individual was defined legally, politically, and theologically as a member of the Jewish community. Although the eastern European Jewish experience was far different, it too was transformed at the beginning of the eighteenth century. As western Europe moved away from the feudal and corporate structure of medieval Europe toward unified and sovereign states, the Habsburg, Ottoman, and Russian empires had absorbed all of the previously independent countries of eastern and central Europe by the end of the eighteenth century. Each of these empires had a corporate structure and was composed of social estates. Among other things, this meant that the eastern European Jewish individual, like their premodern ancestors, was still defined legally, politically, and theologically as a member of the Jewish community. But as a result of the economic and political turmoil of eastern Europe generally, the Jewish community changed dramatically from within.

This chapter explores three new and different conceptions of the Jewish individual that emerged in eastern Europe in the eighteenth and nineteenth centuries: the Hasid, the freethinker, and the yeshiva scholar. A new and particularly modern emphasis on individuality unites these otherwise-different expressions of modern Jewish identity and thought. Each of these new forms of Jewish individuality was created within the broader context of Jewish communal life, which still defined the individual Jew's political and cultural identity. It is for this reason that the category of religion was largely irrelevant to all three. Eastern European Jews in fact were for the most part not emancipated until the early twentieth century. This historical fact underscores the main thesis of this book: the modern concept of religion was created in tandem with the modern nation-state.

THE BIRTH OF HASIDISM

Especially because of their long black coats, black hats, side curls, and overgrown beards, Hasidim today are often seen (and also present themselves) as icons of Jewish traditionalism and authenticity. Yet in its origins, Hasidism, like orthodoxy, was a wholly modern movement (and long black coats and black hats were merely the fashion of seventeenth-century Polish nobility). Hasidism was not just a modern movement but also a revolutionary one that refigured both the institutions and concepts of Jewish authority. If the legacies of Mendelssohn and the Haskalah mark the beginnings of Jewish modernity in the West, that of Mendelssohn's contemporary, Israel ben Eliezer (1700–1760), also known as the Baal Shem Tov (master of the good name), and the movement he inspired, Hasidism, mark the start of Jewish modernity in the East.

Israel ben Eliezer was born in Okopy, now part of the Ukraine. Not much more is known about his early life. According to his disciples, however, he was not a Torah scholar, although he received a traditional Jewish education. Given that he did not seem to be particularly intellectual and was known for his good nature, he initially worked with children, and later traveled throughout Poland and Lithuania, meditating disputes, serving as a ritual slaughterer, running a village tavern, and digging for clay in the woods. By 1740, he was known as a healer and performer of miracles. He settled in the village of Medzhybizh, which became the base for the Hasidic movement. After 1760, Hasidism spread throughout Poland and Lithuania, where it developed into different branches and became a mass movement, which, not surprisingly, greatly disturbed rabbinic authorities.

In the telling of his followers and early scholarship about his life, the Baal Shem Tov is usually portrayed as the founder of a radically new movement. But recent historiography tells a more complicated story: within his historical and social context, Israel ben Eliezer was one of a number of baalei shem tov (masters of the good name) whose teachings reflected a broader early modern trend, the popularization of Jewish mysticism (Kabbalah), which had previously been accessible only to a small, elite group of rabbis. Baaleei shem tov were people who specialized in the more practical, magical dimensions of Kabbalah, and traveled around offering their services to protect people against evil and disease, usually by reciting incantations as well as preparing talismans and amulets. The term hasid was also not unique to the Baal Shem Tov or his followers but instead referred more generally to a pious person, as the word had in earlier periods of Jewish history. Israel ben Eliezer's originality consisted not in his embrace of popular mysticism and magic but rather in his complete rejection of the asceticism that had marked previous Jewish notions of piety. As important, he focused on redeeming the individual Jew as opposed to the entire Jewish people.

These ideas and their popularity greatly threatened the rabbinic establishment. In particular, the *mitnagdim*, or "opposers," as they became known, rejected Hasidism and actively fought against the movement. Among the mitnagdim, we meet a third towering figure of the eighteenth century, Rabbi Elijah ben Solomon (1720–97), known as the Vilna Gaon, whose legacy, along with those of Mendelssohn and the Baal Shem Tov, helped determine the intellectual course of modern Judaism. The Vilna Gaon opposed Hasidism both politically and intellectually. In 1772, the rabbinic council of Lithuania, under the Vilna Gaon's leadership, arrested Hasidic leaders and excommunicated all adherents of Hasidism. The Vilna Gaon also sent letters to neighboring Jewish communities exhorting them to take action against Hasidism. In 1797, after the Vilna Gaon had died, his followers turned to the Russian authorities, urging them to arrest Rabbi Shneur Zalman of Liadi (1745–1812), the founder of Habad, also known as Lubavitch Hasidism, who was subsequently jailed in Saint Petersburg. Despite these efforts, Hasidism continued to attract even more followers.

Why were the mitnagdim so bothered by Hasidism? To begin with, Hasidism stressed ecstatic religiosity and communion with God, and not Torah study. While the Baal Shem Tov did not reject the authority of Jewish law (as is also true of Hasidim today), he nonetheless de-emphasized concern with both the minutia of Jewish law and its theoretical study. In this way, Hasidism broke down the distinction between the elite and the masses, as knowledge and intellectual acumen were no longer the main marks of distinction. The Vilna Gaon and the Baal Shem Tov thus differed fundamentally on what Judaism was. For the former, it was study and observance; for the latter, it was ecstatic experience. The Vilna Gaon and the

Baal Shem Tov also disagreed profoundly about human nature. The Baal Shem Tov emphasized the centrality of joy for Jewish and human experience, and as a result, singing and dancing are staples of Hasidic life. The Vilna Gaon had a far darker view of human nature. As he put it: "This is all of man's purpose [in life]: that he not be left to [satisfy] his own desire, but to be constrained in with bridle and bit, and until his dying day man must chastise himself, not by fasts and self-afflictions, but by restraining his mouth and his appetites."[1]

Beyond intellectual and spiritual differences, Hasidism also challenged the very fabric of traditional Jewish life, which centered on the family and Torah study. The following Hasidic story, titled "Praying in the Field," helps to illustrate the nature of these challenges. While this example is an early twentieth-century reconstruction among the Hasidic tales collected by Buber, it nonetheless illuminates precisely what the Vilna Gaon found so offensive about Hasidism.

> A Hasid who was traveling to Medzhybizh in order to spend the Day of Atonement near the Baal Shem, was forced to interrupt his journey for something or other. When the stars rose, he was still a good way from the town and, to his great grief, had to pray alone in the open field. When he arrived in Mezbizh after the holiday, the Baal Shem received him with particular happiness and cordiality. "Your praying," he said, "lifted up all the prayers which were lying stored in that field."[2]

The first thing we notice in this tale is that the Hasid is alone and traveling to be with the Baal Shem Tov for the most important day of the Jewish liturgical year. From the perspective of traditional Judaism, this situation is highly problematic. Why is the Hasid alone and not with his family (either his parents, or his wife and children)? Among the Vilna Gaon's charges against the Hasidim was that they broke the commandment "Honor thy father and thy mother."[3] Since the Hasid stops his travels before the holiday begins, the Hasid's behavior is still within the bounds of Jewish law. Because he prays alone, however, he cannot recite much of the Yom Kippur liturgy, which must be said with a quorum of at least ten men. The Baal Shem Tov is not disturbed by the fact that the Hasid was unable to pray with a community but instead praises the Hasid, suggesting that what matters most is not one's relation to the community but rather one's individual relation to God. The Baal Shem also implies that a field and nature are optimal places for prayer—a view not shared by rabbinic Judaism. The Baal Shem elevates nature's status all the more by suggesting that the field itself is full of prayers. Finally, this tale reflects the Hasidic stress on prayer over study, which reverses the priorities of traditional Judaism.

Why was Hasidism so successful? One reason is certainly because of its spiritual appeal. Yet it was also successful because of the weakness of Jewish communities and rabbinic authority, which had been decimated during the seventeenth century. During the Thirty Years' War (1618–48), Jews were persecuted and murdered by both Catholics and Protestants. After the war, Ukrainian peasants, who resented the Jewish economic relationship with the Polish nobility, revolted against the Polish-Lithuanian Commonwealth, and in doing so tortured and massacred at least half the Jewish population. Shortly thereafter, a Jew from the Ottoman Empire named Shabbetai Zvi (1626–76) traveled to Egypt and Palestine, declaring in 1665 that he was the Messiah. Shabbetai's followers, who became known as Sabbatians, traveled through Europe, spreading the word that the Messiah had arrived. With an enormous following, which included many prominent rabbis and Jews from all walks of life, Shabbetai journeyed in 1666 to Istanbul (known then as Constantinople), where he expected to take the sultan's crown. He was immediately arrested, and faced with the choice of death or conversion, he converted to Islam and lived another ten years. The twin facts that he was not the Messiah and converted to Islam were devastating to Jews around the world.

On top of this calamity, economic conditions worsened for the Jewish community. Poland's economy especially suffered in the early eighteenth century, and as a result, the Polish kingdom levied even greater taxes on Jewish communities. This left Jewish communities with less money to support their own people and institutions. Certainly at the beginning of the eighteenth century there were still great rabbinic scholars, such as the Vilna Gaon, but Torah study as a central institution of the Jewish community was diminished. As one historian notes, the intellectual standards for becoming a rabbi deteriorated significantly. Whereas in 1719–20, rabbis were required to study for twelve years after they were married before they could be ordained, in 1760–61, ordination only required that the rabbi be older than twenty.[4]

All these events contributed to Hasidism's hold on the Jews of eastern Europe, and two aspects of the movement's success will be especially relevant for the next two sections of this chapter: the threat that Hasidism posed to traditional rabbinic authority, and Hasidism's emphasis on the individual and the individual's experience. These two factors gave rise to the possibility of a perhaps-unlikely pair of new conceptions of Jewish identity: Jewish individuals as freethinkers and authors of their own lives, on the one hand, and the reinvention of rabbinic culture, on the other. I turn first to the extraordinary life of Solomon Maimon (1753–1800), who wrote about his chaotic experiences as an eastern European Jew in search of enlightenment, and then to the Mussar movement.

MAIMON: LOOKING FOR ENLIGHTENMENT
IN AN UNENLIGHTENED WORLD

Maimon was born near Mir in Lithuania, and most of what we know about his life comes from his autobiography, published in 1792–93. It tells the story of his quest for learning, from his seemingly humble intellectual beginnings as a young Lithuanian Jew to his becoming a significant conversation partner in contemporary philosophical discussions with, among others, Kant. Maimon writes that at an early age, his efforts at learning were thwarted by "the general constitution of Poland at the time; the condition of our people in it, who, like the poor ass with double burden, are oppressed by their own ignorance and the religious prejudices connected therewith, as well as by the ignorance and prejudices of the ruling class."[5] Married at age eleven, he becomes a father when he is just fourteen. He soon becomes disillusioned with Talmudic studies, and turns to Hasidism and Jewish mysticism. In keeping with the story discussed above about the Hasid who journeys alone, without his family, to be with the Baal Shem Tov on Yom Kippur, Maimon remarks, "Young people forsook parents, wives and children and went en masse to visit the exalted 'rebbes' and to hear from their lips the new doctrine."[6] Maimon praises the personal character of the Hasidim he meets, but he at the same time finds Hasidic teachings wanting.

In his midtwenties, Maimon abandons his family and travels to Berlin, but he is denied entrance into the city. He wanders around for two years before settling in Posen (Graetz's birthplace), where he remains for about ten years, supporting himself as a tutor and writing a philosophical treatise titled *Heshek Shelomo* (Solomon's Desire). He is finally granted permission to enter Berlin, where despite his rude behavior and uncultured habits, Mendelssohn is impressed with his intellect, and subsequently befriends him and tries to help him in his philosophical quest. Maimon settles in Hamburg for a period, during which time he studies math and science in the hope of becoming a physician.

In 1787 Maimon travels to Berlin again, and after reading Kant's *Critique of Pure Reason*, he writes a critical commentary on it that Kant eventually admitts is the most penetrating analysis of his philosophy. While Maimon continues to move around during the last thirteen years of his life, he publishes an expanded version of his commentary on Kant, a book on philosophical logic, his autobiography, a book in Hebrew on Maimonides, and six other books. In recent years, philosophers have increasingly recognized Maimon's major contributions to the history of philosophy generally and German idealism especially, yet his autobiography remains his best-known work. Reading Maimon together with Mendelssohn, his contemporary, as well as other modern Jewish thinkers, one cannot but be struck by the difference in tone and genre. For one thing, Maimon's autobiography is extremely funny. For another, why does Maimon, a serious philosopher, write an autobiography? Let me first consider the question of genre and then the significance of Maimon's humor.

Like three other prominent eastern European Jews who I will discuss in upcoming chapters, Mendele the bookseller (1836–1917), Sholem Aleichem (1859–1916), and Ahad Ha'am (1856–1927), Maimon was not born with the name under which he wrote; his given name was Solomon son of Joshua, but when he traveled to the West he adopted Maimon as his last name. His act of self-creation by reforming the past through a name change was to become an ever-present theme in the intellectual life of modern eastern European Jews. Sholem Yankev Abramovitsh puts himself in the service of bearing and creating his people's stories, naming himself Mendele the bookseller. Sholem Aleichem, by giving himself a name that means "peace unto you," or more colloquially "hi there, what's up?" makes himself the people's storyteller. Asher Hirsh Ginsberg, in taking the name Ahad Ha'am, or "one of the nation," attempts to re-create the Jewish nation of which he is part. In changing his name, Maimon makes himself a peer of Maimonides (who as discussed in chapters 2 and 3, is also the philosophical hero of Krochmal, Cohen, Soloveitchik, and Leibowitz , though all for different reasons), whose name was Moses son of Maimon. Surely one reason that Maimon attempts to re-create himself in Maimonides's image is that he wants to follow Maimonides in his philosophical quest. Yet in refashioning himself by giving himself a new name and literally writing his own story, Maimon is a distinctly modern person who is, the autobiography shows, first and foremost an individual. His story is his own. Herein lies the significance of the autobiographical genre: Maimon is the author of his own life.

Time and again in his autobiography Maimon accepts the consequences of not being part of any community but instead standing on his own. First he abandons his community of birth and even his own family. But he is not accepted by various Jewish communities in the West because he is both too much an eastern European Jew in manner and too much of a skeptical philosopher to accept any community's authority. At the same time, he is not accepted into the philosophical community because he is a Jew, and an uncultured eastern European one at that. Kant's response to Maimon's philosophical gifts epitomizes this lack of acceptance. On the one hand, Kant writes that "none of my critics understood me and the main questions as well as Herr Maimon does but also very few men possess so much acumen for very deep investigations as he." Yet Kant cannot but add "as regards 'the improvement of critical philosophy' [Maimon's response to Kant's system] by Maimon (Jews always like to do that sort of thing, to gain an air of importance for themselves at someone else's expense), I have never really understood what he is after and must leave the reproof to others."[7]

Since his Jewish identity is such a hindrance to his philosophical pursuits, Maimon decides at one point that in order to gain acceptance, he must convert to Christianity. But like Friedländer, discussed in chapter 1, Maimon says he will only do so without embracing Christian dogma. Again like Friedländer, Maimon is refused and then decides not to convert. In his words, "I must therefore remain what I am—a stiff-necked Jew. My religion enjoins me to *believe* nothing, but to *think* the truth and to practice goodness. If I find any hindrance in this from external circumstances, it is not my fault. I do all that lies in my power."[8] There is also an important difference, though, between Friedländer's and Maimon's consideration and then refusal of conversion. Friedländer, still believing in the ideal of enlightened reason, seeks to call himself an Israelite, in distinction to both a Jew and a Christian. In contrast, Maimon uses an anti-Jewish sentiment—that Jews are stiff-necked in refusing to become Christians— to undercut both Christianity and the pretense of a new enlightened society. On the one hand, Maimon is making fun of himself: he is a stiff-necked Jew and can't do anything about it. On the other hand, Maimon depicts what he takes to be the absurdity of Christian dogma (it does not conform to truth and the practice of goodness) and the idea of a new kind of enlightened society. (It is not his fault, Maimon suggests, if, despite his intellect and attempts to improve himself, society will not accept him.)

I can now turn to Maimon's humor. Maimon continually characterizes eastern European Jews as uncouth and irrational, with depictions that can be somewhat cartoonish. For example, the following story is typical of Maimon's description of his relations with his mother-in-law:

> Once I came home from the academy extremely hungry.... I found a dish of curds and cream, I fell upon it, and began to eat. My mother-in-law came as I was thus occupied, and screamed in rage, "You are not going to devour the milk with the cream!" The more cream the better, thought I, and went on eating, without disturbing myself by her cry. She was going to wrest the dish forcibly from my hands, beat me with her fists, and let me feel all her ill-will. Exasperated by such treatment, I pushed her from me, seized the dish, and smashed it on her head. That was a sight! The curds ran down all over her. She seized in rage a piece of wood and if I had not cleared out in all haste, she would certainly have beat me to death.[9]

Maimon makes fun of himself as much as he does others. His portrait of his initial attempt to enter Berlin is typical:

> They burst into loud laughter. And certainly they were not to be blamed. Imagine a man from Polish Lithuania of about five and

twenty years, with a tolerably stiff beard, in tattered dirty clothes, whose language is a mixture of Hebrew, Yiddish, Polish, and Russian, with their several grammatical inaccuracies, who gives it out that he understands the German language and that he has attained some knowledge of the sciences. What were the young gentlemen to think?[10]

One might conclude from reading the autobiography that Maimon's view of eastern European Jewry is not all that different from the German Jews' disdain for the intellectual and personal characteristics of eastern European Jews, noted in chapter 4. One might also conclude that Maimon's is a tragic story of someone who just could not clean up his act. If only he had learned to shave properly, bought a good suit, and behaved himself, he would have been accepted into both enlightened Jewish and Christian circles. If only he could have been more like Mendelssohn.

Yet to read Maimon this way is to miss the subversive nature of his narrative. It is true that Maimon makes fun of eastern European Jews and himself, but his story also undercuts the western European claim for an enlightened society, Jewish or otherwise. Just as Maimon uses the anti-Jewish caricature of a stiff-necked Jew to double effect, so too his humorous, negative descriptions of eastern European Jews and himself also often have a double meaning. For instance, this is how he describes his encounter with Marcus Herz (1747–1803), a German Jewish physician, friend of Mendelssohn, and student of Kant:

> He [Herz] took great pleasure in my conversation, and we often discussed the most important subjects in Natural Theology and Morals on which I expressed my thoughts quite frankly.... At first, this friend regarded me as a speaking animal and entertained himself as one might with a dog or a starling that has been taught to speak a few words. The odd mixture of the animal in my manners, my expressions and my whole outward behavior with the rational in my thoughts excited his imagination more than the subject of our conversation raised his understanding.[11]

On the surface, it seems that Maimon's lack of culture and manners is preventing him from reaching his true potential. After all, he is able to engage such prominent figures as Herz intellectually, but his animallike appearance and behavior are distracting. One recent commentator explores another level of meaning, however: "If we literally translate this phrase [speaking animal] back into Hebrew (Maimon's language of primary literary and philosophical literacy), it becomes *hai ha-medaber*, which is the medieval Aristotelian designation of man as the rational or speaking animal."[12] Appreciating Maimon's double entendre on the phrase "speaking animal" invites the autobiography's reader to appreciate the depth of Maimon's learning, which stems from his knowledge of medieval Jewish philosophy—a knowledge that Herz, an enlightened German Jew, does not possess. Maimon's implied deprecation of Herz (and not himself) is confirmed all the more by Maimon's claim that Herz's imagination impeded his understanding. For both Kant, Herz's philosophical hero, and Maimonides, Maimon's philosophical hero, it is primarily the understanding, and not the imagination, that can grasp truth.

So too, for all his admiration of and respect for Mendelssohn, Maimon offers a particularly trenchant criticism of the argument that Mendelssohn makes in *Jerusalem*. Like his use of the phrase "talking animal" that I just explored, Maimon's contention about Mendelssohn is not immediately obvious. Maimon begins by writing, "So far as I am concerned, I am led to assent entirely to Mendelssohn's reasoning by my own reflections on the fundamental laws of the religion of my fathers." Yet Maimon continues, "The fundamental laws of the Jewish religion are at the same time the fundamental laws of the Jewish state. They must therefore be obeyed by all who acknowledge themselves to be members of this state, and who wish to enjoy the rights granted to them under condition of their obedience."[13] Mendelssohn's assertion, though, as we know from chapter 1, was essentially the opposite. The reasoning that Maimon describes is not Mendelssohn's but rather Spinoza's (discussed in the introduction), which defines Jewish law in political terms. Mendelssohn invents the ideas that Judaism is a religion and that Jewish law is not political but rather religious precisely in order to counter Spinoza's claim. What, then, is Maimon up to?

Maimon unravels the very tension in Mendelssohn's argument that I examined in chapter 1. Let us recall that Mendelssohn provides a traditional conception of the Jewish obligation to obey Jewish law. Again, as Mendelssohn puts it: "He who is not born into the law need not bind himself to the law; but he who is born into the law must live according to the law; and die according to the law." Yet Mendelssohn also defines religion in general and Jewish religion in particular in terms of its voluntary nature. Religion, Mendelssohn claims, cannot be coerced because "the right to our convictions is inalienable." It is for this reason that Mendelssohn first and foremost rejects the Jewish community's right to excommunication. Maimon puts Mendelssohn's two theses together and then draws out their implications. If Jews are obligated to obey the law, then the Jewish community—that is, the community of the law—has rights. The Jewish community, which Maimon, in a nod to Spinoza, calls the Jewish state, exercises political agency in defining and upholding Jewish law. But Jewish individuals also have a right, as thinking individuals, not to be part of the community. It is thus highly problematic for

Mendelssohn to maintain that Jews are obliged to obey the law and that Jewish individuals have the right to their own convictions, but that the community of the law—that is, the Jewish community—has no rights as a community. In Maimon's words:

> Mendelssohn wanted to cancel the excommunication on the ground that the church has no rights in civil matters. But how can he maintain the perpetuity of the Jewish ecclesiastical state? For what is a state without rights, and wherein consists, according to Mendelssohn, the rights of this ecclesiastical state? ... For excommunication is merely tantamount to saying:—"So long as you put yourself in opposition to the laws of our communion, you are excluded from it; and you must therefore make up your mind whether this open disobedience or the privileges of our communion can most advance your blessedness."[14]

Expressing his respect for Mendelssohn's intellect, Maimon contends that Mendelssohn must have been well aware of this tension in his thought. Yet Maimon also recognizes the rhetorical character of Mendelssohn's arguments: "This surely cannot have escaped a mind like Mendelssohn's, and I leave to others to decide how far a man may be inconsistent for the sake of human welfare."[15] As we saw in chapter 1, Mendelssohn's main goal is to defend the compatibility of Judaism and modernity. To do so, he makes an argument that attempts to preserve both Judaism as a community of law and modernity as the possibility of a new society that makes citizenship possible for all, regardless of private religious belief. But, Maimon suggests, these two ideas don't go together, and each of them is problematic on its own terms. In the case of the Jewish obligation to obey the law, individual Jews can choose not to be part of the community, though the social costs, as seen by Maimon's own life, can be great. At the same time, from Maimon's perspective, no new society exists, and given the beliefs and behavior of the so-called enlighteners, no such society seems likely.

What, then, can a modern Jew who desires consistency do? The quest for real enlightenment, or human perfection, Maimon observes, is in the end only available to the individual. Maimon may "leave it to others to decide how far a man may be inconsistent for the sake of human welfare," but his own choice seems clear: consistency or, perhaps better, the quest for consistency, has a high social cost. If Mendelssohn is the first modern Jewish thinker, perhaps Maimon is the first modern Jewish individual. He is a stiff-necked Jew who only wants to be free to be who he is, whether or not the Jewish community or enlightened society likes it. And his chosen genre, autobiography, allows him to be an individual who can create his own life—a life that will be his and no one else's.

THE REINVENTION OF TRADITION

Maimon was not alone in being disturbed by what he regarded as the growing ignorance of the Jewish masses. Traditionalists themselves were painfully aware of the low intellectual standards that marked Talmudic study in the eighteenth century, which the rise of Hasidism only exacerbated. In this section, I look at the attempt from within traditionalist circles to reinvent the rabbinic tradition as a response to these challenges. This reinvention came to be known as the Mussar movement, which shares with Hasidism and Maimon a focus on the individual. Where Mussar differs is in its insistence that far from hindering the spiritual fulfillment of the individual, the rabbinic tradition properly conceived offers the true path to individual realization.

To understand the Mussar movement, we must begin with the Vilna Gaon's student, Rabbi Hayim of Volozhin (1749-1821), who is best known for the establishment of the Volozhin Yeshiva in 1803. As mentioned in chapter 3, Joseph Soloveitchik's great grandfather, Joseph Baer, was the co-head of the Volozhin Yeshiva and his grandfather, also named Hayim, developed a highly analytic method of Talmudic study that stressed conceptual creativity and innovation. The founding of the Volozhin Yeshiva and the subsequent evolution of new methods of rigorous but creative abstract reasoning marked the start of the expansion of a series of Lithuanian yeshivas that flourished in the nineteenth century. These yeshivas produced great numbers of important Jewish luminaries, within the yeshiva world and beyond; also, students at these yeshivas were some of the founders of Hebrew and Yiddish literature, such as the Yiddish writer Abramovitsh and the Hebrew poet Hayim Nahman Bialik (1873-1934), who are discussed in the next two chapters.

The Volozhin Yeshiva differed from prior traditionalist yeshivas in at least three ways. First, the establishment of the yeshiva was a direct response to the disintegration of Jewish communal life in eastern Europe. Prior to its establishment, local communities had their own local yeshivas. The Volozhin Yeshiva, in contrast, was a centralized institution to which students, having left their hometowns, would migrate. Second, in contrast to the Vilna Gaon, Hayim stressed the social dimension of Torah study and in particular the *hevruta* style. The term hevruta comes from the Hebrew term for friend, *haver*, and a hevruta is made up of two people (traditionally men) who study the Talmud together. The idea is that learning requires a conversation between two people, rather than either the passive reception of knowledge from a teacher or the solitary individual studying alone. Hayim's emphasis on the social dimension of Torah study mitigated the Vilna Gaon's wholly negative view of human nature and existence in light of the Hasidic critique of it. Nevertheless,

Hayim still retained the Vilna Gaon's basic insight that the task of the spiritual life was to improve one's individual nature. In Hayim's words: "'Acquire a friend' [Sayings of the Fathers 1:6] ... with whom one can take counsel also concerning matters of Divine service. For if you are wise in your own eyes, the Evil Impulse can blind your eyes and make the crooked and the hilly [to appear] straight. Therefore, you must take counsel with a friend, for your own evil impulse is not so close to him, as to be misleading."[16] Third, and perhaps most significant, rather than practical training for rabbis, the Volozhin Yeshiva promoted Torah study for its own sake (what is known as *Torah l'shma*). In all these ways, the Volozhin Yeshiva tried to provide an alternative to both Hasidism and the temptation of the Haskalah.

As I will discuss in greater detail in the next chapter, by the second half of the nineteenth century, Hasidism and its opponents had for the most part made peace with one another, as their shared enemies now were Jewish reformers of a variety of different ideological stripes. It was in this context that Rabbi Israel Salanter (1810–83) develops his Mussar approach. "Mussar" is a biblical term, which is variously translated as chastisement, discipline, and instruction (such as in Deuteronomy 11:1–2: "Therefore you shall love the Lord your God, and keep His charge, and His statutes, and His ordinances, and His commandments, always. And know you this day; for I speak not with your children that have not known, and that have not seen the *chastisement* [or discipline or instruction] of the Lord your God, His greatness, His mighty hand, and His outstretched arm.").

Salanter's thought begins with the premise shared by both Hasidism and the Haskalah: that Jewish thought and experience center on the individual. Where Salanter differs is in his insistence that the Jewish tradition itself offers a more compelling alternative than do either of these two newcomers to Jewish thought. Like Hayim, Salanter places Torah study at the center of Jewish life. Yet he differs from Hayim in linking a modern psychological conception of the human being to Torah study. As Salanter puts it:

> Do not say that what God has made cannot be altered, and that because He, may He be blessed, has planted within me an evil force I cannot hope to uproot it. This is not so, for the powers of a human being may be subdued, and even transformed. Just as we see regarding [the nature of] animals, that man is able to tame them and bend their will to his will ... and also to domesticate them ... so has man the power to subdue his own evil nature ... and to change his nature toward the good through exercise and practice.[17]

Self-scrutiny is at the heart of Mussar practice. Whereas Hasidism maintains that the righteous person (the zaddik) is free of sin, Mussar describes the righteous person as struggling deeply and profoundly with sin. In doing so, the righteous person is a model for others, who each must cultivate their own struggle. In cultivating this struggle, Mussar practice underscores ethical responsibility and acts of humility.

A particular story about Salanter allows us to appreciate this aspect of Mussar as well as differences between Mussar and Hasidism, on the one hand, and Haskalah, on the other:

> People had congregated in the synagogue for Kol Nidre [the prayer that begins Yom Kippur]. They waited for Rabbi Israel but he did not appear. Since it was getting late, they recited Kol Nidre without him. Then they sent out to look for him, but no one could find him. The crowd was growing panicky; soon the service would be over. Then, abruptly he entered, took his accustomed place, drew the prayer shawl over his head and began to pray. Everyone was astonished at his appearance: his coat was rumpled; his hair and beard full of down. After he finished his prayers, he recounted what had happened to him.
>
> On his way to the synagogue for Kol Nidre, he heard a child crying. He went in the house, saw an infant crying in its cradle, a bottle of milk just out of its reach. The mother had prepared the bottle and gone off to the synagogue, expecting her six-year-old daughter to give the baby its bottle. But the little girl had fallen fast asleep and did not hear the baby crying. Rabbi Israel fed the baby and put it to sleep. When he was ready to leave, the little girl awoke and begged him not to go for she was afraid to be alone. Reluctant to leave small children alone with low-burning candles, he stayed until the mother returned from the synagogue. He rejoiced he had been given the opportunity to do a good deed at a time as sacred as Yom Kippur. His listeners were amazed: How could one miss the Yom Kippur services because of a child's crying? Rabbi Israel scolded them: "Do you not know that, even in the case of a double doubt about saving a life in jeopardy, Jews are permitted not only to omit the prayers but even to profane the Sabbath?"[18]

At first glance, this story seems similar to the tale of the Hasid mentioned earlier in this chapter; both take place on Yom Kippur and are about missing the opening prayers of Yom Kippur, the most important day of the Jewish year. Despite these similarities in form, however, the stories have different implications. As discussed above, the story about the Hasid challenges both the centrality of family life to traditional Judaism as well as rabbinic authority. The one about Salanter affirms both of these. First, Salanter is delayed because he is giving a baby a bottle. Second, Salanter defends his act on the basis of Jewish law: "Do you not know that, even in the case of a double doubt about saving a life in jeopardy, Jews are permitted not only to omit the prayers but even to profane the Sabbath?" Whereas the story about the Hasid questions the ultimate value (although not the value itself) of following Jewish law to the letter, the story about Salanter affirms the letter of the law.

Just as Mussar challenges Hasidism, it also challenges the Haskalah's commitment to the German idea of Bildung noted in chapter 1: the notion that self-improvement comes about by way of increased adherence to rationality and cultural refinement. From the point of view of Mussar, self-improvement begins not with the outer person but rather with the inner one. At the same time, our obligations to others stem not from a heightened sense of rationality but instead from profound humility resulting from self-scrutiny. Here it is important to notice that it is an act of great humility for Salanter, the great rabbi, to feed a baby a bottle as opposed to taking his place as the congregation's head on the most important day of the Jewish year. This is why the crowd is amazed: How can it be that the most exalted intellect of the day has chosen to feed a baby rather than be on time for the most significant religious moment of the Jewish year? That Salanter's "coat was rumpled; his hair and beard full of down" only confirms his humbled state.

As we have seen, the practical and intellectual rigors associated with Mussar and the yeshiva scholars are predicated on a deep sense of individual responsibility and creativity. Mussar and the Lithuanian yeshivas thus were already in their own period criticized by what we would call today ultraorthodoxy (discussed in the conclusion of this book). Among the complaints launched against the Lithuanian yeshivas were that their students wore short jackets, were clean shaven, and married late. While these may seem to be merely matters of appearance, it is crucial to recognize that they are linked to the deeper issue of the type of learning promoted by the Lithuanian yeshivas—learning that, as mentioned, highlighted creativity and innovation above all else.[19] For the ultraorthodox critics of the Lithuanian yeshivas, the emphasis on intellectual innovation, coupled with some of the outer trappings of modernity, reflects an ultimate concession to modernity and its ideal of a free individual who has the power to create him- or herself. Seen from this perspective, the yeshiva scholar and Maimon, while in many ways worlds apart, are nevertheless on the same spectrum.

Yet here we come to an interesting tension in Salanter's own thought. While he was fully aware of the modern strains in his thinking, such as his reliance on individual psychological accounts of the self, Salanter consciously rejected Hirsch's modern orthodoxy, explored in chapter 2. Salanter spent time in Germany and admired aspects of the modern orthodoxy that he encountered there. He did not believe that Hirsch's modern orthodoxy was appropriate for eastern European Jews, though, because he recognized the limitations placed on Jewish life when Judaism is understood as a religion—that is, as one of a number of dimensions of modern life. Salanter worried especially about the future of Torah study, noting that there were no great Torah scholars in Germany, and in this criticism he included Hirsch. Instead, rabbinic authorities were relegated to adjudicating aspects of Jewish ceremonial law. This was the result of defining Judaism as a modern religion.

Like Mendelssohn, Hirsch had characterized Judaism as a religion of law, yet he also claimed that observance of the law was voluntary. Let us recall Hirsch's description of the genuine Jew: "timeless principles ... will move and guide the genuine Jew, without compulsion ... in every fiber of his heart and every stirring of his will" to observe the law. Strikingly, Salanter and Maimon concur that, in Maimon's words, "the fundamental laws of the Jewish religion are at the same time the fundamental laws of the Jewish state. They must therefore be obeyed by all who acknowledge themselves to be members of this state, and who wish to enjoy the rights granted to them under condition of their obedience." For Salanter's form of orthodoxy, as opposed to Hirsch's, it is only under these conditions that genuine Torah study is possible.

CONCLUSION

We have seen in this chapter that the Hasid, the freethinker, and the yeshiva scholar are all distinctly modern forms of Jewish identity and thought. The upheavals in eastern European Jewish life provided the soil within which each of these new forms took root. Yet while all three can easily be thought of in terms of individual spiritual quests, none of them fit easily into the modern category of religion. Let me return to Schleiermacher's definition of religion: "Religion maintains its own sphere and its own character only by completely removing itself from the sphere and character of speculation as well as from that of praxis."[20] Neither the Hasid nor the freethinker nor the yeshiva scholar removes themselves from the sphere and character of speculation, or from praxis. On the contrary, each of these individual spiritual quests is made possible against the backdrop of a Jewish communal life that however weakened, shares common forms of public practice and speculation, otherwise known as religious law and tradition. The Hasid pursues his spiritual quest within the context of Jewish law even when this law is reconceived as a means to an end rather than as an end in itself. So too, Maimon's freethinking is predicated on a rejection of Jewish communal life, which he defines in terms of adherence to common forms of behavior. And finally, the yeshiva scholar's spiritual quest takes place within the strictures of Jewish law and its study. In the next chapter, I will look at another invention of eastern European Jewry: the creation of modern Jewish culture.

SUGGESTED READINGS

Baal Shem Tov and Hasidism

For Buber's neo-Hasidism, see suggested readings for chapter 4.

For U.S. neo-Hasidism, see suggested readings for chapter 9.

Etkes, Immanuel. *The Besht: Magician, Mystic, and Leader.* Trans. Saadya Sternberg. Hanover, NJ: University Press of New England, 2005.

> Exploring the historical significance of the Baal Shem Tov by considering three central dimensions of his work, Etkes seeks to clarify the sense in which this figure can be seen as the founder of Hasidism—the sense in which the Baal Shem Tov, perhaps unknowingly, set in motion processes that would lead to the Hasidic movement's emergence.

Hundert, Gershon David, ed. *Essential Papers on Hasidism: Origins to Present.* New York: New York University Press, 1991.

> The texts in this volume—ranging from eighteenth-century accounts to twentieth-century essays—analyze the history, beliefs, and practices of the Hasidic movement.

Rapoport-Albert, Ada, ed. *Hasidism Reappraised.* London: Littman Library of Jewish Civilization, 1996.

> The essays in this volume examine the history of Hasidism as well as scholarship on this movement.

Rosman, Moshe. *Founder of Hasidism: A Quest for the Historical Ba'al Shem Tov.* Berkeley: University of California Press, 1996.

> Raising concerns about the reliability of sources often used to reconstruct the Baal Shem Tov's life, Rosman suggests that we should view this figure as "a person of his time"—as reflecting, perpetuating, and developing pre-existing social and religious patterns.

Hayim of Volozhin and Salanter

Etkes, Immanuel. *The Gaon of Vilna: The Man and His Image.* Trans. Jeffrey M. Green. Berkeley: University of California Press, 2002.

> Etkes studies the activity, views, image, and impact of the Vilna Gaon. Chapter 5 devotes particular attention to the life and thought of Hayim, outlining the theological and educational dimensions of his response to Hasidism—namely, the systematic theology that he developed and the influential yeshiva that he established.

———. *Rabbi Israel Salanter and the Mussar Movement: Seeking the Torah of Truth.* Trans. Jonathan Chipman. Philadelphia: Jewish Publication Society, 1993.

> Etkes provides an overview of Salanter's life, thought, and public activity. Chapter 3 concentrates on Hayim's thought, especially this figure's conception of Torah study and views on the fear of God.

Goldberg, Hillel. *Israel Salanter: Text, Structure, Idea: The Ethics and Theology of an Early Psychologist of the Unconscious*. New York: Ktav Publishing House, 1982.
    This study explores the development of Salanter's thought across four pe-riods in his life, presenting him as a "systematic thinker," and focusing on his ethics, psychology, and theology.
Steiner, Mark. "Rabbi Israel Salanter as a Jewish Philosopher." *Torah u-Maddah Journal* 9 (2000): 42–57.
    This essay argues that Salanter should be read as a "Jewish philosopher," because of the problems he addressed and approach he adopted—given that he both addressed issues central to the history of philosophy, and did so in a "systematic" manner.

Historical Context

For the history of eastern European Jewry, see suggested readings for chapter 7.

Maimon

Feiner, Shmuel. "Solomon Maimon and the Haskalah." *Aschkenas* 10, no. 2 (2000): 337–59.
    Looking at the development of Maimon's thought and career, this essay seeks to clarify the nature of his relationship to the Jewish Enlightenment, reassessing the view that this eighteenth-century figure was a paradigmatic representative of that movement.
Franks, Paul W. "Jewish Philosophy after Kant: The Legacy of Salomon Maimon." In *The Cambridge Companion to Modern Jewish Philosophy*, ed. Michael L. Morgan and Peter Eli Gordon, 53–79. Cambridge: Cambridge University Press, 2007.
    Describing Maimon's work as contributing to Jewish thought's involve-ment with Kantian philosophy, Franks argues that Maimon both utilized the resources of medieval Jewish thought to reframe aspects of Kant's phi-losophy, and drew on aspects of Kant's work to refigure medieval Jewish traditions.
Freudenthal, Gideon, ed. *Salomon Maimon: Rational Dogmatist, Empirical Skep-tic: Critical Assessments*. Dordrecht: Kluwer Academic Publishers, 2003.
    The essays in this volume explore various dimensions of Maimon's thought, focusing on issues such as his involvement in eighteenth-century philosophical debates. Freudenthal's introduction devotes particular at-tention to the "intercultural character" of Maimon's writings—the ways in which Maimon not only utilized literary forms more common among premodern thinkers but also drew on resources derived from Jewish and European philosophical traditions.
Librett, Jeffrey S. "Stolen Goods: Cultural Identity after the Counterenlighten-ment in Salomon Maimon's *Autobiography* (1792)." *New German Cri-tique* 79 (2000): 36–66.
    Reading Maimon's autobiography against the backdrop of tensions be-tween Jews and Christians, and between Enlightenment and Counteren-lightenment, this essay suggests that Maimon was unable to discover a

"stable place" among Jews and Germans, and that this position as an outsider helped generate a distinctive account of cultural identity.

Socher, Abraham P. *The Radical Enlightenment of Solomon Maimon: Judaism, Heresy, and Philosophy*. Stanford, CA: Stanford University Press, 2006. Providing an overview of Maimon's life and thought, Socher emphasizes the significance of medieval and early modern Jewish traditions for the development of Maimon's philosophy.

Chapter 7

THE TRANSFORMATION OF TRADITION AND
THE INVENTION OF JEWISH CULTURE

STANDING AGAINST THE MODERN category of Jewish religion invented in western Europe, the modern notion of Jewish culture, which developed in eastern Europe, transformed traditional Judaism. Rather than defining Judaism as a narrow sphere of life among other spheres, however, as happened in the West, Jewish culture became a vibrant form of life that encompassed all aspects of the experience of modern Jews. Let us recall Katz's characterization of the three possible paths that German Jews could have taken after emancipation. First, Jews could have simply left Judaism behind and joined the German cultural tradition. Second, Jews could have used German culture to refigure Judaism and Jewish culture in light of the modern era. And third, as Katz observed above, "Jewish novelists could have depicted contemporary Jewish society as they experienced it, or the Jewish past as they had learned it, and spun their tales around Jewish characters. Jewish poets could have derived their inspiration from the long succession of Jewish poetical tradition, giving it a new lease on life through a new linguistic garb." As we saw in chapter 2, if they wanted to remain identifiably Jewish, German Jews primarily chose the second path, and in doing so implicitly supported the premise that Judaism is a religion. Significantly, most German Jews did not choose the third path because the comprehensive conception of German culture simply did not admit any other type of cultural identity. The creation of modern Jewish culture, therefore, happened mainly in the eastern European context. As we saw in the last chapter, eastern European Jews experienced momentous changes in the eighteenth and nineteenth centuries, but unlike in western Europe, these changes did not include the granting of individual rights of citizenship. Even though eastern European Jews lacked political freedom, they did possess a cultural freedom denied to Jews in western Europe, thereby providing a context for the emergence of modern Yiddish literature.

For many people, the category of Yiddish literature brings to mind *Fiddler on the Roof*, the American theatrical adaptation of several stories by Yiddish writer Sholom Aleichem. *Fiddler* tells the tale of Tevye, a dairyman living in a small village, who laments the loss of tradition as he witnesses the new and different choices open to his five daughters. One daughter marries a Jewish tailor for love, and not the man that her father had chosen for her. A second daughter runs off with a radical revolutionary. The climax of *Fiddler* comes when the third daughter marries a gentile and converts to Christianity. For Tevye, this means his daughter is literally dead. He "sits shiva" for her, observing the traditional week of mourning after the death of a parent, child, or spouse, and Tevye mourns the loss of tradition as well. *Fiddler on the Roof* presents a dichotomy between tradition and modernity, setting an image of an "authentic" eastern European Jewish life centered on the pieties of the past against the choices available to modern individuals. This picture parallels the romantic visions of eastern European Jewry expressed by early twentieth-century German Jews, which I explored in chapter 4.

Yet in contrast, the origins and contents of the genre of modern Yiddish literature (including much of Sholom Aleichem's work) tell a different and far more complex story. I turn in this chapter to Sholom Jacob Abramovitsh, whose literary heir Sholem Aleichem called him "the grandfather of Yiddish literature"; in the following section I will treat Sholem Aleichem himself. As mentioned in chapter 6, both authors wrote under pen names—Abramovitsh under Mendele the bookseller, and Solomon Rabinovitsh under Sholem Aleichem. The fact that Mendele the bookseller and Sholem Aleichem also both appear as characters in their respective authors' stories already suggests a literary genre that calls into question straightforward claims to authenticity. We will see that both Abramovitsh and Sholem Aleichem tell complicated stories about eastern European Jewish life that break down the dichotomies between modernity and tradition as well as self-consciousness and authenticity.

But perhaps most basically in the context of this book's narrative, which concerns the invention of the idea of Jewish religion and its many conceptual aftereffects, Abramovitsh and Sholem Aleichem break down the distinction between the individual and collective implicitly embraced by German Jewish thinkers, and reflected in the Comte de Clermont-Tonnerre's well-known words to the French assembly in 1789, quoted in chapter 2: "One must refuse everything to the Jews as a nation but one must give them everything as individuals; they must become citizens." As discussed in chapter 4, the rejection of the Yiddish language was part and parcel of the invention of Jewish religion. For Mendelssohn, as for the maskilim generally, speaking proper German was the first step toward becoming a rational human being. It was necessary to speak German well, argued the maskilim in the eighteenth century and the reformers in the nineteenth century, because Jews were part of the German nation. The use of Yiddish, in contrast, suggested that the Jews were a people apart. In this way, the claim that Jews were not a nation within a nation went hand in hand with the rejection of Yiddish.

Although Yiddish writers certainly agreed with the maskilim that Yiddish was associated with collective Jewish life, they differed from them in affirming the individual Jew's intimate tie (for better and worse) to that Jewish collective. And they did so by transforming what had historically been a theological vocabulary characterizing God's special relationship with the people of Israel into a cultural lexicon that described only the life of the people themselves. In this connection, we will see in this chapter's conclusion that the modern idea of Jewish culture, like the modern notion of Jewish religion, is not without its own conceptual tensions. But before doing so, I will look at Abramovitsh's and Sholem Alecheim's stories in some detail as well as the historical origins of modern Yiddish literature.

MODERN YIDDISH LITERATURE IN CONTEXT

In order to understand the emergence of modern Yiddish literature and the invention of modern Jewish culture, one must appreciate the complexities of the context in which they developed. Before that, though, I should explain the beginnings of the Russian-Jewish encounter. Prior to 1772, Jews were forbidden to live in Russian territory, but as mentioned in chapter 4, in 1772 the Russian Empire annexed a large part of the Polish kingdom and suddenly thousands of Jews lived under Russian rule. Two subsequent annexations of lands from the Polish kingdom followed, bringing even greater numbers of Jews under Russian rule. This led, in the early 1790s, to the establishment of "the Pale of Settlement," the geographic region in which Jews were allowed to settle. This area roughly corresponded to the historical borders of the former Polish-Lithuanian Commonwealth. Jews were not allowed to settle in the northeastern part of the kingdom, but they were permitted to immigrate to parts of the Ottoman Empire that had been captured by Russia. From 1772 until the Russian Revolution in 1917, Russia's policy toward the Jews vacillated between opening up educational, economic, and migrational opportunities for Jews, and the retraction of such reforms, often in an attempt to integrate Jews fully into Russian culture and the Russian state. Still, whatever the policy at a given time, reforms and retractions of reforms served only to affirm, and not to eliminate, a society built on hereditary social estates and different group (as opposed to individual) identities.

As discussed in part I of this book, in the late eighteenth century, western Europe was dissolving its hereditary social estates, either through revolution, as was the case in France, or reform, as in Prussia. For Jews living in western Europe, this meant that they were granted citizenship rights as individuals but not as a corporate body. Let us recall that this is exactly what Mendelssohn, in contrast to Dohm, had advocated. As we saw in chapter 1, it was by virtue of separating the individual Jew politically, though not theologically, from the Jewish community that Mendelssohn created the idea of Jewish religion. It was also by virtue of separating the individual Jew from the Jewish nation that Jews were granted the individual rights of citizenship, as we saw in chapter 2. The situation in Russia was far different. Rather than moving away from hereditary social estates, the Russian Empire at the end of the eighteenth century moved toward developing such estates on what had been the European model.

We can appreciate the centrality of social estates in the Russian Jewish experience already in the first encounters between the Jews and the Russian Empire. In 1786, the Russian empress Catherine the Great (1729–96) classified Jews as urban residents, with the privileges and obligations of the urban estates (such as artisans and petty traders). Yet the corporate status of the Jewish community remained, which made it possible for Catherine to continue collecting taxes from Jewish communities. Catherine's successor (and grandson), Czar Alexander I (1777–1825), introduced a series of reforms that opened schools and universities to Jews (and other non-Russian minorities), while also encouraging new kinds of Jewish economic activity, such as agriculture. But with the reign of Nicholas I, beginning in 1825, many of these reforms were retracted. As was the case in Germany and France, calls for enlightened reforms, and reforms that benefited the Jews in particular, were met with conservative, nationalist, and anti-Jewish backlash. In the Russian context, this backlash was tied to the Russian Orthodox Church's insistence on the conversion of the Jews. In 1827, with this end in mind, Nicholas I demanded that each Jewish community fill a quota of Jewish boys for conscription into the Russian army. The length of service was twenty-five years. Nicholas I also demanded a quota of cantonists—young boys for premilitary training. Needless to say, most of these recruits never returned to the Jewish community. In 1844, Special Schools for the Education of Jewish Youth were created by the state for the purpose of assimilating Jews into Russian culture. In order to eradicate any distinct Jewish identity, Nicholas I also canceled the rights of corporate Jewish communities. Nevertheless, due to its own disorganization, the Russian Empire was unable to integrate the Jews into an alternative administrative system. Against his own intentions, Nicholas's weakening of the corporate Jewish community thus also weakened Russian control of the Jewish community.

Things seemed to change in 1855 when Czar Alexander II took the throne. Alexander II upended many of Nicholas's policies. First and foremost, he took steps to reform the Russian economy by abolishing the feudal system, and encouraging capitalism and industry. For this purpose, Alexander II allowed Jews of a certain wealth to leave the Pale of Settlement and move to the empire's interior. Jews with advanced academic degrees were also allowed to leave the Pale, as were some artisans (such as mechanics and technicians of various sorts). This policy was known as "selective integration."[1] Perhaps not surprisingly, it was the small group of Jews that benefited from this policy that were most committed to the ideals of enlightenment and cultural integration for Russia's Jews.

The abolition of the feudal system meant that Jews generally had to take up new kinds of trades in order to compete in the new economy. Jewish communities suffered economically during this transition, and there was less financial support for rabbis. Without a community to provide financial contributions, the prestige and practical power of both rabbinic and Hasidic authorities were greatly eroded. As mentioned in chapter 6, by the second half of the nineteenth century Hasidim and their opponents had for the most part made peace with one another, and were united against various types of Jewish reformers. It was also during this period that modern Yiddish literature developed as a distinct genre.

The origins of modern Yiddish literature and what we might call today Jewish secularism are outgrowths of the coupling of the Haskalah and tradition. Abramovitsh began his literary career as a radical maskil devoted to Hebrew literature. But unlike Judah Leib Gordon (1830–92), a Lithuanian-born Jew and perhaps the greatest Hebrew poet of the nineteenth century, who described Yiddish literature as "an ugly symptom of the spread of reaction among us," Abramovitsh did not disdain Yiddish.[2] After publishing in Hebrew for a decade or so, he switched to Yiddish to reach the Jewish masses, who did not read Hebrew but did read Yiddish. In particular, prayer books for women, known as *Tekhines* (supplications), were printed in Yiddish (as opposed to men's prayer books, which were printed in Hebrew). According to his unfinished autobiography, Abramovitsh suggested that when he had written only in Hebrew, he had in effect been writing only for other maskilim and he wanted to reach a broader audience.

Abramovitsh published his first Yiddish novel in serial form in 1864–65 and subsequently wrote five more novels in Yiddish. His progressive turn from Hebrew to Yiddish reflects his growing skepticism and disillusionment with the possibilities of political and cultural progress for Russian Jews. Although he remains dedicated to the intellectual ideals of enlightenment, Abramovitsh's fiction also illuminates the self-delusional and ultimately self-destructive consequences of maskilic belief in an age of historical as well as political progress. So too, Abramovitsh reveals, it is delusional to think that individual Jews, no matter how much they desire it, can separate themselves from the Jewish community. There is simply nowhere to go. To illustrate these points, let me now examine Abramovitsh's story "The Mare," published first in 1873 and then in an expanded edition in 1886.

"THE MARE"

The narrator of Abramovitsh's piece, Mendele the bookseller, begins his story by telling his readers that he has come into possession of a manuscript called "The Mare." A friend gave it to Mendele to replace Mendele's horse, which had just died. According to the narrator, the manuscript holds deep truths and secrets within it. The manuscript's author is Izzy (short for Israel), a young Jewish man whose mother only wants him to get married in accordance with tradition. Izzy, however, has other plans and is studying for his entrance examinations to the Russian university, but his studies seem to be making him sick. This is the context in which he tells of his encounter with a mare who is in bad shape; not only is she thin and weak but she also has been beaten. The mare tells Izzy of her ordeals, and he tries to help her. Izzy then wakes up from what has apparently been a nightmare. It turns out that he has been studying so hard for his entry exams that he has exhausted himself—hence the sleep and nightmare. His mother urges him to give up the studies, which are making him ill, and marry.

But Izzy wants to be "a human being":

Oh, Mother. I curse the day that I was born to be miserable and hated by all the world! My own people, the Jews, are so terrible to me, and so are the "others," the Christians! The Jews hate me for not being a Jew after their own hearts, and the Christians despise me for being a Jew—"Ah, that's the trouble! A Jew!" For the sin with which I and my ancestors were born, and which has been handed down to us from Father Abraham, we are punished with misery, oppression, expulsions, afflictions, sufferings, and every possible torture. I feel it's my foremost obligation to do anything in my power to fight this misfortune. A man who's been expelled from the rest of mankind, in whom God's gift of human dignity has been degraded, who's been crowded into a confining area like a bird in a cage, unable to budge—if that man doesn't give a damn, then it would be better not to have been born at all. I'm a human being, Mama! I'm alive and I want to live. I want to get out of this narrow confinement and live on an equal footing with other human beings in God's great world. I have to do my best to keep my being Jewish from harming me and to improve my condition.[3]

In pursuit of his humanity, he rushes off to take his entrance exams. Facing harsh examiners who are glaring at him and "dressed in uniforms with brass buttons," Izzy is unnerved and fails.[4] Afterward, he meets the mare again and decides to write to the "society for prevention of cruelty to animals," thinking that the society's high-minded principles will save the mare from her sufferings. Izzy also insists that the mare improve herself by cleaning up her appearance and learning to dance. But Izzy's attempts to help are not successful and only make the mare's situation worse, bringing the mare to Ashmedai, king of the demons. When Izzy wakes up, his mother is in tears, because Izzy's effort to improve himself has literally made him sick. Again she begs him to get married.

"The Mare" is an equal opportunity offender. Nobody comes off well, including the traditional Jewish community, the maskilim, Christians, Russia, and the czar. The form of the story reflects its multivalent criticism. How many mares are there? "The Mare" read by the reader, Mendele's dead horse, the manuscript "The Mare," the mare Izzy encounters, and the second mare who may not be the same as the first. What is the relation between these mares? Abramovitsh seems to indicate that they are all intertwined and cannot be separated, just as the problematic nature of traditional Judaism, the Haskalah, Russia, and the czar cannot be separated.

The society for the prevention of cruelty to animals parodies an actual society, the Society for the Spread of Enlightenment among the Jews of Russia (OPE), founded in Saint Petersburg in 1863 by a small group of elite Jews who were the beneficiaries of the selective integration policy mentioned above. Within Abramovitsh's story, the society for the prevention of cruelty to animals represents the emptiness and futility of enlightenment ideals, just as Izzy's attempt to teach the mare to dance makes fun of claims for cultural improvement. As the mare puts it, "Such philosophizing is neither here nor there. All I want to say is that those things aren't essential. When a creature is born, it knows nothing about them. It only wants to eat, breathe, and move freely before it has even the foggiest notion of those contrivances."[5]

The mare's words not only question the existential relevance of philosophy but also point to the morally questionable, if not hypocritical, stance of the OPE. How can the OPE preach the need for enlightenment among Jews when the Jewish masses, like the mare, are hungry and continually threatened with physical violence? Understood within the context of selective integration, Izzy's troubles with his studies also come into sharper focus. As mentioned, his ordeal is the result of his effort to pass his exams and gain entrance into the university system, which for him and all Jews in the Russian Empire was perhaps the main conduit of selective integration. Maybe Izzy's mother is right after all; his studies have made him sick. He should just get married.

Yet Abramovitsh is just as critical of the traditional Jewish community and its ideas. Izzy is continually frustrated with the passivity of the mare, who like the traditional Jewish community, does nothing to defend herself and continually allows herself to be beaten. On another level, "The Mare" overtly satirizes traditional Jewish ideas and practices through ironic references to the book of Job, the holiday of Purim, the Ten Commandments, Ashmedai, and the prophetic call to the orphan, widow, and stranger, among others. Let me look specifically at two examples of Mendele's satirization of the tradition from the preface to the manuscript "The Mare." Mendele begins by praising God:

> Mendele the Book Dealer says unto you: Glory be to the Creator, Who, after making the great universe, took counsel with the angelic hosts and finally fashioned a small world, namely man, who is known as the microcosm for combining within himself—if you take a close look—all manner of creatures and animals. You will find in him all species of wild beasts and all breeds of cattle. You will find a lizard, a leech, a Spanish fly, a Japanese beetle, and similar creeping and crawling pests. You will even find a demon, a devil, a satan, a fiend, an imp, a Jew-baiter, and similar hellhounds, cat toying with a mouse; a fox sneaking into a chicken coop and twisting the necks of the poor fowls ... and similar wondrous things. But that's neither here nor there. Praised be the Good Lord.[6]

Mendele's benediction mimics the form of a Jewish prayer, but in its content, it questions the very belief in a God who loves the people of Israel and mocks the wonders of creation. Mendele continues to describe the manuscript in the following terms:

> The Mare is written in a lofty manner, the style of the ancients. Each reader will comprehend it in accordance with his intelligence and on his own level. For people on the surface level, it will simply be a lovely tale, and they will enjoy the plot. But those on a deeper level will also find an allusion, an application, to us sinful human creatures. I, for example, on my level, found in it nearly all Jewish souls, all our beings, and the secret of what we are doing in this world. I am convinced that during your perusal, a number of you, each according to his nature, will be unable to help himself and will ardently call out: "Why, that's an allusion to Mr. Yossel!" Or: "Oh! That's a

reference to Mr. Nathan! Mr. Zalman-Jacob! Mr. Hershke!" Or else: "Hey! I've discovered the secret behind our kosher-meat tax, our philanthropists, and all our behavior!" And so on.[7]

Mendele implicitly compares "The Mare" to scripture in attributing to it the four levels of meaning found in traditional Jewish interpretation: the plain sense of the text, homiletic exegesis, a hint of a secret, and finally a secret. Mendele mocks the very notion of esoteric meaning by suggesting that the big question for human beings in general and Jews in particular is not, for instance, about God the creator but rather about taxes. The kosher-meat tax also refers to Abramovitsh's own play à la clef from 1869, "The Tax," a satirical work for which he was driven out of town (Berdichev, in the Ukraine) by the local Jewish establishment.

Let me return once more to the context of the origins of modern Yiddish literature. "The Mare" was first published in 1873 and then republished in an expanded version in 1886. Despite the euphoria among maskilim that followed the reforms of Alexander II beginning in 1855, the 1860s already marked the onset of a virulent anti-Semitism, with Russians of varying political persuasions finding reasons to blame the Jews for their perceived ills. On the Right, the Jews were cast as European invaders, and often associated (negatively) with the French and Germans. From this perspective, Jews were blamed for bringing an end to the Russian aristocracy. In contrast, on the Left, Jews were blamed for bringing capitalism to Russia and exploiting various ethnic groups, such as the Ukrainians and Poles. Jews in this case were associated with the old Polish aristocracy in particular and the feudal past in general.

In 1871, two years before Abramovitsh published "The Mare," an anti-Jewish riot broke out in Odessa to devastating effect, both physically and intellectually. Although the Russian authorities did not participate in the violence, they did nothing to stop it. The riot and its aftermath crushed the hopes of Odessa's many Jewish intellectuals who had until then been committed to maskilic ideals. The Russian-language Jewish newspaper closed, as did Odessa's OPE chapter. In 1881, five years before Abramovitsh published an expanded edition of "The Mare," Alexander II was assassinated. Multiple pogroms broke out a month later against Jews and spread to more than two hundred cities, with riots against Jews continuing through 1884. The new czar, Alexander III, blamed the Jews for these riots and imposed new restrictions on them. As a result of these pogroms and more that followed, in 1903–6, many eastern European Jews turned to Zionism, the subject of chapter 8, or immigrated to the United States, the subject of chapter 9. Let me now consider one of the eastern European Jews who immigrated to the United States in response to the Russian pogroms, Sholem Aleichem, and his story "On Account of a Hat."

"On Account of a Hat"

Rabinovitsh was born in the Ukraine, where his father was a merchant attracted to the ideas of the Haskalah and especially the emergence of modern Hebrew literature. The younger Rabinovitsh initially wrote in Hebrew, but then turned to Yiddish, using the pen name Sholem Aleichem for his first published stories because he did not want his father to know that he was publishing in Yiddish. In his lifetime, Sholem Aleichem was enormously popular and read by Jews all over the world, religious and secular alike. He had hoped to support himself in the United States through his writings and work in the theater, but when this proved difficult, he left his family in New York and traveled around Europe to give readings. In 1911 he returned to New York, where he died in 1916.

First, I will briefly recount the story told in "On Account of a Hat." A Jewish traveler meets Sholem Aleichem on a train and tells him a story about a businessperson from Kasrilevke, his hometown, named Sholem Shachnah, or as he is known at home, "Sholem Shachnah Rattlebrain." Determined to get home before Passover begins the next evening, Sholem Shachnah arrives at a train station named Zlodievke (Roguesville) in the middle of the night. He is exhausted after not sleeping for two nights, but also desperately afraid of missing his train. With great trepidation, he takes the only open seat in the station—a small spot on a bench next to a sleeping Russian official, whom he names "Buttons" after the brass buttons of the official's coat. Still afraid of missing his train, Sholem Shachnah pays a Russian peasant to wake him up when the train comes. He falls asleep, and having been awakened in the middle of a bad dream, somewhat dazedly grabs the wrong hat. Now wearing the hat of the Russian official, Sholem Shachnah races to buy a ticket, only to face a huge line. As he approaches, the crowd lets him go first in line, and the ticket agent asks him, "Where to, your Excellency?" Sholem Shachnah is shocked and confused by the deferential behavior of the crowd and the ticket agent, yet he nevertheless insists, despite the ticket agent's protests, that he wants a third-class ticket. Completely unaware that he is wearing the official's hat, Sholem Shachnah finds himself escorted not to the third-class car and not even to a second-class one but instead to first class. He has no idea what is going on. Suddenly he sees himself in the mirror. His response: "Twenty times I tell him [the peasant] to wake me and I even give him a tip, and what does he do, that dumb ox, may he catch cholera in his face, but wake up the official instead! And me he leaves asleep on the bench! Tough luck, Sholem Shachnah old boy, but this year you'll spend Passover in Zlodievke, not at home."[8] Convinced that his real self is asleep at the train station, Sholem Shachnah jumps off the train and returns to Zlodievke, thereby missing not only his train home but also the start of Passover.

On the most basic level, "On Account of a Hat" is funny because the main character, Sholem Shachnah, is not just stupid but absurd as well. Sholem Shachnah is a country bumpkin in a sophisticated city of trains and their schedules. His stupidity turns to absurdity at the climax of the story when Sholem Shachnah doesn't recognize himself in the mirror because he is wearing the official's hat. In search of his real self, he idiotically gets off the train and ends up not making it home for Passover because of his own silliness. But this reading is partial, reflecting only the story within the story. Let us recall that according to Sholem Aleichem's story, a traveler is telling the story to Sholem Aleichem. This traveler, after describing Sholem Shachnah's initial arrival at the train station, comments to the fictional Sholem Aleichem: "When the wise men of Kasrilevke quote the passage from the Holy Book, 'Tov shem meshemen Tov,' [from Ecclesiastes 7:1, 'A good name is better than precious oil'] they know what they're doing. I'll translate it for you: We were better off without the train."[9] In the same way that Abramovitsh implies that the big question for Jews is not about their relation to God but rather about their taxes, Sholem Aleichem suggests that what is of real concern for Russian Jews is not the wisdom of Ecclesiastes but instead the ways in which the technological achievements of the modern world have made life harder. Just look at poor Sholem Shachnah's attempt to get home. The traveler's reference to the Ecclesiastes passage is all the more ironic because he is telling a story that for all intents and purposes gives Sholem Shachnah a bad name—in direct defiance of the passage he quotes. By gossiping about Sholem Shachnah to Sholem Aleichem, who then purportedly writes down and thereby further disseminates this tale of Sholem Shachnah's stupidity, the traveler is violating the very tradition from which he purports to be drawing wisdom.

Given that the story seems to imply that one's identity is reducible to the hat on one's head, "On Account of a Hat" might be read as suggesting that there is no real distinction between the Jew, represented by Sholem Shachnah, and the Russian, represented by Buttons. Yet at least from the perspective of the traveler telling the story, the narrative is only funny because of the underlying assumption that it would be absurd to think that a Jew could be mistaken for a Russian official. In fact, the only imaginable relationship between Jews and Russian officialdom in the story within the story is the tremendous fear that Sholem Shachnah exhibits toward Buttons. Let us also recollect Izzy's alarm as he faces his university examiners who are dressed in uniforms with brass buttons—a fear so intense that it makes him sick and he cannot perform, and in the end fails his exams. Brass buttons alarm both Izzy and Sholem Shachnah, who worry that they are not safe when brass buttons are nearby. The ridiculousness of Sholem Shachnah's character—he looks in the mirror and because he is wearing the wrong hat, sees not himself but instead the Russian official—is only matched by the incongruity of the idea that a Jew and a Russian could be mistaken for one another.

The nervous anxiety that produces the humor in "On Account of a Hat" is all the more evident in the story's setting, where Sholem Shachnah is in a great hurry because he needs to get home in time for Passover. For his readers, this story, published in 1913, would call to mind a terrifying event of two years earlier, when a Jewish man named Menachem Mendel Beilis was accused of murdering a thirteen-year-old Ukrainian boy in order to use the boy's blood to bake matzo for Passover. Such accusations had been common, especially in the Middle Ages, when Jews were periodically accused of killing Christian children in order to use their blood for Jewish rituals. Anti-Jewish riots often accompanied or were accompanied by such accusations (these accusations and their violent aftermaths have continued into the twentieth and twenty-first centuries, first in Poland after the Holocaust and today in parts of the Islamic world). There was no evidence that Beilis was in any way involved in the boy's murder, but the accusation helped fuel and was fueled by Russian anti-Semitism. As one government agent put it, Beilis's "guilt" makes "glaringly clear how this all-powerful international Jewry organizes its forces, and how incapable the Russian government is in its serious struggle against the Jews."[10] After two years of an investigation that did not produce any compelling evidence against him, Beilis was finally tried in Kiev in September and October 1913. Remarkably, largely due to the glowing testimonies to Beilis's good character from his Russian neighbors, a jury acquitted him.

Given that his readers would immediately associate Passover with the Beilis trial, Sholem Aleichem's framing of "On Account of a Hat" with Sholem Shachnah's desperate attempt and then ultimate failure to get home in time for Passover enacts again the complex interplay between humor and anxiety that marks the story. To make it home in time for Passover is not just to be home for the holiday but it is also to escape the great perils of Russian Jewish life, if only briefly. Sholem Shachnah fails to make it home, and though the story's readers may laugh because he is so silly, Sholem Aleichem at the same time offers readers of the story a grim picture of the Jewish present and future in Russia.

CONCLUSION

As we have seen in this chapter, modern Yiddish literature, as exemplified by two of its founders, Abramovitsh and Sholem Aleichem, is quite different from the philosophical, historical, and theological writings that emerged in western Europe. For one thing, modern Yiddish literature, like Maimon's autobiography, is filled with humor. One would be hard pressed to find anything funny or entertaining in German Jewish thought (and the reader is welcome to reread the first four chapters of part I of this book to double-check). This difference in tone is significant for what it reveals about the contrasting perspectives of western and eastern European Jews. German Jewish thought is sober but optimistic. All the German Jewish authors discussed in part I seemed sure that they had some access to truth and certainty, and that they could find their way in the modern world as both modern Jews and modern people. My examination of Abramovitsh and Sholem Aleichem in this chapter as well as Maimon in the last chapter reflects a far more ironic as well as less certain vision of the Jewish and non-Jewish worlds. One may debate the virtues and veracities of each of these perspectives, but what is not debatable is that for all they lacked in modern political and individual rights, eastern European Jews created a vibrant culture out of the stuff of Jewish life and experience. Modern Yiddish literature both creatively describes eastern European Jewish life as its denizens experienced it and, as we will see further below, transforms what had formerly been theological categories into cultural ones. By way of conclusion, let me consider briefly the category of Jewish culture, which like the category of Jewish religion, is not without its own tensions and internal contradictions.

In both "The Mare" and "On Account of a Hat," theological vocabulary turns into a cultural lexicon. In the case of "The Mare," we saw that Abramovitsh parodies mainstays of traditional Jewish life (such as formulaic blessings and exegetical formulas) to suggest that the meaning of Jewish existence does not stem from a relationship between God and the Jewish people but rather from the life experiences of the Jewish people themselves. In the case of "On Account of a Hat," Sholem Aleichem also transforms language about God and the Jewish people into language about only the Jewish people. At the beginning of the story, for instance, the traveler tells the fictional Sholem Aleichem that "one day God took pity on Sholem Shachnah, and for the first time in his career as a real-estate broker ... he actually worked out a deal."[11] Yet God's pity turns out not to have been merciful at all. In the first place, as the traveler tells it, Sholem Shachnah's brethren cheat him. In the second place, Sholem Shachnah is in his perilous situation—trying to get home in time for Passover—as a result of God's pity.

Perhaps most fundamentally, the underlying conceit of "On Account of a Hat"—that a Jew could be taken for a Russian official—is based on what was a well-known Jewish joke, which was not about a Jew and a government official but rather about a Jew and a priest. In one critic's retelling of the original joke, a Jew "falls asleep next to an Eastern Orthodox priest, is rudely awakened when the time comes, and in his confusion exchanges his kapote, or gaberdine, for a reverentke, a priestly habit. When the Jew washes his face ... he stops dead and exclaims, 'That idiot! I asked him to wake me up, and what does he do? He wakes the priest up instead!'"[12] In retelling the joke about a Jew and a Russian official, and not a Jew and a priest, Sholem Aleichem further secularizes Jewish tradition, thus following Abramovitsh in transforming theology into culture.

We see, then, that the notion of Jewish culture is predicated on a transformation of an underlying religious culture whose concern is not with the Jewish people alone but rather with the Jewish people's relation to the divine. To put it a bit more strongly, the notion of Jewish culture, or Jewish secularism, is parasitic on a religious culture. Abramovitsh's and Sholem Aleichem's literary genius comes from their adaptation of theological language to new circumstances. Their social commentary and humor emerge from transfiguring what had been a theological framework into a cultural one, thereby calling into question what had been the authoritative status of this theological framework. The question becomes, What happens when this theological language and tradition are no longer common literary bodies of reference for Jewish people?

Here again, I must return to the historical and political context that gave rise to the emergence of modern Yiddish literature: the weakening of the traditional Jewish community without an accompanying alternative political structure for Jews. This meant that despite the enormous changes wreaked on eastern European Jews in the eighteenth and nineteenth centuries, it was still possible to speak of a common culture deriving from the Jewish tradition. Once this common culture can no longer be taken for granted, what does it then mean to speak of or create a living Jewish culture? Put another way, What happens when no one gets the joke because no one appreciates the reference? I will continue to explore this issue in the next two chapters—first in the context of Ahad Ha'am's cultural Zionism and advocacy of Hebrew culture, and then in relation to Mordecai Kaplan's attempt to reconstruct Judaism as civilization (as opposed to religion) in the United States.

Suggested Readings

Abramovitsh

Miron, Dan. *A Traveler Disguised: The Rise of Modern Yiddish Fiction in the Nineteenth Century.* Foreword Ken Frieden. Syracuse, NY: Syracuse University Press, 1996.

Addressing a variety of issues relating to the emergence of modern Yiddish literature, Miron's study focuses primarily on the figure of Mendele in Abramovitsh's writings, suggesting that this character allowed Abramovitsh to navigate the relationship between a modern identity and the traditional Jewish world—to mediate between the Westernized writer and their "dark Jewish other."

Miron, Dan, and Anita Norich. "The Politics of Benjamin III: Intellectual Significance and Its Formal Correlatives in Sh. Y. Abramovitsh's *Masoes Benyomin Hashlishi*." In *The Field of Yiddish: Studies in Language, Folklore, and Literature*, ed. Marvin I. Herzog, Barbara Kirshenblatt-Gimblett, Dan Miron, and Ruth Wisse, with Alan Huffman, 1–115. 4th ed. Philadelphia: Institute for the Study of Human Issues, 1980.

The authors explore the relationship between the formal, aesthetic, and political dimensions of Abramovitsh's *The Abridged Travels of Benjamin the Third*. Miron and Norich show that the text begins by criticizing the weakness and stagnation of Jewish society relative to western Europe, but concludes by offering a more suspicious view of politics and mobility.

Pinsker, Sanford. "Mendele Mocher Seforim: Hasidic Tradition and the Individual Artist." *Modern Language Quarterly* 30 (1969): 234–47.

This essay provides an overview of Abramovitsh's writings, treating his work against the backdrop of earlier traditions in Yiddish literature.

Schwarz, Jan. *Imagining Lives: Autobiographical Fiction of Yiddish Writers*. Madison: University of Wisconsin Press, 2005.

Linking Yiddish autobiographical fiction to a consciousness of being exiled from life in the shtetl, Schwarz explores the ways in which Yiddish authors transformed U.S. and European models of autobiographical writing. Chapter 1 deals extensively with Abramovitsh's work, addressing issues such as his significance for "life writing" and treatments of the self in later Yiddish literature.

Seidman, Naomi. *A Marriage Made in Heaven: The Sexual Politics of Hebrew and Yiddish*. Berkeley: University of California Press, 1997.

Considering Abramovitsh within a broader study of gender and language among eastern European Jews, Seidman analyzes the social dimensions of the complex relationship between Hebrew and Yiddish—more specifically, the ways in which this relationship reflected and strengthened the gender structures within Jewish communities.

Shaked, Gershon. *Modern Hebrew Fiction*. Trans. Yael Lotan. Ed. Emily Miller Budick. Bibliography Jessica Cohen. Bloomington: Indiana University Press, 2000.

Chapter 2 of this study addresses topics such as Abramovitsh's use and transformation of classical Hebrew sources, appropriation and adaptation of existing literary traditions, and disillusionment with the worldview of the Jewish Enlightenment.

Aleichem

Miron, Dan. *The Image of the Shtetl and Other Studies of Modern Jewish Literary Imagination*. Syracuse, NY: Syracuse University Press, 2000.

Miron's essays explore the emergence and function of representations of the shtetl in Yiddish literature, portraying such accounts as a way to reconcile attachment to the past with life in the present, thereby remembering an "idealized" home while justifying participation in the modern world.

Roskies, David G. *A Bridge of Longing: The Lost Art of Yiddish Storytelling.* Cambridge, MA: Harvard University Press, 1995.
  Chapter 5 of this text provides an overview of Aleichem's life and writings.

"Sholem Aleichem: The Critical Tradition." In *Prooftexts* 6, no. 1 (1986).
  The essays in this issue—drawn from early twentieth-century criticism and contemporary literary scholarship—look at topics such as Aleichem's characters, humor, and use of quotations.

Wisse, Ruth R. *The Modern Jewish Canon: A Journey through Language and Culture.* New York: Free Press, 2000.
  Examining issues ranging from Aleichem's cultural and historical context to the autobiographical dimensions of his work, Wisse links *Tevye the Dairyman*—one of Aleichem's well-known works—to the project of creating a Yiddish "comic hero."

———. *Sholem Aleichem and the Art of Communication.* B. G. Rudolph Lectures in Judaic Studies. Syracuse, NY: Syracuse University, 1980.
  Exploring Aleichem's literary artistry and view of modernization, Wisse suggests that this author recognized a "common human denominator within arbitrary national distinctions," but nevertheless imposed a "limit" on processes of cultural transformation.

Historical Context

Abramsky, Chimen, Maciej Jachimczyk, and Antony Polonsky, eds. *The Jews in Poland.* Oxford: Basil Blackwell, 1986.
  The essays in this volume examine the history of Polish Jewry from the Middle Ages to the twentieth century.

Dawidowicz, Lucy S. "Introduction: The World of East European Jewry." In *The Golden Tradition: Jewish Life and Thought in Eastern Europe.* Ed. Lucy S. Dawidowicz, 5–90. Syracuse, NY: Syracuse University Press, 1996.
  Focusing on the period between the late eighteenth and early twentieth centuries, Dawidowicz offers an overview of eastern European Jewry's cultural and intellectual life as well as the broader historical context in which this life took shape.

Hundert, Gershon David. *Jews in Poland-Lithuania in the Eighteenth Century: A Genealogy of Modernity.* Berkeley: University of California Press, 2004.
  Hundert seeks to illuminate the life of Polish and Lithuanian Jewry in the eighteenth century as well as the continuities between this life and the experience of later eastern European Jews. Emphasizing the presence among Polish and Lithuanian Jews of a positive attitude toward Jewish identity, Hundert identifies a variety of historical factors that contributed to this "social-psychological translation of the concept of chosenness."

Klier, John Doyle. *Russia Gathers Her Jews: The Origins of the "Jewish Question" in Russia, 1772–1825.* Dekalb: Northern Illinois University Press, 1986.
  Klier explores the emergence of the "Jewish Question" in Russia during the late eighteenth and early nineteenth centuries, devoting particular attention to the transformation of "Russian Judeophobia" during this

period—and more specifically, to the ways in which concepts imported from the West played a central role in this transformation.

Nathans, Benjamin. *Beyond the Pale: The Jewish Encounter with Late Imperial Russia*. Berkeley: University of California Press, 2002.

Based on encounters between Russians and Jews during the nineteenth and early twentieth centuries, Nathans argues that aspirations for civic emancipation and social integration played a key part in shaping Russian Jewish history, and that the integration of Jews into Russian society began well before the revolution of 1917—indeed, that this process had its origins in reforms initiated by the imperial state and Jewish elites.

Pipes, Richard. "Catherine II and the Jews: The Origins of the Pale of Settlement." *East European Jewish Affairs* 5, no. 2 (1975): 3–20.

Pipes describes and assesses Russian policy toward the Jews during the second half of the eighteenth century, contending that the treatment of Jews by Catherine II was "remarkably enlightened" in crucial respects.

Stanislawski, Michael. "Russian Jewry, the Russian State, and the Dynamics of Jewish Emancipation." In *Paths of Emancipation: Jews, States, and Citizenship*, ed. Pierre Birnbaum and Ira Katznelson, 262–83. Princeton, NJ: Princeton University Press, 1995.

Focusing primarily on the period between the late eighteenth and early twentieth centuries, Stanislawski explores the nature of "Jewish emancipation" in the context of the Russian state, outlining the regime's gradual and "incoherent" extension of authority over the Jews as well as the impact of such efforts on the life of Russian Jewry.

———. *Tsar Nicholas I and the Jews: The Transformation of Jewish Society in Russia, 1825–1855*. Philadelphia: Jewish Publication Society of America, 1983.

Stanislawski studies the connection between Russian policy toward the Jews during the first half of the nineteenth century and developments that subsequently occurred in Russian Jewish life.

Weissler, Chava. *Voices of the Matriarchs: Listening to the Prayers of Early Modern Jewish Women*. Boston: Beacon Press, 1998.

Utilizing Yiddish devotional prayers, Weissler's essays seek to illuminate the religious lives of Jewish women.

Chapter 8

THE REJECTION OF JEWISH RELIGION AND
THE BIRTH OF JEWISH NATIONALISM

THE TERM ANTI-SEMITISM, coined in the late nineteenth century, implies that all Jews are Semites. Why, at this time, were Jews defined as such, and not, for instance, as German, French, Russian, or Polish? As we saw in chapters 2, 6, and 7, in the first half of the nineteenth century, in both western and eastern Europe, Jews had achieved some measure of success integrating into their various societies. This success, however, was met by non-Jewish society not with openness to further integration but rather with anti-Semitic backlash, from both the Right and Left. While they had their different reasons, both conservatives and liberals, in both western and eastern Europe, claimed that Jews did not conform to the correct national type, be it German, French, Russian, or Polish. Instead, despite the fact that Jews had lived in Europe for centuries, conservatives and liberals alike alleged that Jews were a foreign people, that they were Semites, the predominant ethnicity in the biblical lands of Judaism's origin. Hence the term anti-Semitism.

The Zionist movement arose in the context of nineteenth-century European nationalism and defined itself in opposition to the idea that Jews could be full members of a modern nation-state, whether French, German, or Russian, while adhering to their Jewish religion in their private lives. Rather, Zionists argued, the Jews themselves constituted a nation of their own. In making these claims, Zionists also rejected the traditional Jewish belief that the Jews will only return to the land of Israel en masse when the Messiah comes. (This point is often obscured by the rise of religious Zionism, discussed in chapter 5, but as we will see in this chapter, as a historical movement Zionism was distinctly secular and even antireligious.) Perez Smolenskin (1842–85), a Hebrew writer and Zionist polemicist, concisely captured the Zionist rejection of a modern concept of Jewish religion along with traditional Jewish belief and practice. Whether fairly or not, Smolenskin blamed Mendelssohn for what he regarded as the worst parts of Jewish modernity: the decline of Jewish national feeling among Jews, and what Smolenskin considered irrational devotion to Judaism's legal tradition. In Smolenskin's words, it was Mendelssohn "who doubly ensnared our people by weakening its sense of national unity and insisting on the continued total obligation of the religious laws."[1] Zionists aimed to restore the Jewish national feeling that they believed the idea of Jewish religion had weakened.

At least two creative tensions lie at the heart of Zionism. First, Zionism was perhaps unique as a historical, nationalist movement in that the Jews, unlike, for example, the English, French, Germans, or Russians, had neither a land of their own nor a national spoken language. Let us recall that Hebrew was a sacred language for Jews and, increasingly in the eighteenth century, a literary language. But Hebrew was not yet a modern, spoken language. Second, Zionism was at the same time a revolutionary movement that rejected the history of Jewish exile and a conservative movement that sought to preserve the Jewish people. Zionism thus had to account for the continuity between the Jewish past and Zionist present. As we will see in this chapter, this tension between radical change and fundamental continuity would and in fact continues to play itself out in the question, What is *Jewish* about the Jewish state? I will explore this question by turning first to Theodor Herzl's explicit rejection of Jewish religion, and then to Ahad Ha'am's cultural Zionism and attempt to refigure traditional Jewish religious concepts as part of a secular renaissance of Jewish culture. The chapter will conclude by considering the thought of Ahad Ha'am's critic, the Jewish Nietzschean Michah Josef Berdichevsky (1865–1921), examining in particular another dimension of the issue with which I ended the last chapter: Who has the authority to define the parameters of a culture when the authority of the tradition on which the culture is built has been undermined?

The Advent of the Zionist Movement

Herzl is the founder of the Zionist movement. But Herzl's ideas were in no way original, and much of what he had to say was based on his ignorance of modern Jewish life. We might even say that Zionism became a modern movement because of Herzl's profound unawareness of contemporary Jewry. Herzl claimed that the idea for a Jewish state had just come to him in a moment of inspiration: "Just how I got from the fictional to the practical ideas is already a mystery to me.... It all transpired in the unconscious."[2] He believed his ideas were wholly original and therefore needed to be heard. Had Herzl known that others before him, in the recent past, had argued, often far more eloquently than he would, for the necessity of creating a Jewish state, Herzl may not have written his manifesto, *The Jewish State*, in 1896, and Zionism may have just remained a notion discussed by a few Jewish intellectuals here and there. What Herzl brought to Zionism were not ideas or knowledge of Judaism, or the history of the Jews. What he gave it was a relentless energy and imagination, which inspired not intellectuals but rather the masses. Herzl died in 1904, at the age of forty-four, having literally worked himself to death. But in the eight years between the publication of *The Jewish State* and his death, Herzl had irrevocably changed modern Judaism by creating a Jewish national movement that redefined Judaism not as a drama between God and the Jewish people but instead as one between the Jewish people and the nations of the world. Before turning to Herzl's ideas and biography in some detail, though, let me briefly consider two of Herzl's Zionist predecessors: Moses Hess (1812–75) and Leon Pinsker (1821–91).

In 1862, Hess, born in Bonn and raised as an Orthodox Jew, published *Rome and Jerusalem: A Study in Jewish Nationalism*. In this book, Hess criticizes and rejects the idea that Judaism is a religion, calling this notion a modern and particularly Protestant invention. Hess maintains that the denial of Judaism's national dimension is a "recent German invention" that cannot be taken seriously.[3] Emancipation, argues Hess, has decimated the fullness of Jewish identity, reducing Judaism and Jewishness to an unsustainable individualism. This problem is not limited to Reform Judaism but applies to Orthodox Judaism as well:

> In Jewry, as well as in the entire modern world, there are to be discovered at present two main tendencies which, though diametrically opposed to each other, still originate from the same source, namely, the need of objective religious norms and the inability to create them. One tendency ... expresses itself on the part of some people in turning back to the old uncritical belief which, however with them, lost its naïve and true character.... [I]t is represented by Hirsch ... and other less gifted spirits, as well as by a host of ignoramuses and hypocrites.... As an antidote against this reaction, the negative reform aspirations may possess some justification, even though ... they did not succeed in creating any stable solid life forms. The characteristic trait of the negative spiritual tendency ... is its extreme individualism and incoherence.... Each of our Jewish Protestants has his own code.[4]

In a manner reminiscent of his German Jewish contemporary Graetz, Hess contends not only that Judaism conforms to current ideals of nationalism but also that it is the original nationalism that European nationalisms ought to try to emulate. As Hess puts it, "Nothing is more foreign to the spirit of Judaism than the idea of the salvation of the individual which, according to the modern conception, is the corner-stone of religion. Judaism has never drawn any line of separation between the individual and the family, the family and the nation, the nation and humanity as a whole."[5]

Hess is both a Zionist and socialist. What links the two? As we see in the two quotations above, Hess views the problem experienced by modern Jews—the need of norms, and the inability to create them—as one for the entire world. His friend Marx argued in 1844 (most likely influenced by Hess) that the problems of capitalism and religion are one and the same: both value the individual above the collective and reduce human society to individual self-interest. For both Hess and Marx, the right to one's own religious beliefs amounts to "the right to enjoy one's fortune and to dispose of it as one will; without regard for other men and independently of society."[6]

Spinoza, for Hess, understood what modern Jews ought to do: "Spinoza conceived Judaism to be grounded in Nationalism, and held that the restoration of the Jewish kingdom depends entirely upon the will and courage of the Jewish people."[7] Modern Jews need to return to their homeland and form a socialist commonwealth. Jewish nationalism, Hess declares, is not one of many choices for Jews. Hess is cognizant of growing anti-Semitism and therefore believes that Jewish nationalism is a necessity. His explanation for anti-Semitism is simple: the Jewish people get in the way of other national projects. If the Jewish people were a normal nation among nations, anti-Semitism would disappear. Hess's argument is captured in the title of his book: *Rome and Jerusalem*. Rome refers to the Italian nationalism of Giuseppe Mazzini (1805–72), and Jerusalem refers to Hess's call for Jewish nationalism.[8] Jerusalem is like Rome, Hess's title implies. Rome and Jerusalem are two nationalities in the age of nationalism. *Rome and Jerusalem* did not have much of an immediate effect. Hess's fellow socialists found his interest in Jewish nationalism strange, if not problematic. Reform and Orthodox Jews alike were outraged by Hess's criticisms of them. But perhaps the most basic reason *Rome and Jerusalem* did not find an immediate audience is that the book is written for intellectuals. Indeed, *Rome and Jerusalem*, like much of Hess's other work, is a meditation on Hegel's philosophical system.

Pinsker, writing in Odessa, wrote for the masses and not for intellectuals. In 1882, in the wake of the pogroms of 1881, he anonymously published a pamphlet called *Auto-Emancipation*. Like Hess's, Pinsker's argument is found in his title: emancipation has failed modern Jewry; Jews therefore need to emancipate themselves—that is, they need to start acting and determining their own fate rather than allowing others to do so for them. Although Pinsker's pamphlet is not a philosophical work, his assertion in many ways parallels Hess's. Like Hess, Pinsker identifies the Jewish problem with the idea that Judaism is a religion. But whereas Hess claims that the notion that Judaism is a religion is a modern invention,

Pinsker maintains that the problem is not just the modern, Protestant idea of religion but also traditional Jewish belief since the exile:

> The belief in a Messiah, the belief in the intervention of a higher power to bring about our political resurrection, and the religious assumption that we must bear patiently a punishment inflicted upon us by God, caused us to abandon every care for our national liberty, for our unity and independence. Consequently, we really gave up every thought of a fatherland.... The people *without a fatherland forgot their fatherland.* Is it not high time to realize what a disgrace this state of things is to us?[9]

According to Pinsker, the modern political project of Jewish emancipation only intensifies this passive strain in Jews and Judaism; in waiting to be emancipated, Jews both behave and are treated, by their friends and enemies alike, as passive objects.

Pinsker, a graduate of the University of Moscow, was a physician, and he characterizes anti-Semitism (which he calls "Judeophobia") as a disease: "Judeophobia is a form of demonopathy, with the distinction that the Jewish ghost has become known to the whole race of mankind.... Judeophobia is a psychic disorder. As a psychic disorder it is hereditary, and as a disease transmitted for two thousand years it is incurable.... He must be blind indeed who will maintain that the Jews are not the chosen people, the people chosen for universal hatred."[10] As would be the case for Herzl, Pinsker defines the need for Zionism entirely in terms of the reality of anti-Semitism. In keeping with his view of Jewish passivity, Pinsker describes Jews as ghostlike, a shadow of the living. Although he depicts Judeophobia as a "psychic disorder," Pinsker nevertheless thinks that anti-Semites rightly recognize the pathology of modern Jewish life. Unlike anti-Semites, however, Pinsker believes that Jews can change themselves as soon as they understand their disgraceful situation and passive complicity in it.

Given the tight link that he posits between anti-Semitism and the need for a Jewish state, Pinsker, as would Herzl after him, does not see the need for much continuity between the Jewish past and Zionist future. Rather, for both Pinsker and Herzl, the Jewish past and Zionist future have only the Jews in common, and the Jews, aside from their experience of anti-Semitism, are just like everybody else. In this connection, Pinsker is not especially committed to Palestine as the future homeland for the Jews. Given its historical meaning, Palestine is certainly one option for a homeland, but, suggests Pinsker, so is the United States. Pinsker cares less about the particular location and more about the need for concrete action on the part of the Jewish people to begin the logistical work for the Jewish state's creation. Enter Herzl.

HERZL AND THE JEWISH STATE

Born in Budapest in 1860 to an assimilated Jewish family, Herzl studied law in Vienna, but his real interest was in writing plays and novels, for which, it turned out, he did not have much talent. Yet he did have tremendous talent for journalism, and in 1892 was appointed Paris correspondent for Vienna's *New Free Press*. In Paris, the French had increasingly warmed to Russia following Germany's annexation of Alsace-Lorraine in 1871, and in this context, the support of French Jews for their Russian brethren and criticism of Russia in the aftermath of the Russian pogroms in 1881 was interpreted as pro-German, and hence anti-French. With this came a rise in French anti-Semitism, which culminated in the infamous Dreyfus affair.

In November 1894, Captain Alfred Dreyfus, an assimilated Jew who had risen in the ranks of the French military, was accused of treason, and Herzl was assigned to report on the case. Dreyfus's trial was closed to the public and journalists, and despite his unwavering declarations of innocence and the lack of any concrete evidence against him, Dreyfus was unanimously found guilty and sentenced to life imprisonment on Devil's Island. After the verdict, mobs crowded the streets of Paris for days, shouting "Death to the Jews." Herzl claimed that the Dreyfus affair proved once and for all that assimilation was impossible. As he observed, "And where? In France. In republican, modern, civilized France, one hundred years after the declaration of the Rights of Man." Herzl famously proclaimed, "The Dreyfus trial ... which I witnessed in Paris in 1894, made me a Zionist."[11] Herzl no doubt saw the Dreyfus affair as a seminal event, but his ambivalence about the possibility of assimilation and his own Jewish identity long predated the affair. At the same time, recent scholarship suggests that Herzl's claim about the pivotal role of the Dreyfus affair for his Zionism was a belated contrivance on his part.

Whatever the case, months before the Dreyfus affair Herzl wrote a play that reflected his ambivalences. The play, *The New Ghetto*, centers on a young Jewish man who is trapped into marrying the daughter of an ostentatiously wealthy and crude Jewish family with questionable morals (a thinly veiled reference to Herzl's wife and in-laws, whom he despised). The family attempts to buy a mine from a German aristocrat just when the mine's workers are protesting their unsafe working conditions. The hero disassociates himself from the financial dealings of his wife's family and tries to help the workers. Tragically, the strike organized by the hero ends in a mining accident, and the German aristocrat accuses the hero of being part of a Jewish conspiracy to ruin him. The hero tries to save his honor by entering a duel, in which he dies, uttering in his last breath and as the final sentence of the play, "Jews, my brothers, they won't let you live again, until you learn how to die.... I want out! Out of the ghetto!"[12]

In Herzl's play, the German aristocrat's accusation is presented as only natural. Herzl, in contrast, depicts the Jewish hero as unusual in having a social conscience. The Jewish hero's recourse to honor also has nothing to do with his Jewishness but instead is the adoption of an aristocratic rite, defending his honor by dueling, as well as the notion that passively dying is more honorable than continuing to fight. The notion that Jews must "learn to die" indicates that if Jews want to get out of the ghetto, they must fully cease to be Jews. In a letter from 1892, Herzl portrays his Jewish brethren in rather uncomplimentary terms: "I do not consider the anti-Semitic movement altogether harmful. It will inhibit the ostentatious flaunting of conspicuous wealth, curb the unscrupulous behavior of Jewish financiers, and contribute in many ways to the education of the Jews." Herzl does not think much more highly of the Jewish religion: "Perhaps also as regards religion. I consider religion indispensable for the weak. There are those who, weak in willpower, mind, or emotions, must always be able to rely on religion."[13] Both of these comments show that in his self-perception, Herzl is an enlightened European. What changes with the Dreyfus affair is not Herzl's identification with Europe (as we will see, he embraces European culture through and through) or his interest in Judaism (he never shows more than passing interest in Jewish religion, culture, or history). Rather, what changes is Herzl's sense that the Jews are to blame for their own suffering. As Herzl realizes, there is nothing the Jews could do in Europe to make anti-Semitism go away. Even if every Jew were to behave like the hero in *The New Ghetto*, there simply is no getting out of the ghetto. What the Jews need to do is to get out of Europe and create a state for themselves.

The Jewish State follows this line of thinking and its argument goes as follows. Europe will never accept the Jews, and this has been proven. Jews must therefore form their own state and govern themselves in accordance with the best of Europe's traditions. The formation of a Jewish state is good not only for the Jews but will also help Europe's nations. Anti-Semitism is caused by economic competition, and once the Jews have left Europe, economic competition will disappear, as will anti-Semitism. Thus, Herzl believes, Europe's leaders along with well-known anti-Semites ought to and would support the Zionist cause. The formation of a Jewish state is after all in their best interests as well.

In the eight years after the publication of *The Jewish State* until his death, Herzl negotiated with, among others, the sultan of Turkey, Kaiser Wilhelm, the king of Italy, and Pope Pius X on behalf of the establishment of a Jewish state. Herzl was not successful. He also did not have any success with Jewish philanthropists, who were already giving aid to suffering Jewish communities. As Herzl reports, a year before publishing *The

Jewish State, he had approached Baron Maurice de Hirsch as well as the famous Jewish philanthropic and banking family, the Rothschilds. They were not persuaded.[14] Eastern European Jews, perhaps to Herzl's surprise, rather than their western counterparts, made Zionism an actual political movement. Herzl, unknowingly, had answered Pinsker's call for logistical organization when, in 1897, he organized the first Zionist Congress. Like his western European predecessors, Herzl viewed eastern European Jews as the real thing. Describing the first Zionist Congress, Herzl wrote:

> Brothers have found each other again. They possess that inner unity which has disappeared from among westerners. They are steeped in Jewish national sentiment without betraying any national narrowness and intolerance. They are not tortured by the idea of assimilation. They do not assimilate into other nations, but exert themselves to learn the best in other peoples. In this way they manage to remain erect and genuine. Looking on them, we understood where our forefathers got the strength to endure through the bitterest times.[15]

The Jewish people were not closer to having their own state in 1904, when Herzl died, but, with a mass following made up largely of eastern European Jews, he had in fact created the Zionist movement.

What is Jewish about Herzl's vision of the Jewish state? Not much. Though translated as *The Jewish State*, Herzl's title in German is *Der Judenstaat*, which literally means a state of Jews, rather than a state that is Jewish. And that sums up Herzl's view: the state is for the sake of the survival of Jews, and not for the sake of the survival of Judaism or some form of Jewishness. As I have discussed, Herzl had little knowledge of, or more important, interest in, Judaism or any cultural sense of Jewishness. A few practical issues explored in *The Jewish State* are especially telling. First, what language would be spoken in the Jewish state? Herzl immediately rules out both Hebrew and Yiddish. About Hebrew, Herzl notes, "We cannot converse with one another in Hebrew. Who amongst us has a sufficient acquaintance with Hebrew to ask for a railway ticket in that language? Such a thing cannot be done."[16] It is true that Hebrew was not yet a modern spoken language, but as mentioned in chapters 4 and 7, from the late eighteenth century forward, maskilim, in both western and eastern Europe, had developed Hebrew into a modern literary language, and there was no reason that Hebrew could not be converted into a modern spoken language (which was actually happening as Herzl was writing). At the same time, Herzl's contemporary Ahad Ha'am, to whom I will turn in the next section, was advocating a revival of Hebrew culture. But Herzl did not know any of this. He also rejects Yiddish. Sounding like a maskil, Herzl states, "We shall give up using those miserable stunted jargons, those Ghetto languages which we still employ, for these were the stealthy tongues of prisoners."[17] As a solution, Herzl suggests that the Jewish state ought to be like Switzerland, with several European languages coexisting as national languages.

What about religion? Herzl writes, "We shall keep our priests within the confines of their temples in the same way as we shall keep our professional army within the confines of their barracks."[18] On the one hand, Herzl seems merely to posit a liberal distinction between church and state. Yet it is striking how devoid of content Herzl's notion of Jewish religion is in *The Jewish State*. The picture is somewhat different in Herzl's utopian novel of 1902, *Old New Land*, in which he envisions life in the Jewish state. In the novel, Jews celebrate Passover and go to the synagogue. Perhaps most intriguingly, Herzl, a great lover of opera, imagines an opera about Shabbetai Zvi, the seventeenth-century false messiah, discussed briefly in chapter 6. These descriptions in the novel notwithstanding, Herzl does not have a sustained interest in Judaism or Jewish culture. This, for instance, is Herzl's proposal for a flag and its symbolism: "I would suggest a white flag, with seven golden stars. The white field symbolizes our pure new life; the stars are the seven golden hours of our working-day. For we shall march into the Promised Land carrying the badge of honor."[19] (Here I may note, by the way, the name of the big mall in the city of Herzliya, the small coastal city in Israel named after Herzl: "the seven-hour mall.")

Most telling of all perhaps is the question of the land itself. For Herzl, the Jewish state need not have been in the land of Israel. At the first Zionist Congress, Herzl accepts the definition of Zionism as seeking "to secure for the Jewish people a publicly recognized, legally secured, home in Palestine."[20] His vision of a state for Jews, however, is in no way dependent on a connection to the land of Israel—a connection that was essential for most Zionists. Although these Jews were quite pronounced in their opposition to traditional Judaism, they saw Zionism as continuous with their Jewish identity, which unlike Herzl, they defined not just in terms of anti-Semitism. The issue of land came to a head at the sixth Zionist Congress in 1903, subsequently known as the "Uganda Congress." In response to the brutal pogrom in Kishinev, Russia, the British government had offered Herzl and the Zionist Congress some land in Uganda, East Africa. Herzl wanted to accept this offer, although only provisionally. But many eastern European Jews opposed Herzl and insisted that only the land of Israel would do.

AHAD HA'AM AND CULTURAL ZIONISM

Notwithstanding his significant success in mobilizing the Zionist movement, Herzl had his detractors. First and foremost among his critics was Ahad Ha'am. Born in 1856 in Skvrya, a small town in the Ukraine where

two Hasidic dynasties fought for control, Ahad Ha'am turned away from
Hasidism at an early age, and sought to educate himself in classical Jewish sources, medieval Jewish philosophy, and maskilic literature. Having
taught himself the Russian alphabet from reading storefronts, he also
studied philosophy, literature, and history on his own. Unlike almost all
his contemporaries, from both the East and the West, Ahad Ha'am was
not enamored with German philosophy but instead preferred British philosophers, especially Jeremy Bentham, John Locke, and John Stuart Mill.
He also was a fan of Charles Darwin. Although Ahad Ha'am sympa-
thized with the Haskalah's attempt to modernize Jews and Judaism, he
believed that the Haskalah had done so at too high a cost.

Ahad Ha'am explicitly rejects the modern idea that Judaism is a religion because he believes that Jews have attempted to eliminate their
communal identity for the false promise of the modern liberal state. In a
well-known and aptly titled essay, "Slavery in Freedom," he writes:

> Do I envy these fellow Jews of mine their emancipation? I answer in
> all truth and sincerity: No! A thousand times No.... I have at least
> not sold my soul for emancipation.... I at least know "why I remain
> a Jew"—or, rather, I can find no meaning in such a question, any
> more than if I were asked why I remain my father's son. I at least can
> speak my mind concerning the beliefs and the opinions which I have
> inherited from my ancestors, without fearing to snap the branch
> that unites me to my people. I can even adopt that "scientific heresy
> which bears the name Darwin," without any danger to my Judaism.
> In a word, I am my own, and my opinions are my own.[21]

Western European Jews are slaves in their freedom, argues Ahad Ha'am,
because political rights have come at the cost of Jewish collective identity.
As such, western European Jews are slaves to European culture. In their
so-called freedom they are forced to imitate European intellectual and
social habits; they simply cannot be themselves. Ahad Ha'am points out
that the notion that Judaism is a religion makes Jews slaves to the politics
and culture of the modern nation-state.

Ahad Ha'am also opposes the idea that Judaism is a religion on contemporary scientific grounds. He contends that it simply is no longer
tenable to believe in a supernatural God. If Judaism has any hope of
survival, it has to transform itself in accordance with modern science and
particularly Darwin's theory of evolution. In this regard, Ahad Ha'am
thinks Judaism has a real advantage over Christianity. Since the Jews are
a people, claims Ahad Ha'am, they can easily understand their traditions
as having evolved for the sake of Jewish collective survival. In a sentiment
that would be picked up by Kaplan in the United States, to be discussed
in chapter 9, Ahad Ha'am famously contends that "one can say without

any exaggeration that more than the Jewish people has kept the Sabbath, the Sabbath has kept [the Jewish people]."[22] The future of Christianity, in contrast, argues Ahad Ha'am, is far more precarious in that Christianity emphasizes the individual's belief in a supernatural God. In this way, Ahad Ha'am, at one and the same time, discredits the notion of an individual apart from the community and the belief in supernaturalism.

Ahad Ha'am's critique of Jewish life in western Europe does not mean of course that he sees Jewish life in eastern Europe as an ideal. Continually denied the freedoms of modern people, Jews are not allowed to live freely in eastern Europe, where they are also subject to increasing mob violence. For Ahad Ha'am, only the establishment of Jewish collective life in Palestine can revive Judaism and the Jewish people. This is the crux of his cultural Zionism. His aim is not the establishment of the external political structures of a nation-state, as is the case for Herzl and political Zionism, but rather the inward transformation of Jews—and Judaism— as they gather in the land of Israel.

Turning for a moment to Herzl, we might wonder why survival of the Jews and Judaism is necessary at all. Indeed, Herzl does not have a well-developed answer to this question; for him, Jewish survival, which a state for Jews would ensure, is an end in itself. Yet at a deeper level Herzl's analysis suggests that Jews are a people (and therefore entitled to survive as such) only because anti-Semites have made them so. The European nations simply will not allow the Jews to assimilate, which from Herzl's perspective would have been the best course of action. If Jews could assimilate, then the survival of the Jewish people, as opposed to individuals of Jewish descent, would not be necessary. It is for these reasons that Ahad Ha'am despises Herzl's political Zionism, which he sees not as an intrinsically Jewish enterprise but rather as a product of anti-Semitism. Where Herzl sees Zionism as necessary because of decay in the world in which Jews live (anti-Semitism), Ahad Ha'am believes Zionism to be essential because of decay in Jews themselves (assimilation to modern liberal culture). As such, Herzl proposes an external solution, the establishment of a state, while Ahad Ha'am proposes an internal solution, the spiritual rebirth of the Jewish nation.

Jewish survival matters to Ahad Ha'am for the sake of the spiritual renaissance of the Jewish people and Judaism. He is not opposed to the possibility of establishing a Jewish state at some future point, but he believes that Herzl's vision is bound to fail since it only concerns material and not spiritual ends:

> Judaism needs at present but little. It needs not an independent state, but only the creation in its native land of conditions favourable to its development: a good-sized settlement of Jews working without

hindrance in every branch of culture, from agriculture and handi-
crafts to science and literature. This Jewish settlement, which will
be a gradual growth, will become in the course of time the center of
the nation, wherein its spirit will find pure expression and develop
in all its aspects up to the highest degree of perfection of which it is
capable. Then from this center the spirit of Judaism will go forth to
the great circumference, to all the communities of the Diaspora, and
will breathe new life into them and preserve their unity; and when
our national culture in Palestine has attained that level, we may be
confident that it will produce men in the country who will be able,
on a favorable opportunity, to establish a state which will be truly a
Jewish state, and not merely a state of Jews.[23]

The settlement, and perhaps eventual state, would, for Ahad Ha'am, em-
body the prophetic tradition of justice and truth. Ahad Ha'am does not
believe that the Jewish people are chosen by God to be the bearers of the
prophetic message (again, he concludes that belief in a supernatural God
is an idea that modern people cannot accept) but instead contends that
history has made the Jewish people the chosen people who literally carry
with them the prophetic message.

How should we understand the prophets in the modern age, according
to Ahad Ha'am? Answering this question brings us to the heart of Ahad
Ha'am's understanding of culture. A prophet, for Ahad Ha'am, is not a
messenger from God but rather an idealist concerned with "the universal
dominion of absolute justice."[24] In contrast, a priest, for Ahad Ha'am, is
not an intermediary between the human and God but rather one who organizes national and political life. Whereas "prophets" are unbending in
their pursuit of perfection, "priests" are realists who recognize that they
must speak the language of their people. In making these distinctions,
Ahad Ha'am offers an account of the prototypes of the prophet and
priest. He analyzes how these figures have been understood historically
and how a modern person may understand them. It is necessary, according to Ahad Ha'am, to transform what historically have been theological
concepts into secular ones. It is this very process of transformation that
is key to Ahad Ha'am's understanding of Judaism as a national culture.
The point here is not to choose between prophet and priest but instead to
appreciate, in contemporary secular guise, the dialectical and productive
tension between the two.

The revivification of the Hebrew language is, in Ahad Ha'am's view,
the most central and pressing transformation incumbent on those working for a renaissance of Jewish national culture. Once again, he uses implicitly theological language to make a secular point. He likens political
redemption for the Jews—that is, Zionism—to the resurrection of the

dead (*t'hiyat ha-metim*). And cultural Zionism, he maintains, would lead to the "resurrection of the hearts" (*t'hiyat ha-levavot*) of the Jewish people.[25] The resurrection of the dead Hebrew language would lead the way from the deadened life of exile to the revival of the Jewish nation, in both flesh and spirit. According to Ahad Ha'am, this is something that Yiddish simply cannot do: "Hebrew has been our language ever since we came into existence; and Hebrew alone is linked to us inseparably and eternally as part of our being."[26]

In 1897, Ahad Ha'am founded the Hebrew periodical *Ha-Shiloah*, in which he published a number of his harsh criticisms of Herzl's Zionism. In 1903, Bialik, who would become the most important Hebrew poet of the twentieth century, became the editor of *Ha-Shiloah*. An adherent of Ahad Ha'am's cultural Zionism, Bialik also calls for the translation of theological concepts into secular ones and indeed for a new Hebrew canon to emerge from the old one. As he puts it, "Every closure [*hatimah*] announces the sealing [*ne'ilah*] of an old period, and at the same time it proclaims the opening of a new one."[27] Here Bialik plays on references to the Day of Atonement liturgy. Hatimah refers to the closing of the book of life. (A common greeting right before the Day of Atonement is *gmar hatimah tovah*, "finish with a good closure," which means, more idiomatically, "may your name be sealed in the book of life.") Ne'ilah is the final prayer before the end of Yom Kippur and ushers in the sealing of the book of life—that is, God's final judgment. In transforming these inherently theological terms into new, secular ideas, Bialik performs the cultural transformation for which Ahad Ha'am hopes.

Nevertheless, as Bialik recognizes, this transformation of the religious to the secular is easier said than done. In a well-known essay of 1917, "Halakhah and Aggadah" (Jewish law and narrative), Bialik expresses the tension between secular Zionism's new theory of culture and its practice. He writes, "Any aggadah which does not ... issue halakhah ... is mere sentimental babble."[28] In other words, reinterpretation is all well and good, but if it does not tell us what we should be doing, it is meaningless. To return to Bialik's wordplays on hatimah and ne'ilah, what does it mean to speak of a new, Hebrew canon without the divine authority on which the old canon is predicated? Can we meaningfully speak of hatimah and ne'ilah if we no longer believe in a God who passes judgment? If it is we who judge—as a secular conception of Jewish culture would suggest—on what basis do we judge?

I will return to these tensions in this chapter's conclusion, but before doing so let me consider Ahad Ha'am's legacy, given that the Zionist movement continued to concentrate not on Hebrew culture but rather on the establishment of a state. Let us recall the context of Jewish immigration to Palestine at the twentieth century's opening. Prior to Hitler's rise to power in 1933, Jewish immigration to Palestine, beginning in 1882 as a response to the pogroms in Russia, came in five large waves. Ahad Ha'am's cultural programs simply did not speak to the practical needs of Jews coming to Palestine during the second wave of immigration (known as the "second Aliyah") who had fled Russia after yet another deadly series of pogroms (1903–6) and whose ideological commitments were strongly socialist. Despite his pen name—again, meaning "one of the nation"—Ahad Ha'am did not have a popular following and, given the intellectualist character of his cultural Zionism, was often considered an elitist.

Ahad Ha'am is perhaps most remembered for the legacy of an essay he published in 1891 called "Truth from the Land of Israel." In this piece, he worries that the Arabs in Palestine will not tolerate a growing Jewish community. Like cultural Zionism generally, this concern did not speak to most Jews or Arabs at the time, but Ahad Ha'am did have intellectual adherents to his vision of Hebrew culture as well as the possibility of establishing a binational confederation of Jews and Arabs in Palestine. Proponents of binationalism never had much political influence, but this idea was a significant intellectual preoccupation, primarily among German Jewish intellectuals and émigrés to Palestine in the 1920s (including Shmuel Hugo Bergmann, Buber, Scholem, Judah Magnes, Arthur Ruppin, and Ernst Simon). In 1925, Brit Shalom (association for peace), a group focused on discussion about and the promotion of binationalism, was established in Jerusalem. For many advocates of binationalism, the Hebron riots of 1929, during which Palestinian Arabs brutally attacked and murdered Jewish civilians in Hebron and elsewhere, called much of Brit Shalom's mission into question. Still, Buber in particular continued to advocate binationalism long after the Israeli state was established in 1948, carrying Ahad Ha'am's mantle with him until his death in 1965.

Finally, while Ahad Ha'am's political influence was minimal, his vision directed the eleventh Zionist Congress, held in Vienna in 1913. This was the first time that Ahad Ha'am officially joined the Zionist party, and he did so because the focus of the Zionist Congress was on the establishment of the Hebrew University, which would be the institutional conduit for the creation and preservation of Hebrew culture. With the establishment of the Hebrew University of Jerusalem in 1925, Ahad Ha'am's ideas were brought to fruition.

CONCLUSION

In this chapter, I have explored the advent of the Zionist movement. As we have seen, political and cultural Zionism both oppose the idea that Judaism is a religion. Both forms of Zionism recognize that this concept is a modern invention that arises together with the modern nation-state, and both reject the idea that Jews can be citizens of the modern state while maintaining their religion in their private lives. As we saw, Herzl, the founder of the Zionist movement, opposes this notion on the basis of anti-Semitism's persistence. Ahad Ha'am, in contrast, rejects the idea that Jews can be citizens of modern nation-states while practicing their religion in private, because, he argues, this arrangement makes Jews slaves to the modern nation-state and perverts the fullness of Jewish life.

By way of conclusion, let me return to the question I asked of Herzl earlier in this chapter: What is Jewish about the Jewish state? Ahad Ha'am would seem to have answered this question by insisting that without a reinvigorated Jewish culture there could be no Jewish state but only a state of Jews. As we saw in the context of my discussion of Bialik, however, the implications of Ahad Ha'am's conception of Judaism and Jewish culture are not all that clear. If Hebrew culture relegates authority to the Jewish people themselves, and not to God or tradition, how is it possible to determine what the aggadah and halakhah should be? This was one of the charges that Berdichevsky, Ahad Ha'am's younger contemporary and critic, brings against him.

Berdichevsky's biography reflects many of the themes I examined in the last three chapters. Born in Medzhybizh, the headquarters of the Baal Shem Tov, Berdichevsky was attracted by the ideas of the Haskalah, and left Hasidism to study at the Volozhin Yeshiva. But his skeptical nature led him away from the yeshiva world to the study of philosophy in Germany and Switzerland. Berdichevsky used Hebrew, Yiddish, and German in his writings, which included fiction and essays on a variety of issues of the day; he also edited anthologies of folktales. Like Maimon, Abramovitsh, Sholom Aleichem, and Ahad Ha'am, Berdichevsky created a new pen name for himself: Bin Gorion.

The possibility of self-transformation is at the heart of Berdichevsky's thought; as he puts it, "We are Hebrews, worshiping only our own hearts."[29] Ahad Ha'am's conception of Hebrew culture is basically conservative. For him, the creation of a Hebrew culture at one and the same time preserves the vital elements of Judaism and the Jewish tradition. Berdichevsky draws different conclusions from the premise that he shares with Ahad Ha'am: that the Jews and Judaism are in need of revival. For Berdichevsky, the creation of a Hebrew culture is radical. If Jewish people themselves authorize their own transformation, as Ahad Ha'am suggests that they historically have and ought now to do again, Berdichevsky concludes that there are no clear boundaries as to what is Jewish and what is not.

In this vein, Berdichevsky also opposes Ahad Ha'am's ethical vision of Jews and Judaism. The Jewish people, argues Berdichevsky, are not a light unto the nations and indeed are no different from other peoples. What the Zionist project needs to recognize, he claims, is that Zionism and Hebrew culture should be aiming for normalization. For Berdichevsky, Zionism and cultural Zionism especially must understand the importance of power. As he explains, "There is a time for men and nations who live by the sword, by their strong arm, by vital boldness. This time is the hour of intensity, of life in its essential meaning. But the book is no more the shade of life, life in its senescence."[30]

Berdichevsky's criticism of Ahad Ha'am would seem to bring us back to the title of Herzl's manifesto: *Der Judenstaat*. Should we translate it as "the Jewish state" or "the state for Jews"? While all of the authors discussed in this chapter write before the establishment of the state of Israel in 1948, the actual existence of the state has in no way resolved this question. Here too we see that the category of Jewish nationality, like the categories of Jewish culture and Jewish religion, is not without its own tensions and internal contradictions.

SUGGESTED READINGS

Ahad Ha'am

"Forum: Perspectives on Ahad Ha-'Am." *Jewish History* 4, no. 2 (1990).
  The essays in this issue of *Jewish History* explore various dimensions of Ahad Ha'am's work, ranging from his political activity to his views on Jewish culture.
Kornberg, Jacques, ed. *At the Crossroads: Essays on Ahad Ha-Am*. Albany: State University of New York Press, 1983.
  The essays in this volume examine issues such as Ahad Ha'am's views on Hebrew and political activity.
Zipperstein, Steven J. *Elusive Prophet: Ahad Ha'am and the Origins of Zionism*. Berkeley: University of California Press, 1993.
  Zipperstein looks at Ahad Ha'am's writings, public activity, and status among Zionists, linking him to the context of eastern European Jewish life, emphasizing his role as Zionism's "chief internal critic," and suggesting that we can discover a consistent vision of the Jewish future in his work.

Background

Almog, Shmuel, Jehuda Reinharz, and Anita Shapira, eds. *Zionism and Religion*. Hanover, NH: University Press of New England, 1998.
  The essays in this volume explore the relationship between Zionism and religion in Europe, the United States, and the Yishuv.
Avineri, Shlomo. *The Making of Modern Zionism: The Intellectual Origins of the Jewish State*. New York: Basic Books, 1981.
  Based on various nineteenth- and twentieth-century thinkers, Avineri seeks to illuminate the diversity of Zionist thought as well as Zionism's relationship with modern political philosophy.

Brenner, Michael. *Zionism: A Brief History*. Trans. Shelley Frisch. Princeton, NJ: Markus Wiener Publishers, 2003.
    Brenner outlines the history of Zionism from the emergence of nationalist projects in the nineteenth century to recent developments in the state of Israel.
Halpern, Ben. *The Idea of the Jewish State*. 2nd ed. Cambridge, MA: Harvard University Press, 1969.
    Halpern analyzes the development of modern conceptions of Jewish sovereignty, describing the background and emergence of the Zionist movement as well as subsequent reconceptualizations of Jewish sovereignty—more specifically, reconceptualizations linked to developments within world Jewry and Zionism's relations with the international community.
Hertzberg, Arthur. Introduction to *The Zionist Idea: A Historical Analysis and Reader*, 15–100. Ed. Arthur Hertzberg. Foreword Emanuel Neumann. New York: Atheneum, 1979.
    Emphasizing the importance of understanding Zionism as a postemancipation phenomenon, Hertzberg traces the development of Zionist thought during the nineteenth and early twentieth centuries.
Laqueur, Walter. *A History of Zionism*. New York: Holt, Rinehart, and Winston, 1972.
    Lacquer surveys the history of Zionism, beginning with European developments during the era of emancipation and continuing through the establishment of the Israeli state.
Reinharz, Jehuda, and Anita Shapira, eds. *Essential Papers on Zionism*. New York: New York University Press, 1996.
    The essays in this volume examine intellectual, social, political, economic, and cultural dimensions of Zionist history.
Stanislawski, Michael. *Zionism and the Fin de Siècle: Cosmopolitanism and Nationalism from Nordau to Jabotinsky*. Berkeley: University of California Press, 2001.
    Stanislawski links the embrace of Zionism by key figures to the nature of European culture in late nineteenth century, illuminating the ways in which diverse thinkers turned to nationalism after an engagement with cosmopolitanism, and highlighting similarities between the various Zionisms that these individuals went on to endorse.
Vital, David. *The Origins of Zionism*. Oxford: Clarendon Press, 1975.
    Vital's books, here and just below, study the history of Zionism between the late nineteenth and early twentieth centuries.
———. *Zionism: The Crucial Phase*. Oxford: Clarendon Press, 1987.
———. *Zionism: The Formative Years*. Oxford: Clarendon Press, 1982.

Berdichevsky

For Buber's cultural Zionism, see suggested readings for chapter 4.
For the religious Zionist political party, Agudat Israel, see suggested readings for chapter 5.
    For nonstatist conceptions of Zionism in Kaplan's thought and that of two other Jewish thinkers, the historian Simon Rawidowicz (1897–1957) and the political theorist Hans Kohn (1891–1971), see suggested readings for chapter 9.
Golomb, Jacob. *Nietzsche and Zion*. Ithaca, NY: Cornell University Press, 2004.

Golomb considers Berdichevsky within a broader study of Zionist think-ers' attraction to the work of Friedrich Nietzsche. Chapters 3 and 4 devote particular attention to Nietzsche's role in Berdichevsky's intellectual devel-opment and dispute with Ahad Ha'am.

Shapira, Anita. "Herzl, Ahad Ha-'Am, and Berdichevsky: Comments on Their Nationalist Concepts." *Jewish History* 4, no. 2 (1990): 59–69.
Shapira compares the versions of Jewish nationalism articulated by Herzl, Ahad Ha'am, and Berdichevsky, outlining the ways in which the latter two figures break with Herzl's conception of Zionism, while also identifying a variety of issues that separate Ahad Ha'am from Berdichevsky—issues such as the nature of Jewish history, significance of Jewish tradition, and status of the diaspora.

Bialik

Aberbach, David. *Bialik*. London: P. Halban, 1988.
Aberbach provides an overview of Bialik's life, work, and historical context.

Breslauer, S. Daniel. *The Hebrew Poetry of Hayyim Nahman Bialik (1873–1934) and a Modern Jewish Theology*. Lewiston, ME: Edwin Mellen Press, 1991.
Exploring Bialik's life and work, Breslauer seeks to reconstruct the con-ception of Judaism emerging from the poet's writings.

Herzl

Gelber, Mark H., and Vivian Liska, eds. *Theodor Herzl: From Europe to Zion*. Tübingen: M. Niemeyer, 2007.
The essays in this volume examine issues ranging from Herzl's historical context to the nature of his nationalism.

Kornberg, Jacques. *Theodor Herzl: From Assimilation to Zionism*. Bloomington: Indiana University Press, 1993.
Challenging the widespread identification of the Dreyfus affair as the pri-mary cause of Herzl's turn to Zionism, this study ascribes to Herzl a long-standing ambivalence regarding his Jewish identity, and argues that Zion-ism addressed this ambivalence by providing a new ideal of Jewishness.

Robertson, Ritchie, and Edward Timms, eds. *Theodor Herzl and the Origins of Zionism*. Edinburgh: Edinburgh University Press, 1997.
The essays in this volume look at issues such as Hezl's German Jewish context, political activities, and relationships with various figures.

Shimoni, Gideon, and Robert S. Wistrich, eds. *Theodor Herzl: Visionary of the Jewish State*. Jerusalem: Hebrew University Magnes Press, 1999.
The essays in this volume scrutinize Herzl's early career as well as his later work on behalf of Zionism.

Hess

Avineri, Shlomo. *Moses Hess: Prophet of Communism and Zionism*. New York: New York University Press, 1985.

This study provides an overview of Hess's thought, focusing on—and considering the relationship between—the socialist and "proto-Zionist" aspects of his work.

Koltun-Fromm, Ken. *Moses Hess and Modern Jewish Identity*. Bloomington: Indiana University Press, 2001.

Calling attention to dimensions of Hess's Jewish thought beyond his well-known anticipation of Zionism, Koltun-Fromm argues that works such as *Rome and Jerusalem* continue to possess relevance for contemporary Jews, that Hess attempted to bring together a variety of conflicting commitments, and that these tensions help illuminate the complex nature of modern Jewish identity.

Pinsker

Ginsburg, Shai. "Politics and Letters: On the Rhetoric of the Nation in Pinsker and Ahad Ha-Am." *Prooftexts* 29, no. 2 (2009): 173–205.

Delving into the relationship between Pinsker and Ahad Ha'am, Ginsburg contends that we can discover in the politics and rhetoric of the latter an attempt to struggle with the claims of the former.

Netanyahu, Benzion. Introduction to *Road to Freedom: Writings and Addresses by Leo Pinsker*, by Leo Pinsker, 7–73. New York: Scopus Publishing Company, 1944.

Netanyahu provides an overview of Pinsker's life and thought.

Chapter 9

JEWISH RELIGION IN THE UNITED STATES

MANY IMMIGRANTS to the United States saw themselves as the new Israel who had escaped the bondage of their past enslavements and respective Egypts, and Jewish immigrants felt no differently. As the nineteenth century turned into the twentieth, many Jews looked to the United States as the new Promised Land, and their hopes for their new home are captured in striking literary testimonies. In his play *The Melting Pot*, Israel Zangwill (1864–1926), a British Jew who ran an emigration society that helped thousands of Jews emigrate to the United States and actually coined the term "melting pot," describes a society in which the differences among its immigrants would mesh to create something new and unprecedented. Mary Antin (1881–1941), who had fled czarist Russia as a young girl, testifies in her autobiography, *The Promised Land*, to the transformative possibilities of life in the United States; as she writes in its opening pages, "I have been made over. I am absolutely other than the person whose story I have to tell."[1] Perhaps most widely known are the words of the Jewish American poet Emma Lazarus (1849–87), now inscribed on the Statue of Liberty: "Give me your tired, your poor, Your huddled masses yearning to breathe free, The wretched refuse of your teeming shore, Send these, the homeless, tempest-tost to me, I lift my lamp beside the golden door!"[2]

How does the story of how Judaism became a religion change in the U.S. context? In the United States, Jewish thought has seen a number of reiterations of the themes discussed in part I of this book, especially among the ideological inheritors of the German Jewish philosophical tradition: the reform, conservative, and orthodox movements. Yet Jewish thinkers have also been more willing to move beyond a sharp separation between the concept of Jewish religion and U.S. politics. Two possible reasons for this shift immediately come to mind: the dominance in the United States of descendants of eastern European Jews who, as we have seen in the last three chapters, had different conceptions of Judaism than their western European counterparts; and the complicated interplay between religion and political life that has marked the United States since its founding. In distinction especially to the French and more generally the European model in which religious claims made in the public sphere are by definition in conflict with the state's claims, in the United States religious assertions

can at times conflict with governmental authority, at other times complement it, and at still other times be completely irrelevant to the state.

This chapter considers American Jewish attempts to rethink the relation between religion and politics. To do so, I will focus on an unlikely
pair of American Jewish thinkers: Mordecai Kaplan, an émigré from
eastern Europe who became the intellectual founder of Reconstructionist
Judaism, and Leo Strauss, a German Jewish émigré who became one of
the most important American political philosophers of the twentieth century. Despite their significant political and theological differences, Kaplan
and Strauss both reject the modern category of religion as it applies to
Judaism, blaming this categorization for the continued demise of Judaism in the modern period. This chapter will explore their different views
of modern Judaism and U.S. liberal democracy as both rethink as well
as oppose the classical liberal distinction between the private and public
realms, and between religion and politics.

JEWS AND JUDAISM IN THE UNITED STATES

Before turning to Kaplan and Strauss, let me first consider briefly the
history of Jews and Jewish religion in the United States. Prior to 1836,
not many Jews migrated to the United States, but in 1836, German Jews
began to immigrate, primarily for economic reasons. The next big influx
began in 1881 in response to the outbreak of pogroms in Russia, discussed in chapter 7; that year approximately 5,700 Jews immigrated to
the United States, with about 13,200 Jews in 1882. The most devastating
pogrom year was from mid-1905 to 1906, and from 1904 through 1908
approximately 64,000 Jews arrived on U.S. shores. In all, from 1881
through 1910, about a million and a half Jews came into the country.[3]

The German Jews who arrived in significant numbers after 1836 were
sympathetic to reforming Judaism. In 1873, Rabbi Isaac Mayer Wise
(1819–1900) formed the Union of American Hebrew Congregations,
which became the Union of Reform Judaism. In 1875, the Hebrew Theological Institute, which would later become Hebrew Union College, the
flagship of the U.S. reform movement, was founded in Cincinnati. Since
there were no preexisting traditionalist communities in the United States,
the reform movement was able to quickly carry out changes that were far
more radical than was possible in Germany, such as allowing men and
women to sit together during religious services. Perhaps most famously,
or infamously, Hebrew Union College celebrated its first graduating class
in 1883 with what became known as the "Trefah [not kosher] Banquet,"
at which soft-shell crabs, shrimp salad, and frogs' legs were served (all of
these foods are not kosher), and meat was mixed with milk.

Kaufmann Kohler (1843–1926), one of the U.S. reform movement's early rabbis, intensified the universalist message of the German reform movement by inspiring what became known as the Pittsburgh Platform; in this document, the movement declared that Reform Jews "accept as binding only the moral laws [of Judaism], and maintain only such ceremonies as elevate and sanctify our lives, but reject all such as are not adapted to the views and habits of modern civilization." The platform also explicitly affirmed the idea that Judaism is a religion, while categorically rejecting the notion that Jews in any way constitute a nation: "We consider ourselves no longer a nation, but a religious community, and therefore expect neither a return to Palestine, nor a sacrificial worship under the sons of Aaron, nor the restoration of any of the laws concerning the Jewish state."[4]

Prior to 1880, approximately 250,000 Jews lived in the United States, and most were reform. By 1920, some 3,500,000 Jews lived in the United States, and most were orthodox. The Jewish Theological Seminary Association, which would become the Jewish Theological Seminary of America, the flagship of the conservative movement (what was known in Germany as the positive-historical school), was founded in 1886 in response to the influx of traditionalist Jews from eastern Europe. The seminary sought to maintain the tradition, while also recognizing that Judaism always has and must continue to adapt to its present-day circumstances. Much in keeping with the vision of positive-historical Judaism, discussed in chapter 2, the Jewish Theological Seminary sought to preserve in the United States "the knowledge and practice of historical Judaism, as ordained in the law of Moses and expounded by the prophets and sages of Israel in Biblical and Talmudic writings."[5] Eastern European Jewish immigrants founded two other schools, Yeshivat Eitz Chaim in 1886 and the Rabbi Isaac Elchanan Theological Seminary in 1889; these would eventually merge to become Yeshiva University, the institutional base of U.S. orthodoxy, which in keeping with Hirsch's vision, defines itself in terms of the unchanging nature of Jewish law. Soloveitchik, discussed in chapter 3, followed his father, Moshe, in leading Yeshiva University's rabbinical school.

In the United States, Reform and Orthodox Judaism altered their relations to Jewish nationalism. In its Columbus Platform of 1937 the reform movement revised its original lack of support for a Jewish homeland in Palestine. In recognition of the precarious situation of world Jewry, the movement called for "the obligation of all Jewry to aid in its upbuilding as a Jewish homeland by endeavoring to make it not only a haven of refuge for the oppressed but also a center of Jewish culture and spiritual life."[6] Modern orthodoxy, in turn, has had a complicated relationship with Zionism. For example, Soloveitchik broke with other prominent members of his family who lived in Palestine by endorsing political Zionism, although Soloveitchik's position on Zionism is still debated (some think he merely endorsed the political necessity of a Jewish state, while others believe he actually saw the establishment of the state as the beginning of a redemptive process). Nevertheless, notwithstanding these and other important differences and developments, Reform, Conservative, and Orthodox Judaism in the United States conform to the conceptual and political framework introduced by their German predecessors in understanding Judaism as a religion. (Let us recall, for instance, Soloveitchik's insistence, noted in chapter 3, that Jews are fully committed to U.S. society with regard to political and ethical matters, but not so when it comes to theology or religion, where there are no grounds for commonality; as a result, Judaism as a religion remains separate from both politics and ethics.) I will now consider the thought of Kaplan, who criticized all three movements precisely because they start with the premise that Judaism is a religion.

KAPLAN: FROM RELIGION TO CIVILIZATION

Kaplan was born in Lithuania in 1881, the son of a distinguished Talmudist, and at the age of eight immigrated with his family to New York City. When Kaplan was twelve, his father, Isaac, a rabbinical judge (*dayan*) in the office of Jacob Joseph, the chief rabbi of New York, enrolled his son in the Jewish Theological Seminary. At that time, in 1893, the seminary's faculty members were traditional Jews with some secular learning. Kaplan himself was taken with modern scholarship in general and biblical criticism in particular, and when he graduated from the seminary at age twenty-one, he was plagued by severe doubts about Judaism's relation to modernity. Still, after receiving his rabbinic ordination from the Jewish Theological Seminary, Kaplan became the associate rabbi of an orthodox congregation, Kehillat Jeshurun in New York. Kaplan remained troubled by the relation of modern life and scholarship to traditional Judaism, however. When he proposed changes to his congregation, he faced tremendous resistance, and so when he was invited to become the first dean of the newly formed Teachers Institute of the Jewish Theological Seminary, he enthusiastically accepted. Soon afterward Kaplan became a professor of homiletics at the same institution—a position that he held for more than fifty years.

Kaplan's thought developed in the context of the social and political climate of the United States from its entry into World War I through the decades that followed. His thought was especially affected by American wariness of new immigrants, as the country contemplated entering the war. As one well-known government study of immigration put it in 1916:

> With startling suddenness, the effects flowing out of the war have brought to public attention aspects of immigration that heretofore have been regarded with unruffled complacency. It has consciously become all of a sudden of the greatest importance to us as a nation that the immigrants whom we have welcomed into our society … should be an integral part of that society and not foreign to it. We have found that our forces for assimilating this foreign element have not been working…. We have suddenly been made to realize that … many of these … are not strangers to the hand that stabs in the dark or the lips that betray with a kiss.[7]

Jews, like other immigrant groups, increasingly needed to prove their loyalty and "Americanize." While a number of immigrant groups suffered unfair prejudice in the decades following World War I, Jews were especially affected. Colleges and universities as well as professional schools began using quotas to restrict Jewish admission. Whereas in 1927, 50 percent of Jewish applicants were accepted to medical school, by 1930 only 20 percent were accepted. Jews were also increasingly granted only limited admission to other professional schools, including law, engineering, architecture, and dentistry. Even if they were lucky enough to be among those within the Jewish quota, Jews were then denied jobs after graduation. By the late 1920s, for example, Jews were excluded from 90 percent of the office jobs available in New York City. Want ads frequently included the proviso that Jews need not apply.[8] By 1923, Jewish immigration to the United States had been severely restricted.

Kaplan continually struggles with the question of how to make Jewish life meaningful in a U.S. environment that he sees as producing either assimilation or growing self-hatred among Jews. In 1917, he founded the Jewish Center, located at West 86th Street in New York, which provided its members not only with a sanctuary to pray in but also with a swimming pool, gym, club rooms, library, and meeting rooms. The Jewish Center would become the model for Jewish community centers around the country. In 1934, Kaplan published what would be his magnum opus, *Judaism as a Civilization*. His argument is captured in the title: Judaism is a civilization and as such concerns the whole of life—not one mere slice of it. Just as a Jewish communal center ought to replace the synagogue, so too the notion that Judaism is a civilization must replace the idea that Judaism is a religion. For Kaplan, nothing less than the future of Judaism is at stake: "*Paradoxical as it may sound, the spiritual regeneration of the Jewish people demands that religion cease to be its sole preoccupation.*"[9]

Kaplan spends a portion of *Judaism as a Civilization* criticizing the three movements of modern Judaism. With regard to Reform Judaism he argues: "Only in Wonderland can there be a cat which leaves its grin behind it. In the world of reality it is not feasible to try to have the grin without the cat. That experiment has been undertaken by Reformism in trying to have the Jewish religion without the living entity to which that religion belongs—without a living, functioning Jewish people." He is equally harsh about modern orthodoxy: "What, in short, is this law of God which no longer regulates our workaday life, and which, outside of marriage and divorce laws, functions only in matters which least affect social relationships and the adjustment of conflicting interests." And Kaplan is perhaps harshest on the movement with which he is affiliated, Conservative Judaism, which, he maintains, cannot make up its mind about the most essential matters: "On the one hand we are told that 'the message entrusted to Moses contained a standard of living for all times.' ... On the other hand we are told that 'important changes in the life of all the Jewish people made many of the Biblical laws inapplicable or entirely obsolete.'"[10]

He proposes that Judaism must be reconstructed as a civilization. First and foremost this means that Judaism must be understood in terms of the collective life of the Jewish people. A civilization encompasses all avenues of life, including land, language, literature, mores, laws, and folkways. Both Palestine (and later the state of Israel) and the United States offer Jews an opportunity to reconstruct Jewish civilization. Much in keeping with Ahad Ha'am's thought, Kaplan suggests that Jewish religious life be understood in what he calls "functionalist" terms. For instance, the Sabbath must be seen in terms of how it preserves the collective life of the Jewish community rather than as a commemoration of God's resting on the seventh day of creation. Summarizing his vision of the task ahead, Kaplan asserts that it is

> necessary to recall that Judaism as a civilization is not a form of truth, but a form of life. The higher the organism is in the scale of life, the more intricate and complex its structure. To survive, Judaism must become complex.... [T]hose who look to Judaism in its present state to provide them with a ready-made scheme of salvation in this world, or in the next, are bound to be disappointed. The Jew will have to save Judaism before Judaism will be in a position to save the Jew.... He [the Jew] must rediscover, reinterpret and reconstruct the civilization of his people. To do that he must be willing to live up to a program that spells nothing less than a maximum of Jewishness.... If this be the spirit in which Jews will accept from the past the mandate to keep Judaism alive, and from the present the guidance dictated

by its profoundest needs, the contemporary crisis in Jewish life will prove to be the birth-throes of a new era in the civilization of the Jewish people.[11]

Although Reconstructionist Judaism would become, in the hands of Kaplan's son-in-law, a fourth movement of U.S. Judaism, Kaplan does not intend to start a new movement, maintaining that

Judaism as a civilization admits of more than one religious viewpoint. Orthodox Jews may continue to insist that Jewish civilization is supernaturally revealed, and Reformists may cultivate the modernist attitude toward the content of Judaism, without thereby altering the nature of Judaism as a civilization, or denying themselves that place in the life and future of civilization which they may earn and deserve.[12]

Kaplan views U.S. democracy as fertile ground for reconstructing Jewish civilization. Against what he considers to be a narrow view of U.S. society, instituted in both Theodore Roosevelt's and Woodrow Wilson's campaigns, Kaplan seeks to give credibility and legitimacy to what he calls cultural hyphenates, or independently functioning cultures within the larger society. Cultural hyphenates do not represent divided loyalties, he argues, but rather the best that a democratic society has to offer: the merging and interaction of the particular and the general. As Kaplan observes:

Under what political concept or category can the Jews be integrated into the nation of which they are citizens and at the same time remain sufficiently autonomous to be identifiable as a group? ... The only group category that can render their position tenable is one that will recognize the moral and spiritual right to cultural hyphenisms.... [Religious freedom] ought to include the freedom to foster whatever other civilization besides the one of the majority, which affords consolation or supports the human spirit in the same way as does conventional religion.... Fundamentally, Catholics and Jews are hyphenates. What is needed to normalize their state is to have the cultural hyphenism of minority groups accepted as legitimate.[13]

Strikingly, Kaplan compares Jews to Catholics, and not, as was the case in the German context, to Protestants. Judaism and Catholicism have historically been civilizations in that they both encompass public and not only private life. Kaplan contends that U.S. democracy uniquely creates the possibility of multiple and overlapping identities. It is not necessary, and certainly not desirable, to be a Jew in private and an American in public. Just as he claims that Jewish civilization admits more than one point of view, so too Kaplan describes U.S. civilization as allowing, indeed encouraging, multiple identities.

But viewing Judaism as a civilization is not only a matter of adding spheres of life to the sphere of religion. Instead, declares Kaplan, Jews and Judaism must also rid themselves of certain elements. Most famously, Kaplan contends that a rethinking, if not a disavowal, of both a supernatural conception of God and any notion of Jewish chosenness is necessary. In his words: "The modern man who is used to thinking in terms of humanity as a whole can no longer reconcile himself to the notion of any people, or body of believers, constituting a type of society which may be described as belonging to a supernatural order. This is essentially what the doctrine of 'election' has hitherto implied." Kaplan proposes replacing the idea of election with vocation, or calling. Such a substitution would, he suggests, avoid "invidious distinctions implied in the doctrine of election."[14] Kaplan's disavowal of Jewish election does not mean that he does not consider Jewish civilization unique. Jews are specially drawn to their own rituals and customs, but other civilizations are equally drawn to theirs. For Kaplan, anything nondemocratic is "a menace ... to civilization in general."[15] The notion of vocation, then, is a democratic solution to the problem of election.

Kaplan published a new prayer book in 1945. In it, he changed the blessing that a Jew says when called to the Torah. Instead of the traditional blessing that thanks God "who has chosen us from among all peoples [*asher bahar banu mikol ha-amim*]," Kaplan eliminated the reference to chosenness and replaced it with "who has drawn us to his service [*asher kervanu l'avodato*]." In the eyes of the orthodox, Kaplan's offense was so great that they met in the McAlpin Hotel in New York and formally excommunicated him. This excommunication of course was only symbolic, since the orthodox rabbinate had no political or social jurisdiction over Kaplan, or anyone else. Indeed, this lack of jurisdiction is the very issue I have been exploring throughout this book. The modern Jewish world is one in which the corporate Jewish community has lost its authority over the individual Jew. It remains to be seen, though, whether Kaplan's democratic proposal for how to reconcile Judaism and U.S. democracy does in the end move Judaism beyond the status of a modern religion. I will return to this question in this chapter's conclusion, but first let me examine Strauss's criticism of the modern idea that Judaism is a religion.

STRAUSS AND THE THEOLOGICO-POLITICAL PREDICAMENT OF MODERNITY

The pairing of Kaplan and Strauss at first seems unlikely, due to both their political and philosophical differences. Strauss, a German Jewish émigré to the United States, became one of the most important figures in twentieth-century political philosophy, as mentioned above. While he was never involved in any official way with political life, friends and foes alike have claimed him as the intellectual predecessor of U.S. neoconservatism. Kaplan, as we saw in the last section, began his life as an Orthodox Jew and became the intellectual founder of the only distinctly Jewish American denomination, Reconstructionist Judaism. Like Strauss, Kaplan was not officially involved in U.S. political life but nonetheless was active in building American Jewish institutions, and clearly saw himself as a progressive Democrat. These real biographical differences pale in comparison to Strauss's and Kaplan's philosophical ones. Whatever Strauss's personal politics may have been, his life's work was dedicated to questioning the assumed superiority of modernity to the ancient world. In contrast, Kaplan was a champion of what he regarded as modernity's superiority to the premodern world. Yet despite these differences, Strauss and Kaplan both reject the modern relegation of Judaism to a nonpolitical, indeed merely religious status as untrue to the historical Jewish tradition, and even more important, as destructive to any possibility of future Jewish life. But whereas Kaplan proposes a program to ensure the future of U.S. Judaism, Strauss believes that the most critical and in fact feasible task remained the diagnosis of the problem, which he identifies as the "theologico-political predicament of modernity."[16] Let me attempt to explain this diagnosis by turning to Strauss's early work in Germany, where he was influenced by and engaged with many of the Jewish thinkers discussed in the first part of this book.

Strauss was born in 1883 to an orthodox family in Kirchhain, a small town in rural Germany. He attended a gymnasium, where he was first introduced to the study of philosophy and the classics, and then moved on to the University of Marburg, where he studied with Cohen and wrote his dissertation under the supervision of Cohen's student, Ernst Cassirer (1874–1945). Like Levinas, Strauss later studied with Edmund Husserl (1859–1938) and Heidegger. In 1925 Strauss worked under Julius Guttmann (1880–1950), at the Academy for the Science of Judaism in Berlin, coediting Mendelssohn's papers. It was in this context that he began to engage with Spinoza's philosophy in light of Cohen's attack on him and in 1930 published *Spinoza's Critique of Religion*, which he dedicated to the memory of Rosenzweig, who had died in 1929. In 1932, anxious to leave Germany, Strauss received a fellowship to study in France. He then spent four years in England—the last three on a fellowship at Cambridge University. In an increasingly desperate quest to get out of Europe, Strauss came to the United States in 1937, teaching at Columbia University for a year and then at the New School for Social Research for a decade. In 1949, he became a professor of political science at the University of Chicago. He spent the last five years of his life at Claremont Men's College and St. Johns University.

Looking back on his intellectual development in the early 1920s in Germany, Strauss writes that he was a young German Jew in the throes of the theologico-predicament of modernity. This predicament was simply, though profoundly, whether to choose liberalism or Zionism, with the former representing the political culmination of Spinoza's separation of theology from politics, and the latter representing the utter failure of this project. The young Strauss chose Zionism. After writing his book on Spinoza, Strauss published a book on Maimonides and his predecessors titled *Philosophy and Law*. This book focuses on the tension between modern Jewish accommodations to the idea that Judaism is a religion and premodern Jewish conceptions of the authority of law. From Strauss's point of view, Mendelssohn's strained attempt to defend the necessity and centrality of Jewish law for the Jewish people while denying that the law has any political hold on individual Jews embodies this tension, which culminates in Cohen's philosophy. Strauss comes to identify this especially Jewish problem with that of modernity as such: "Liberalism stands or falls by the distinction between state and society, or by the recognition of the private sphere protected by the law but impervious to the law, with the understanding that, above all, religion as particular religion belongs to the private sphere."[17]

For Strauss, this is not of mere academic interest. Rather, he links the tension to an analysis of the rise of modern tyrannies and the unprecedented evils that they are able to perpetuate. The private sphere, simply put, "protected by the law but impervious to the law," fosters prejudice, including the murderous prejudices of modernity such as anti-Semitism. As Strauss puts it:

> Liberal democracy had originally defined itself in theologico-political treaties as the opposite of ... "the kingdom of darkness," i.e., of medieval society.... [The German Jews] were given full political rights for the first time by the Weimar Republic. The Weimar Republic was succeeded by the only German regime—by the only regime that ever was anywhere—which had no other clear principle except murderous hatred of the Jews.[18]

There is no doubt that Strauss is a critic of liberal democracy, yet he also does not seek, as some of his interpreters have maintained, to return to a premodern political order. He instead considers himself a friend of liberal democracy precisely because he is willing to honestly and rigorously consider its weaknesses.

Like Kaplan, Strauss believes that modern Jews, and modern people generally, have to be honest about the break between the premodern Jewish past and the modern Jewish present. Yet unlike Kaplan, Strauss does not believe there are clear solutions to the problem of how to be a modern

Jew and modern citizen. Rather, he thinks that a grasp of the tensions inherent in being a modern Jew and living with these tensions is the best that modern Jews can do. But the problem of Judaism's relation to modernity does not point to an inherent weakness in Judaism. As he shows at length in his studies of medieval Jewish philosophy, an appreciation and embrace of tensions is instead at the heart of medieval rationalism. One of modernity's major problems, according to Strauss, is the conviction that all problems can be solved and that solutions are always at hand. This belief, contends Strauss, can of course be a good thing as human beings seek, for example, to eradicate disease through the progress of science. Yet this belief can also be tremendously dangerous for it can lead to immoderate political programs such as fascism and totalitarianism.

Strauss admires the ancient Greek philosophers for their philosophical and political moderation. His focus is also on the recovery of medieval Jewish and Islamic philosophical traditions that had developed readings of Plato significantly different from those of the Christian Scholastics. First and foremost among the divergences are different accounts of the relationship between divine revelation and philosophy. Medieval Jewish and Islamic thought identify revelation with divine law, while the Christian Scholastics in general and Thomas Aquinas in particular understand revelation as doctrinal knowledge that humans must believe. In keeping with these definitions of revelation, medieval Jewish and Islamic thought insist on a distinction between philosophy and revelation, while the Christian Scholastics emphasize the complementary natures of philosophy and revelation.

Like other modern scholars with a high regard for Maimonides—Krochmal, Cohen, Soloveitchik, Leibowitz, and Maimon—Strauss has his own interpretation of the medieval rationalist. On Strauss's reading, Maimonides protects the public necessity of law while maintaining the integrity of the philosophical life. Perhaps most famously, or in many circles infamously, Strauss contends that from a political point of view Maimonides is able to balance the necessity of the divine law and integrity of the philosophical life by writing between the lines—that is, by writing in such a way that only the philosophically gifted can appreciate the tension between divine law and philosophy, while the masses can understand more simply that they ought to follow the law.

Needless to say, this is not a democratic idea, at least not in the sense that Kaplan understands democracy. Let us recall that Kaplan rejects the idea of election because he contends that it is undemocratic to suggest that one people, and not everyone, is chosen. Strauss's reading of Maimonides, on the contrary, holds that people are not inherently equal, at least when it comes to comprehending philosophical truths. Strauss extends this line of reasoning in what is perhaps his best-known American book, *Natural Right and History*, in which he compares classical notions of natural right, which are consistent with his reading of Maimonides, and modern views of natural right, beginning with Hobbes, which Strauss argues lead ultimately to modern liberalism's own demise. Much of Strauss's mature work in the United States focuses on the tension between the modern quest for egalitarianism and the philosophical difficulties involved in justifying this quest. In other words, on what philosophical basis can we say that all people are created equal? In an important sense, we are not created equally. Different people have different talents. For instance, it is obvious that some people are smarter than others, better looking than others, or more athletic than others. One might reply to this point by saying that while all of this is true, all people should be treated equally, regardless of their different talents and deficits. Strauss does not object to this idea but also argues that the notion that all people are created equal can only be justified on theological grounds—that is, by the theological idea that all human beings are created in the image of God. For Strauss, this notion is a central component of U.S. political life, yet it is ultimately an idea that cannot be justified through reason but instead only through the faith of the American people.

Here we come to another significant difference between Kaplan and Strauss. We saw above that Kaplan absolutely rejects the idea of a supernatural God, which he believes has been discredited once and for all by the progress of reason. For Strauss, who is not a believer in such a God, the notion of a supernatural God is not something that reason can ever definitively disprove. How, Strauss asks, could reason or science *disprove* the existence of God? It is one thing to say that it is not possible to prove God's existence (this is something Strauss would agree with); it is another to declare that one can disprove God's existence. At the same time, as believers themselves fully acknowledge, God's existence is not something that can be definitively proved. This is why belief in God is a matter of belief (which nonetheless may be subjected to rational inquiry, although it cannot be proven only by means of rationality). Ironically, it is Strauss the nonbeliever who emerges as the defender of the ultimate value of Jewish revelation as it has been classically understood. As he puts it in a direct criticism of Ahad Ha'am, one of Kaplan's greatest influences:

> I believe, by simply replacing God by the creative genius of the Jewish people, one gives away, one deprives oneself—even if one does not believe—of a source of human understanding.... Now I do not wish to minimize folk dances, Hebrew speaking, and many other things— I do not want to minimize them. But I believe that they cannot possibly take the place of what is most profound in our tradition.[19]

What is most profound, for Strauss, in the Jewish tradition is a belief in a transcendent God who reveals himself to the Jewish people by way of the Torah.

What, according to Strauss, is the solution? For Strauss, there is no solution—but this is precisely the point. It is actually in recognizing the irresolvable problem of Judaism's relation to the modern world that Strauss sees the relevance of Judaism and indeed Jewish chosenness for modern, political life. He notes that

> finite, relative problems can be solved; infinite, absolute problems cannot be solved. In other words, human beings will never create a society which is free from contradictions. From every point of view it looks as if the Jewish people were the chosen people, at least in the sense that the Jewish problem is the most manifest symbol of the human problem insofar as it is a social or political problem.[20]

For Kaplan, the Jewish problem is not an absolute problem, and neither are there absolute human problems. U.S. society, in fact, provides for Kaplan the very possibility for the simultaneous resolution of Jewish and human problems. In his words, "[The American Jew] must be willing to live up to a program that spells nothing less than a maximum of Jewishness. True to his historic tradition he should throw in his lot with all movements to further social justice and universal peace, and bring to bear upon them the inspiration of his history and religion."[21] For Strauss, in contrast, the United States offers the possibility, and only the possibility, of a society and political order that would not demand or even strive for the resolution of the Jewish problem in particular, or human problems in general.

Conclusion

We have seen that Kaplan and Strauss present two different views of Judaism and U.S. democracy. For Kaplan, Judaism is whatever Jewish people do. It is, as he writes, not a form of truth but rather a form of life. This form of life needs to be democratized in the United States so that it is in accord with U.S. democracy. U.S. democracy, for Kaplan, simultaneously preserves differences among the civilizations that make up U.S. civilization while also demanding egalitarianism. Each civilization is unique in its own way, and no civilization may claim superiority to another. Strauss, in contrast, views Judaism as making truth claims about a transcendent God and this God's relation to the Jewish people. These claims may be difficult for the modern person to embrace, but, argues Strauss, that does not detract from their profundity and indeed their relevance to modern political life, especially when it comes to notions of human equality. U.S. democracy, for Strauss, is fundamentally egalitarian, but that is because of its religious basis. As such, this religious basis is not something certain but instead must always be reaffirmed by the American people. At the same time, U.S. democracy for Strauss is a meritocracy, meaning that all people are given the opportunity to succeed, yet success is dependent on natural talent. In keeping with Strauss's reading of Maimonides, the elite are not those born to privilege but rather those who achieve excellence by virtue of their own talents. There can be tensions between American conceptions of equality and the notion of merit. But, for Strauss, the American embrace of these tensions is a sign of strength, not weakness.

Kaplan's and Strauss's divergent views of U.S. democracy and the role of religion in U.S. political life no doubt reflect larger, ongoing debates about the nature of the modern meanings of a transcendent God, egalitarianism, and U.S. democracy. But what do their different claims say in connection with the story here about the invention of Jewish religion and its conceptual aftermath? Once again, the starting points for both of their thoughts is the rejection of the German Jewish paradigm that had defined Judaism as a modern religion, and the demand for honest and sober recognition of the break with the Jewish past that modernity brings. Taken together, Strauss and Kaplan do suggest a perhaps-counterintuitive point about the engagement between modern Judaism and democratic politics. As they transform, if not reject, their German Jewish predecessors, Strauss and Kaplan, despite their profound differences, agree that Judaism may thrive in a democratic society in which politics is the site of legitimate disagreement. So too, as the case of Germany as well as arguably the rest of Europe shows, Judaism may fail to thrive in a society that demands consensus to the point of denying any political disagreement.

SUGGESTED READINGS

Historical Context

Dash Moore, Deborah, ed. *American Jewish Identity Politics*. Ann Arbor: University of Michigan Press, 2008.
   The essays in this volume cover issues such as the role of the Holocaust in—and the relevance of gender to—conceptions of American Jewish identity
Diner, Hasia R. *The Jews of the United States, 1654 to 2000*. Berkeley: University of California Press, 2004.
   Diner provides a history of U.S. Jewry between the seventeenth and twentieth centuries, emphasizing the importance of understanding this history in its U.S. and Jewish contexts.
Eisen, Arnold M. *The Chosen People in America: A Study in Jewish Religious Ideology*. Bloomington: Indiana University Press, 1983.
   Focusing on the period between 1930 and 1980, Eisen explores the ways in which American Jewish thinkers articulated new self-understandings by reimagining the concept of chosenness.

Goldstein, Eric L. *The Price of Whiteness: Jews, Race, and American Identity.* Princeton: Princeton University Press, 2006.

    Goldstein traces the complex ways in which American Jews came to identify and be identified as white, and the social and psychological tensions they experienced along the way.

Kaplan, Dana Evan, ed. *The Cambridge Companion to American Judaism.* Cambridge: Cambridge University Press, 2005.

    The essays in this volume provide an overview of Jewish life in the United States, looking at topics ranging from the differences between Jewish denominations to the role of the Holocaust in U.S. life.

Katznelson, Ira. "Between Separation and Disappearance: Jews on the Margins of American Liberalism." In *Paths of Emancipation: Jews, States, and Citizenship,* ed. Pierre Birnbaum and Ira Katznelson, 157–205. Princeton, NJ: Princeton University Press, 1995.

    Devoting particular attention to the impact of U.S. political and economic liberalism on Jewish life in the United States, Katznelson suggests that such liberalism created a situation in which Jews were both welcomed and marginalized, and he examines the strategies adopted by Jewish groups in response to this state of affairs.

Sarna, Jonathan D. "American Jews and Church-State Relations: The Search for 'Equal Footing.'" In *Religion and State in the American Jewish Experience,* ed. Jonathan D. Sarna and David G. Dalin, 1–38. Notre Dame: University of Notre Dame Press, 1997.

    Linking American Jewish views to broader developments in U.S. society, Sarna analyzes the quest for equal rights in early U.S. history, the evolution of views in the nineteenth and twentieth centuries, and a variety of issues that have garnered attention among U.S. Jews—for example, the role of religion in public schools, relationship of the state to parochial schools, and meaning of the "free exercise" of religion.

———. *American Judaism: A History.* New Haven, NJ: Yale University Press, 2004.

    Sarna provides a history of U.S. Judaism between the colonial period and the early twenty-first century.

Jewish Feminism

Jewish feminism, a major current of U.S. Jewish life, is not discussed in this chapter, but the following primary texts may be of interest to readers.

Adler, Rachel. *Engendering Judaism: An Inclusive Theology and Ethics.* Philadelphia: Jewish Publication Society of America, 1998.

    Emphasizing the values of justice and equality, Adler offers a feminist theology of reengagement with Jewish texts, culture, and history.

Greenberg, Blu. *On Women and Judaism: A View from Tradition.* Philadelphia: Jewish Publication Society of America, 1981.

    In this collection of essays, Greenberg attempts to bring together her feminist and Orthodox Jewish commitments, seeking out possibilities within Jewish law "for bringing women to a position of full equality."

Hauptman, Judith. *Rereading the Rabbis: A Woman's Voice.* Boulder, CO: Westview Press, 1998.

    Hauptman analyzes views of women in the Hebrew Bible and Talmud. While recognizing the patriarchal character of classical rabbinic thought, she argues that the Talmud provided women with rights and status that had not been accorded to them in the Bible.

Plaskow, Judith. *Standing again at Sinai: Judaism from a Feminist Perspective.* San Francisco: Harper San Francisco, 1991.
Addressing what she describes as the silencing of women in Jewish tradition and history, Plaskow seeks to reconstruct and reenvision crucial aspects of Jewish life and give Jewish women voices of their own.

Kaplan

Goldsmith, Emanuel S., Mel Scult, and Robert M. Seltzer, eds. *The American Judaism of Mordecai M. Kaplan.* New York: New York University Press, 1990.
The essays in this volume address issues such as the context and development of Kaplan's views, his relationship to other thinkers, and his thoughts on the nature of Judaism.

Gurock, Jeffrey S., and Jacob J. Schachter. *A Modern Heretic and a Traditional Community: Mordecai M. Kaplan, Orthodoxy, and American Judaism.* New York: Columbia University Press, 1997.
Exploring the question of why Kaplan was hesitant to formally break with Orthodox Judaism, the authors suggest that he may have been motivated by a desire to win acceptance for his views as well as by a belief in the power of religious authorities, even in a voluntaristic context.

Magid, Shaul. "The Spinozistic Spirit in Mordecai Kaplan's Revaluation of Judaism." *Modern Judaism* 20, no. 2 (2000): 159–80.
Magid contends that the central premises of Kaplan's thought bear a striking affinity with key Spinozistic claims—especially with respect to the nature of God, idea of "the sacred," and distinction between piety and philosophy.

Pianko, Noam. *Zionism and the Roads Not Taken: Rawidowicz, Kaplan, Kohn.* Bloomington: Indiana University Press, 2010.
Pianko links Kaplan to a group of Jewish thinkers who articulate Zionisms that resist the identification of Jewish nationhood with the existence of a state, and who therefore seek to develop alternative conceptions of Jewish collective identity.

Scult, Mel. *Judaism Faces the Twentieth Century: A Biography of Mordecai M. Kaplan.* Detroit: Wayne State University Press, 1993.
Scult provides an account of Kaplan's life and career.

Neo-Hasidism

Although neo-Hasidism is also among the significant developments in U.S. Jewish life not discussed in this chapter, the following are a few primary sources for interested readers.

Green, Arthur. *These Are the Words: A Vocabulary of Jewish Spiritual Life.* Woodstock, NY: Jewish Lights Publishing, 1999.
Utilizing a list of more than one hundred terms that he takes to be crucial to understanding Jewish life, Green emphasizes Hasidic attention to the inner life and spiritual quest, seeking to resist what he considers overly rationalistic and intellectualist approaches to Judaism.

Heschel, Abraham Joshua. *God in Search of Man: A Philosophy of Judaism.* New York: Farrar, Straus and Giroux, 1976.
Descended from prominent Hasidic rabbis, Heschel attempts to articulate a theological vision for twentieth-century Americans, focusing on themes such as prayer, joy, and communion with God and the Torah.
———. *Moral Grandeur and Spiritual Audacity: Essays.* Ed. Susannah Heschel. New York: Farrar, Straus and Giroux, 1996.
Introduced and edited by Susannah Heschel, the essays in this volume study topics such as holiness, justice, and the nature of religion.

Strauss

Batnitzky, Leora. *Leo Strauss and Emmanuel Levinas: Philosophy and the Politics of Revelation.* Cambridge: Cambridge University Press, 2006.
Identifying historical and conceptual links between the work of Strauss and Levinas, Batnitzky argues that Levinas—unlike Strauss—affirms a modern posture that ascribes social and political relevance to philosophy, while Strauss offers provocative accounts of the possibility of revelation and the limits of philosophy.
Deutsch, Kenneth L., and Walter Nicgorski, eds. *Leo Strauss: Political Philosopher and Jewish Thinker.* Lanham, MD: Rowman and Littlefield Publishers, 1993.
The essays in this volume examine Strauss's views on topics such as Judaism, classical philosophy, and U.S. politics.
Green, Kenneth Hart. *Jew and Philosopher: The Return to Maimonides in the Jewish Thought of Leo Strauss.* Albany: State University of New York Press, 1993.
Highlighting Strauss's writings on Maimonides, this book maintains that grasping Strauss's Jewish thought is central to understanding his philosophical project, and that his views on Judaism and Jewish thinkers continue to be relevant for contemporary discussions.
Sheppard, Eugene R. *Leo Strauss and the Politics of Exile: The Making of a Political Philosopher.* Hanover, NH: University Press of New England, 2006.
Underscoring the significance of the category of exile, Sheppard reconstructs the development of Strauss's thought through the 1940s.
Smith, Steven B. *Reading Leo Strauss: Politics, Philosophy, Judaism.* Chicago: University of Chicago Press, 2006.
The essays in this volume argue that Strauss urges his readers to be open to the claims emerging from both reason and revelation, that he understands politics and philosophy to aim at "irreconcilable" ends, and that he treats philosophy not as the source of concrete answers to specific political questions but rather as a mode of reflecting on inherently contestable issues.
Udoff, Alan, ed. *Leo Strauss's Thought: Toward a Critical Engagement.* Boulder, CO: Lynne Rienner Publishers, 1991.
The essays in this volume address issues ranging from Strauss's reading of Maimonides to his views on reason and revelation.

CONCLUSION

I BEGAN this book with the questions: Is Judaism a religion? Is Jewishness a matter of culture? Are the Jews a nation? In the last nine chapters, we have seen that Jewish thinkers of a variety of religious and ideological stripes have answered these questions by emphasizing one way of understanding Judaism or Jewishness, whether religion, culture, or nationality, instead of others. By way of conclusion I turn to ultra-Orthodox Judaism, which can be understood as a wholesale *rejection* of all these modern attempts to divide human life into different spheres, and thereby as a refusal to engage the question of whether Judaism is or is not a religion.

If, as we saw in chapter 2, modern orthodoxy was created as a response to the reform movement, ultraorthodoxy fashioned itself as a response to modern orthodoxy, which affirms modernity, maintaining that there is no inherent conflict between Judaism and the modern world. Ultraorthodoxy, in contrast, rejects the modern world and any accommodation to it. Yet ultraorthodoxy is of course just as much modernity's child as is modern orthodoxy as well as Reform Judaism, cultural Judaism, and Jewish nationalism, all of which were made possible and continue to flourish because of the freedom of religion granted by the modern nation-state.

In both Israel and North America, the ultraorthodox are able to reap the benefits of two different worlds that they claim are irreconcilable: the modern political world of nation-states that allows for religious freedom, and their own worldview, which holds that they are wholly separate from the world outside them. Ironically, as we will see, it is by reconciling what they claim is irreconcilable that ultraorthodoxy thrives in contemporary society. Let me briefly turn first to the historical origins of ultraorthodoxy in late nineteenth-century Hungary and then to a U.S. Supreme Court case in 1994 involving the ultra-Orthodox Satmar Hasidim that reflects some of the central themes of this book.

In early nineteenth-century Hungary, Rabbi Moses Sofer (1762–1839), widely known as the Hatam Sofer, coined the phrase that still defines multiple streams of ultra-Orthodox Judaism today: "All innovation is prohibited by the Torah."[1] Although this phrase does come from the Talmud, the Hatam Sofer's interpretation of it was, ironically perhaps, rather innovative. The Talmudic context is a discussion of Leviticus 23:14: "And you shall eat neither bread, nor parched corn, nor fresh ears, until this selfsame day, until you have brought the offering of your God; it is a statute forever throughout your generations in all your dwellings." Talking about the law of *hadash*, which refers to new produce, the rabbis use the phrase "anything new [hadash] is prohibited by the Torah" to mean that before enjoying any new fruits of a harvest, a portion must be offered to God. The Hatam Sofer's interpretation, however, creatively suggested that this means that Jews and Judaism can in no way accommodate themselves to the modern world.

The Hatam Sofer consciously recognized that Jewish law in some cases could be open to a number of interpretations, and he also made a number of innovative rulings that implicitly acknowledged that the law could change over time. Nevertheless, he stressed that strict and rigid adherence to Jewish law was necessary in a day and age when Jewish reformers were calling for Jewish accommodation to modernity. Jewish tradition and law demanded that the tradition remain wholly intact. Nothing, no matter how seemingly tangential or minor, could be added or subtracted from the tradition (though the Hatam Sofer himself did precisely this, as we see from the example above). The Hatam Sofer was first and foremost an opponent of the Haskalah and religious reform. Yet within just three decades of his death, his writings would be used against modern orthodoxy in Hungary, and the seeds of ultraorthodoxy would begin to flower, and continue to do so.

The ultra-Orthodox Jews who followed in the Hatam Sofer's footsteps were especially incensed by the attempt of German Jews to bring modern orthodox schools and rabbis to Hungary. In particular, in 1851, the German-born and German-educated Rabbi Esriel Hildesheimer (1820–99), a contemporary of Hirsch, established a Jewish school that also included instruction in German and secular subjects. Hildesheimer, like Hirsch, also preached in German, not Yiddish. While Hildesheimer and Hirsch both saw an enormous gulf between their orthodoxy and the reformers, the ultra-Orthodox Jews viewed them as one of a kind, recognizing that modern Orthodox and Reform Judaism were both attempts to harmonize Judaism with the modern world and nation-state. The ultra-Orthodox Jews recognized that modern orthodoxy, despite its contestations to the contrary, implicitly rendered Judaism a religion, just as Reform Judaism had.

But what could the ultraorthodox do? After all, they, like other Jews, found themselves living within the reality of the modern nation-state, which meant, among other things, that Jewish communities had lost their political autonomy. As a matter of strategy, the ultraorthodox took a cue from the modern orthodox. The modern nation-state had brought with it religious liberty, and the state simply could and would not force individuals to believe what they did not believe. Mendelssohn's vision had, in this sense, come to pass. Religious liberty gave the ultraorthodox the right and means to self-segregate. While modern Orthodox Jews sought to segregate themselves from non-Orthodox Jews, but not from the German or

Hungarian state, the ultra-Orthodox Jews sought to self-segregate from the outside world as such.

The ultraorthodox, though, do *not* perceive the modern world as problematic per se but rather view it as the purview of non-Jews. In contrast, Jews are meant to be a people apart from all others. It is helpful here to turn again to the Hatam Sofer, whose interpretation of Deuteronomy 26:5–8 (verses that appear quite prominently in the Passover Haggadah) would be definitive for ultraorthodox self-understanding. These verses read as follows:

> My father was a wandering Aramean. And he went down into Egypt and sojourned there, few in number, and there he became a nation, great, mighty, and populous. And the Egyptians treated us harshly and humiliated us and laid on us hard labor. Then we cried to the Lord, the God of our fathers, and the Lord heard our voice and saw our affliction, our toil, and our oppression. And the Lord brought us out of Egypt with a mighty hand and an outstretched arm, with great deeds of terror, with signs and wonders.

The Hatam Sofer follows a commentary on this passage, which emphasizes that "became a nation" means that the Israelites separated themselves from the Egyptians by way of their names, language, and attire. In keeping with this interpretation, the Hatam Sofer offers a mnemonic, *shalem*, which combines three words: *shem*, for "name"; *lashon*, for "language"; and *malbush*, for "attire."[2]

The Hebrew word *shalem* literally means "whole" or "complete," and appears in the Hebrew Bible in Genesis 33:18. Jacob has just left his brother Esau, after which we read, "And Jacob came in peace to the city of Shekhem, which is in the land of Canaan, when he came from Paddan-aram; and encamped before the city." The Hebrew original is ambiguous. It reads: *shalem ir shekhem*. Ir means city, and Shekhem is a city. The question then becomes: What does shalem mean? Different commentators over the ages have offered varying interpretations. Some argue that shalem is indeed the name of another city. Some suggest, as the translation above does, that shalem means "peace" (shalem is understood as a variant of shalom, meaning "peace"). For the Hatam Sofer, shalem in this verse is best translated as "whole" or "complete" (also related to peace); to him, the term suggests a wholeness granted by God. And for the ultraorthodox such wholeness is embodied in names, language, and clothing. For this reason, the ultraorthodox retain their Jewish names, continue to speak Yiddish, and wear distinctive clothing (black hats and suits for men; long skirts and head coverings for women).

Let us recall two aspects of the discussion about Salanter and the Mussar movement in chapter 6. First, Salanter consciously rejected

Hirsch's modern orthodoxy because he recognized that Hirsch, despite his protestations and attempts to the contrary, had turned Judaism into a modern religion. Second, Mussar proponents were deemed too modern by the ultraorthodox, who criticized the Lithuanian yeshivas' stress on intellectual innovation as well as adoption of the dress and customs of modern society (they wore short jackets, shaved, and married later). In the context of the Hatam Sofer's motto, all innovation is prohibited by the Torah, and emphasis on shalem (names, language, and clothing), we can now better appreciate the relevance of these perhaps seemingly minor matters for the ultraorthodox. Far from mere matters of appearance, clothing in the ultraorthodox worldview is at once theological and political—theological because clothing represents the Jewish people's special mission to the world, and political because clothing represents the Jewish people's self-segregation from the world (and other Jews).

We have now come full circle. I began this book by noting that before Jews received the rights of citizenship, Judaism was not a religion, and Jewishness was not a matter of culture or nationality. Rather, Judaism and Jewishness were all of these at once: religion, culture, and nationality. The ultraorthodox rejection of the Jewish religion is an attempt to return Judaism to a preemancipation wholeness. It is worth noting, however, that several important historical studies have shown in great detail that ultraorthodoxy is quite unorthodox in its understanding of many tenets of Judaism as it has been historically understood and practiced, including first and foremost its conception of Jewish law (and as we saw above, the Hatam Sofer is an innovative reader of the tradition). My concern here is not with the question of whether ultraorthodoxy is authentic Judaism. If anything, these last chapters have demonstrated that what we call Judaism is something that is dynamic and changes (and this point only becomes clearer when one studies the history of Judaism prior to modernity). My interest is instead in the conceptual challenge that ultraorthodoxy brings to the claim that Judaism is a religion. While I want to examine *Board of Education of Kiryas Joel Village School District v. Grumet*, which illustrates the difficulty of defining Judaism as a religion or not, let me briefly consider Kiryas Joel and the Satmar Hasidim who reside there more generally.

Kiryas Joel is a village in upstate New York, founded by Satmar Hasidim from Williamsburg, Brooklyn, and named after the late Satmar Rebbe, Joel Teitelbaum (1887–1979). The Satmar Hasidim take their name from the German and Yiddish name for what was the Hungarian town of Satmar (which today is the town of Satu Mare in Romania), where their rabbi, Teitelbaum, served as the town's rabbi. In 1944, the Hungarian Zionist Rudolf Kastner negotiated with the Nazis to allow a small group of Hungarian Jews to travel to Switzerland and thereby escape what would have been almost certain annihilation (in 1944, almost half a million Hungarian Jews were deported to Auschwitz). Among this small group was Teitelbaum, who after the war immigrated to Palestine, where he worked to establish a number of yeshivas. When the state of Israel was created, Teitelbaum, who at the time was in New York raising money for his yeshivas, denounced the founding of the Israeli state (this episode is fictionalized in Chaim Potok's popular work *The Chosen*). Teitelbaum decided to remain in the United States, although he did travel to Israel after it was established. Whereas the late nineteenth-century ultraorthodox vehemently opposed the modern orthodox, Teitelbaum directed his ire mainly at Zionism. In Teitelbaum's mind, the desire of Jews to be a nation like all others was a profound perversion of Judaism, which, he maintained, mandated that Jews not be like other nations, even if this means that Jews are persecuted and murdered by the nations of the world.

In the United States, the Satmar Hasidim have taken isolationism to a new level. They are so isolationist that they have had conflicts (often physical) with other ultraorthodox groups whom they consider too integrationist. If success is to be measured by numbers, the Satmar Hasidim have been extremely successful in the United States. In fact, by the 1970s the Satmar Hasidim needed more physical space for their ever-growing community and purchased land in Monroe County, New York, where fourteen families settled. By 2008, approximately twenty-two thousand Satmar Hasidim lived in Kiryas Joel, where the median age of residents was 15 years old, in contrast to New York State's median age of 35.9 years.

I can now look at the court case, which begins with Kiryas Joel's need to educate its children. Although most of Kiryas Joel's children are educated in religious schools, which are not state funded, the town has a disproportionately large number of children with special needs. The question became: Where should they be educated? The obvious answer was the public school district. The residents of Kiryas Joel did send their children to public school, in a neighboring town, but they also contended that the children's experience in public school was traumatic because the culture of public school, and life outside the village generally, was so foreign—and the residents of Kiryas Joel wanted to keep it this way. Rather than continuing to send their children to the public schools to receive the services they needed, parents in Kiryas Joel preferred to have their children go without such services.

In response to this difficult situation, the New York Legislative, in 1989, passed a statute declaring that

> the territory of the village of Kiryas Joel in the town of Monroe, Orange county, on the date when this act shall take effect, shall be and hereby is constituted a separate school district, and shall be known as the Kiryas Joel village school district and shall have and enjoy all the powers and duties of a union free school district under the provisions of the education law.[3]

A few months before the Kiryas Joel village school district was to begin its operations, the New York State School Boards Association challenged this statute as violating the First Amendment to the U.S. Constitution, known as the establishment clause, which holds that "Congress shall make no law respecting an establishment of religion."[4] Simply put, wasn't the New York Legislature implicitly endorsing Satmar Hasidism by giving Kiryas Joel its own school district?

Before turning to the Supreme Court's ruling, let me note how successfully the Satmar Hasidim were able to use their political and religious freedoms to self-segregate. The Satmars, of course, freely purchased and settled their land, which at the time was a subdivision within a town called Monroe. After a zoning dispute with the town, the Satmars successfully petitioned to form a new village. Because non-Satmars living in Monroe did not want to become part of the new village, the village's boundaries included only the Satmars. This allowed the Satmars to create exactly the living arrangements they desired. In the court's summary of the matter, the Satmars

> segregate the sexes outside the home; speak Yiddish as their primary language; eschew television, radio, and English-language publications; and dress in distinctive ways that include head-coverings and special garments for boys and modest dress for girls. Children are educated in private religious schools, most boys at the United Talmudic Academy where they receive a thorough grounding in the Torah and limited exposure to secular subjects, and most girls at Bais Rochel, an affiliated school with a curriculum designed to prepare girls for their roles as wives and mothers."[5]

It may not be an exaggeration to suggest that the residents of Kiryas Joel live not just in their own village but also in a country of their own. They have their own language, educational system, and religious culture, which dictate all aspects of their lives. In 2008, only 6.3 percent of Kiryas Joel's residents spoke English at home, and of males twenty-five years and older, only 356 had graduated from high school. No one in Kiryas Joel had a professional or doctoral degree. What, then, one may ask, do residents of Kiryas Joel have in common with other U.S. citizens? The answer, it seems, is that they share great freedom with their compatriots, so much so that they have used the freedoms granted to citizens of the United States to isolate themselves. Yet the Satmar Hasidim's existence is nevertheless dependent on the United States in both theory and practice. According to the U.S. Census Bureau in 2008, Kiryas Joel also had the highest poverty rate in the country. Sixty-eight percent of Kiryas Joel's residents lived below the poverty rate, and 40 percent received food stamps.[6]

In the Supreme Court case, the court ruled that the statute granting Kiryas Joel its own school district went too far. It agreed that the state may not interfere with the religious freedom of the Satmar community to freely associate only with other Satmars and thereby create their own village. Yet in Justice David Souter's words, "Accommodation is not a principle without limits, and what petitioners seek is an adjustment to the Satmar's religiously grounded preferences.... It therefore crosses the line from permissible accommodation to impermissible establishment." As Justice Anthony Kennedy put it, "There is more than a fine line between the voluntary association that leads to a political community comprised of people who share a common religious faith, and the forced separation that occurs when the government draws explicit political boundaries on the basis of peoples' faith. In creating the district in question, New York crossed that line."[7]

The important thing to notice about these arguments is that they proceed from the assumption that Judaism is a religion. Note Kennedy's causal claim: voluntary association can lead to a political community. On this reading the Satmars are a bunch of individuals who, based on their convictions about God—that is, their religious faith—have chosen to live together. The same principle that allows the Satmars to establish a village of their own—the individual's freedom of religious conscience and association—is also the principle that ought not to allow the Satmars to have their own school district. The problem is that in the latter case, as opposed to the former, the government, and not the individual, is drawing the boundaries.

There is of course much to be said about the U.S. Constitution, the establishment clause, and freedom of conscience more generally in the United States. But for the purposes of my story about how Judaism became a religion, the significance of the Supreme Court's opinion lies in the attempt to put Judaism (and here ultra-Orthodox Judaism) into the category of religion defined primarily in terms of individual belief. As we have seen throughout this book, Judaism does not quite fit into this category. Justice Anthony Scalia recognized this to some extent in his dissenting opinion in *Board of Education of Kiryas Joel Village School*

District v. Grumet. Scalia argued, "On what basis does Justice Souter conclude that it is the theological distinctiveness rather than the cultural distinctiveness that was the basis for New York State's decision? The normal assumption would be that it was the latter, since it was not theology but dress, language, and cultural alienation that posed the educational problem for the children."[8]

Scalia is right that dress, language, and cultural alienation constitute Satmar Hasidism. But if Souter and Kennedy err on the side of reducing Satmar Hasidism to religious faith, surely Scalia goes too far in separating the Satmars' cultural distinctiveness from their theological distinctiveness. As discussed above, the theological, cultural, and indeed political dimensions of ultraorthodoxy are inextricably intertwined. They simply cannot be separated. The Satmars dress as they do, speak the language that they speak, and educate their children as they do because they conceive their identity as a whole, as shalem—that is, as complete. The attempt to define Judaism as a religion (or culture or nationality) is to fragment this wholeness.

As I conclude my story about the invention of the idea of Jewish religion and its conceptual aftermaths, let me be clear once again that I am not suggesting that the ultraorthodox have reclaimed a wholeness that all other Jews have lost (though this is certainly the ultraorthodox position). As we see in the Kiryas Joel case, ultraorthodox wholeness is wholly dependent on the nation-state's protection of religious freedom. The interesting question here is not about ultraorthodoxy per se but rather about this rather odd modern category of religion. We have seen that in the case of Judaism, the category of religion, defined as a sphere of life separate from other spheres (such as politics, morality, and science, just to name a few), simply does not quite fit. Modern Jewish thought may be understood as the story of the attempt by Jewish thinkers to fit Judaism into this category and the rejection of this effort, which in turn inspires subsequent attempts to place Judaism into yet another category, such as culture or nationality, which as we have seen, does not quite fit either.

The reader should not decide that the difficulty, if not impossibility, of reaching a conclusion as to what Judaism is renders Judaism and modern Jewish thought irrelevant or dead. On the contrary, in my view it is, among other things, the difficulty of answering the question of what Judaism is in the modern world that makes modern Jewish thought so interesting and vibrant. Modern Jewish thought lives because these are questions that are difficult to answer.

At the same time, the modern Jewish attempt to fit Judaism into the category of religion is far from a quaint story relevant to Jews alone. Certainly in eighteenth-century Prussia, Mendelssohn's profound problem of how to fit Judaism into a Protestant conception of religion and the private sphere seemed to involve only the Jewish people. Today, the question of whether religion is a private or public matter is critical not just for Jews but also Christians and Muslims as they try to rethink their relation to the modern nation-state. The question of religion's private or public status—the question of whether religion is indeed what our modern Western forebears have largely told us it is—has thus returned to the center of discussions about the nature of the nation-state, as we have seen most recently in current debates about the relation between religion and public life. For instance, France's "headscarf affair" in 1989 in which three Muslim girls were expelled for coming to school in Islamic dress led to a bill in 2004 that banned all conspicuous religious symbols in schools. Yet far from settling the matter, debate about the state's right to ban religion from the public square has only intensified in France and abroad as Europe slowly comes to face the reality that millions of Muslim immigrants do not believe that Islam can be relegated to the private sphere. So too, Americans continue to struggle with public policy on such issues as abortion and gay marriage in large part because of unsettled arguments about the role of religion in U.S. public life. While the story of the invention of Jewish religion does not provide any neat solutions for how to resolve these debates, this story does offer more than three hundred years' worth of conversation about the very problems that, incorrectly, appear unprecedented to so many of us today.

SUGGESTED READINGS

Background

Greenawalt, Kent. *Religion and the Constitution.* 2 vols. Princeton, NJ: Princeton University Press, 2008.
  Greenawalt explores the U.S. Constitution's treatment of the free exercise and establishment of religion, outlining the history of the relevant legal doctrines, considering a variety of specific controversies, and emphasizing the importance of understanding these issues as involving multiple political and legal values.
Heilman, Samuel C. *Sliding to the Right: The Contest for the Future of American Jewish Orthodoxy.* Berkeley: University of California Press, 2006.
  Considering the history and future of Orthodox Judaism in the United States, Heilman contrasts the approaches of and examines the relationship between two distinct subsets of U.S. orthodoxy: a group committed to participating in U.S. society and its institutions, and a group wary of the modern world and committed to preserving Jewish life in cultural "enclaves."

Katz, Jacob. "Towards a Biography of the Hatam Sofer." Trans. David Ellenson. In *Profiles in Diversity: Jews in a Changing Europe, 1750–1870*, ed. Frances Malino and David Sorkin, 223–66. Detroit: Wayne State University Press, 1998.

Katz provides an overview of the life and work of the Hatam Sofer.

Mintz, Jerome R. *Hasidic People: A Place in the New World*. Cambridge, MA: Harvard University Press, 1992.

Focusing on Hasidic Jews in the New York City area, Mintz looks at the history and social life of these communities as well as their relations with various ethnic groups.

Silber, Michael K. "The Emergence of Ultra-Orthodoxy: The Invention of a Tradition." In *The Uses of Tradition: Jewish Continuity in the Modern Era*, ed. Jack Wertheimer, 23–84. New York: Jewish Theological Seminary of America, 1992.

Exploring the development of ultraorthodoxy in nineteenth-century Hungary, Silber outlines the challenges that confronted Hungarian orthodoxy, the diversity of orthodox reactions to such challenges, and the innovative nature of the ultraorthodox response.

Satmar Hasidism and Kiryas Joel

Eisgruber, Christopher L. "The Constitutional Value of Assimilation." *Columbia Law Review* 96, no. 1 (1996): 87–103.

Based on the Supreme Court's decision in the Kiryas Joel case, this piece considers the constitutional and political significance of assimilation.

Glinert, Lewis, and Yosseph Shilhav. "Holy Land, Holy Language: A Study of an Ultra-Orthodox Jewish Ideology." *Language in Society* 20, no. 1 (1991): 59–86.

The authors examine the content, relationship, and implications of conceptions of language and territory in Satmar thought.

Greene, Abner S. "'Kiryas Joel' and Two Mistakes about Equality." *Columbia Law Review* 96, no. 1 (1996): 43–51.

This essay, assessing the Kiryas Joel case, explores the granting of quasi-governmental powers to private groups.

Kaplan, Zvi Jonathan. "Rabbi Joel Teitelbaum, Zionism, and Hungarian Ultra-Orthodoxy." *Modern Judaism* 24, no. 2 (2004): 165–78.

Kaplan analyzes the anti-Zionism of Teitelbaum, considering the historical and textual factors that shaped Teitelbaum's political views—for example, those factors that influenced his opposition to Israel's existence as a democratic nation-state.

Lupu, Ira C. "Uncovering the Village of Kiryas Joel." *Columbia Law Review* 96, no. 1 (1996): 104–20.

This essay delves into the sociological realities of the Kiryas Joel community.

Minow, Martha. "The Constitution and the Subgroup Question." *Indiana Law Journal* 71, no. 1 (1995): 1–25.

Focusing on (potentially) competing commitments to particularity and inclusion, Minow explores and assesses the Kiryas Joel case by considering what she calls the "subgroup question"—the question of what a group must give up in order to obtain benefits from the state, and whether a democratic and secular polity "require[s] assimilation as the price of membership."

NOTES

INTRODUCTION

1. Jonathan Z. Smith, "Religion, Religions, Religious," in *Relating Religion: Essays in the Study of Religion* (Chicago: University of Chicago Press, 2004), 179–96.
2. Baruch Spinoza, *Theologico-Political Treatise*, trans. R. H. M. Elwes (New York: Dover, 1951), 69.
3. In this book I have for the most part employed the more familiar transliterations of certain Hebrew names, but have at the same time tried to maintain internal consistency in the English spelling of other Hebrew and Yiddish names and terms.

CHAPTER 1
MODERN JUDAISM AND THE INVENTION OF JEWISH RELIGION

1. Gotthold Ephraim Lessing, *The Jew in the Modern World: A Documentary History,* ed. Paul Mendes-Flohr and Jehuda Reinharz, 2nd ed. (New York: Oxford University Press, 1995), 63.
2. For a comprehensive account of Mendelssohn's life, see Alexander Altmann, *Moses Mendelssohn: A Biographical Study* (Tuscaloosa: University of Alabama Press, 1973).
3. Christian Wilhelm Dohm, *Über die bürgerliche Verbesserung der Juden* (Berlin: Stettin, 1781–83), 1:28.
4. Ibid., 1:142.
5. Ibid., 1:143.
6. Ibid., 2:56.
7. Moses Mendelssohn, *Gesammelte Schriften Jubiläumsausgabe* (Berlin: F. Frommann Verlag, 1929–84), 8:21.
8. August Friedrich Cranz, in Mendes-Flohr and Reinharz, *The Jew in the Modern World*, 93; translation modified.
9. Moses Mendelssohn, *Jerusalem: Or on Religious Power and Judaism*, trans. Allan Arkush (Hanover, NH: University of New England Press, 1983), 90.
10. Ibid., 97.
11. Ibid., 102–3.
12. Ibid., 87, 113, 114, 111.
13. Ibid., 97.
14. Ibid., 61.
15. Ibid., 130.
16. Immanuel Kant, letter to Moses Mendelssohn on August 16, 1789, in *Kant: Philosophical Correspondence*, ed. and trans. Arnulf Zweig (Chicago: University of Chicago Press, 1967), 107.
17. David Friedländer, cited in Michael A. Meyer, *The Origins of the Modern Jew* (Detroit: Wayne State University Press, 1967), 61.

18. Immanuel Kant, *Religion within the Limits of Reason Alone*, trans. Theodore M. Greene and Hoyt H. Hudson (New York: Harper and Brothers, 1960), 115, 154.

19. Friedrich Schleiermacher, *On Religion* (New York: Cambridge University Press, 1996).

20. Ibid., 22, 23.

21. Ibid., 113–14.

22. Friedrich Schleiermacher, *Briefe bei Gelegenheit der politisch theologischen Aufgabe und des Sendschreibens jüdischer Hausväter. Von einem Prediger außerhalb Berlin* (Berlin: Friedrich Franke, 1799), 36–37.

23. Mendelssohn, *Jerusalem*, 100–103.

24. Ibid., 134.

CHAPTER 2

RELIGION AS HISTORY

1. Jacob Katz, "German Culture and the Jews," in *The Jewish Response to German Culture*, ed. Jehuda Reinharz and Walter Schatzberg (Hanover, NH: University Press of New England, 1985), 93.

2. Ibid., 94.

3. Comte de Clermont-Tonnerre, cited in Arthur Hertzberg, *The French Enlightenment and the Jews* (New York: Columbia University Press, 1968), 360.

4. Moses Mendelssohn, *Jerusalem: Or on Religious Power and Judaism*, trans. Allan Arkush (Hanover, NH: University Press of New England, 1983), 97.

5. Abraham Geiger, in *Abraham Geiger and Liberal Judaism*, ed. Max Wiener (Philadelphia: Jewish Publication Society, 1962), 178.

6. Ibid.,, 155.

7. Ibid., 156–57.

8. Ibid., 133.

9. Abraham Geiger, *Was hat Mohammed aus dem Judenthume aufgenommen?* (Bonn: F. Baaden, 1833); translated as Abraham Geiger, *Judaism and Islam*, trans. F. M. Young (Madras: M.D.C.S.P.C.K. Press, 1898; New York: Ktav Publishing House, 1970).

10. Ibid., 42, 45–46.

11. Samson Raphael Hirsch, in Paul Mendes-Flohr and Jehuda Reinharz, eds., *The Jew in the Modern World: A Documentary History*, 2nd ed. (New York: Oxford University Press, 1995), 199.

12. Samson Raphael Hirsch, in *Judaism Eternal*, ed. Isadore Grunfeld (London: Soncino Press, 1956), 103.

13. Ibid.

14. Samson Raphael Hirsch, "Die Trennungsfrage in Carlsruhe," *Jeschurun* 25 (1870): 128.

15. Samson Raphael Hirsch, in Grunfeld, *Judaism Eternal*, 100.

16. Samson Raphael Hirsch, *Nineteen Letters* (Jerusalem: Feldheim, 1995), 224.

17. Samson Raphael Hirsch, *Collected Writings* (New York: P. Feldheim, 1984), 6:75.

18. Hirsch, *Horeb*, 20.

19. Saint Augustine, *City of God* (New York: Image Books, 1958), 304; Hirsch, *Collected Writings*, 6:206–7.

20. Hirsch, *Collected Writings*, 6:206–7, 299.

21. Heinrich Graetz, *The Structure of Jewish History*, ed. Ismar Schorsch (New York: Jewish Theological Seminary of America, 1975), 100.

22. Ibid., 93–94.

23. Georg Wilhelm Friedrich Hegel, *Reason in History* (Indianapolis: Bobbs-Merrill Company, 1953), 92.

24. Georg Wilhelm Friedrich Hegel, *Introduction to the Philosophy of History* (Indianapolis: Hackett, 1988), 21.

25. Graetz, *The Structure of Jewish History*, 70.

26. Ibid., 91.

27. Heinrich von Treitschke, cited in Michael Meyer, *Judaism within Modernity* (Detroit: Wayne State University Press, 2001), 72.

CHAPTER 3
RELIGION AS REASON AND THE SEPARATION OF RELIGION FROM POLITICS

1. Hermann Cohen, *Jüdische Schriften*, ed. Bruno Strauss (Berlin, 1924), 2:212.

2. Hermann Cohen, *Religion of Reason out of the Sources of Judaism*, trans. Simon Kaplan (New York: Frederick Ungar, 1972), 67.

3. Ibid., 357.

4. Hermann Cohen, *Ethik des reinen Willen* in *Werke*, ed. Hermann-Cohen-Archiv am Philosophischen Seminar Zürich unter der Leitung von Helmut Holzhey (Hildesheim: G. Olms, 1984), 7:267–68.

5. Cohen, *Religion of Reason*, 366–67.

6. Ibid., 313.

7. Ibid., 234.

8. Ibid., 235.

9. Ibid., 234–35.

10. Cohen, *Jüdische Schriften*, 208.

11. Heinrich Graetz, *The Structure of Jewish History*, ed. Ismar Schorsch (New York: Jewish Theological Seminary of America, 1975), 70. Hermann Cohen, cited in Uriel Tal, *Christians and Jews in Germany: Religion, Politics, and Ideology in the Second Reich, 1870–1914*, trans. Noah J. Jacobs (Ithaca, NY: Cornell University Press, 1975), 60.

12. Cohen, *Jüdische Schriften*, 207.

13. Joseph Soloveitchik, *Halakhic Man* (Philadelphia: Jewish Publication Society, 1984), 55.

14. Aaron Rakeffet-Rothkoff, *The Rav: The World of Rabbi Joseph B. Soloveitchik* (Hoboken, NJ: Ktav, 1999), 247.

15. Soloveitchik, *Halakhic Man*, 86.

16. Ibid., 57.

17. Ibid., 134.

18. Joseph Soloveitchik, *Lonely Man of Faith* (New York: Three Leaves, 2006), 36.

19. Ibid., 39.

20. Soloveitchik, *Halakhic Man*, 113, 107.

21. Joseph Soloveitchik, "Hark, My Beloved Knocks," in *In Aloneness, In Togetherness* [Hebrew], ed. Pinchas Peli (Jerusalem: Orot, 1976), 339–40.

22. Hermann Cohen, cited in Tal, *Christians and Jews in Germany*, 60.

23. Joseph Soloveitchik, "Confrontation," *Tradition: A Journal of Orthodox Thought* 6, no. 2 (Spring–Summer 1964): 6.

24. Yeshayahu Leibowitz, *Judaism, Human Values, and the Jewish State* (Cambridge, MA: Harvard University Press, 1995), 71–74.

25. Yeshayahu Leibowitz, cited in Joel Greenberg, "Yeshayhu Leibowitz, 91, Iconoclastic Israeli Thinker" (obituary), *New York Times*, August 19, 1994.

26. Leibowitz, *Judaism,* 116.

27. Ibid., 117, 95.

28. Ibid., 97.

29. Yeshayahu Leibowitz, *The Faith of Maimonides* (New York: Adama Books, 1987), 14.

30. Leibowitz, *Judaism,* 113–14.

31. Ibid., 93.

32. Ibid., 91.

33. Ibid., 137.

34. Ibid.

35. Moses Mendelssohn, *Jerusalem: Or on Religious Power and Judaism,* trans. Allan Arkush (Hanover, NH: University of New England Press, 1983), 58.

36. Ibid., 45.

CHAPTER 4

RELIGION AS EXPERIENCE

1. Eliezer Liebermann, in *The Jew in the Modern World: A Documentary History,* ed. Paul Mendes-Flohr and Jehuda Reinharz, 2nd ed. (New York: Oxford University Press, 1995), 163.

2. Steven Ascheim, *Brothers and Strangers: East-European Jew in German and German-Jewish Consciousness, 1800–1923* (Madison: University of Wisconsin Press, 1982), 13–14.

3. Heinrich Graetz, *History of the Jews* (Philadelphia: Jewish Publication Society, 1895), 5:392.

4. For Cohen on this issue, see Hermann Cohen, "The Polish Jew," in *The Jew: Essays from Martin Buber's Journal Der Jude, 1916–1928,* ed. Arthur A. Cohen (Tuscaloosa: University of Alabama Press, 1980), 52–60.

5. Moses Mendelssohn, cited in Michael A. Meyer, *The Origins of the Modern Jew* (Detroit: Wayne State University Press, 1967), 44.

6. Franz Rosenzweig, *On Jewish Learning,* ed. Nahum N. Glatzer (New York: Schocken Books), 78.

7. On Rosenzweig's life, see Nahum N. Glatzer, *Franz Rosenzweig, His Life and Thought* (New York: Schocken Books, 1953).

8. Martin Buber, *Hasidism and Modern Man,* trans. Maurice Friedman (New York: Harper, 1966), 54.

9. For more on Buber's life, see Maurice Friedman, *Martin Buber: The Life of Dialogue* (Chicago: University of Chicago Press, 1955).

10. Buber, *Hasidism and Modern Man,* 46, 51.

11. Ibid., 165.

12. Martin Buber, *I and Thou,* trans. Walter Kaufmann (New York: Touchtone, 1971), 104.

13. Martin Buber, in *The Martin Buber Reader,* ed. Asher Biemann (New York: Palgrave Macmillan), 44.

14. Franz Rosenzweig *The Star of Redemption,* trans. William W. Hallo (New York: University of Notre Dame Press, 1985), 156.

15. Franz Rosenzweig, *Der Mensch und sein Werk: Gesammelte Schriften* (The Hague: Martinus Nijhoff, 1974–84), 3:169.

16. Rosenzweig, *Star*, 298.

17. Franz Rosenzweig, cited in Glatzer, *Franz Rosenzweig*, 214.

18. Ibid., 102.

19. Friedrich Schleiermacher, *Sämtliche Werke* (Berlin: G. Reimer, 1846), 3:2:218.

20. Franz Rosenzweig, *Scripture and Translation*, trans. Lawrence Rosenwald and Everett Fox (Bloomington: Indiana University Press, 1994), 56–57.

21. Martin Buber, in Biemann, *The Martin Buber Reader*, 115.

22. Buber, *I and Thou*, 158–60.

23. Rosenzweig, *Der Mensch und sein Werk*, 1:2:770–71.

24. Martin Buber, *The Knowledge of Man* (Amherst, NY: Humanity Books, 1998), 117.

25. Franz Rosenzweig, *On Jewish Learning* (New York: Schocken Books, 1955), 116.

26. Rosenzweig, *Star*, 300.

27. Ibid., 306–7.

28. Franz Rosenzweig, in Nahum N. Glatzer and Paul Mendes-Flohr, eds., *The Letters of Martin Buber: A Life of Dialogue* (Syracuse, NY: Syracuse University Press, 1996), 278–90, 280; emphasis added.

29. Rosenzweig, *On Jewish Learning*, 66.

30. Franz Rosenzweig, *Judaism despite Christianity* (Tuscaloosa: University of Alabama Press, 1969), 114.

CHAPTER 5:
JEWISH RELIGION AFTER THE HOLOCAUST

1. Emil Fackenheim, *To Mend the World* (Bloomington: Indiana University Press, 1994), 23.

2. Emil Fackenheim, *God's Presence in History* (New York: HarperCollins, 1972), 90.

3. Ibid., 92.

4. Emil Fackenheim, *The Jewish Return into History* (New York: Schocken Books, 1978), 22; see also Fackenheim, *To Mend the World* , 299–300.

5. Emil Fackenheim, *The Jewish Thought of Emil Fackenheim: A Reader*, ed. Michael Morgan (Detroit: Wayne State University Press, 1987), 289.

6. Emil Fackenheim, *Encounters between Judaism and Modern Philosophy* (New York: Basic Books, 1973), 167–68.

7. Fackenheim, *The Jewish Return into History*, 101.

8. Emil Fackenheim, *What Is Judaism? An Interpretation for the Present Age* (Syracuse, NY: Syracuse University Press, 1999), 35.

9. Ibid.

10. Isaac Reines, *Sefer ha-Tzionut ha-datit* (Jerusalem, 1977), pt. 1, 339; originally published in *Ha-Melitz* 78 (1900), cited in Aviezer Ravitzky, *Messianism, Zionism, and Jewish Religious Radicalism* (Chicago: University of Chicago Press, 1996), 34.

11. Abraham Isaac Kook, "On Zionism" [Hebrew], in *Ha-Devir* (Jerusalem, 1920), cited in Ravitzky, *Messianism, Zionism, and Jewish Religious Radicalism*, 87.

12. Abraham Isaac Kook, *The Lights of Penitence, the Moral Principles, Lights of Holiness, Essays, Letters, and Poems* (New York: Paulist Press, 1978), 53, 51–52.

13. Ibid., 56.

14. Zvi Yehudah Kook, cited in Ravitzky, *Messianism, Zionism, and Jewish Religious Radicalism*, 127.

15. Emmanuel Levinas, *Otherwise Than Being or Beyond Essence*, trans. Alphonso Lingis (The Hague: Martinus Nijhoff, 1981), 75.

16. Emmanuel Levinas, *Totality and Infinity: An Essay on Exteriority*, trans. Alphonso Lingis (Pittsburgh: Duquesne University Press, 1969).

17. See especially "The Prohibition against Representation and 'The Rights of Man'" and "The Rights of the Other Man," in Emmanuel Levinas, *Alterity and Transcendence*, trans. Michael B. Smith (New York: Columbia University Press, 1999).

18. Levinas, *Otherwise Than Being or Beyond Essence*, 159.

19. Emmanuel Levinas, *Difficult Freedom: Essays on Judaism*, trans. Sean Hand (Baltimore: Johns Hopkins University Press, 1997), 218.

20. Ibid., 218–19.

21. Ibid., 221.

22. Ibid., 263.

CHAPTER 6

THE IRRELEVANCE OF RELIGION AND
THE EMERGENCE OF THE JEWISH INDIVIDUAL

1. Elijah ben Solomon, cited in Immanuel Etkes, *Rabbi Israel Salanter and the Mussar Movement*, trans. Jonathan Chipman (Philadelphia: Jewish Publication Society, 1993), 21.

2. Martin Buber, *Tales of the Hasidim*, forward Chaim Potock (New York: Schocken Books, 1991), 65.

3. Elijah ben Solomon, cited in Gershon Hundret, *Jews in Poland-Lithuania in the Eighteenth Century: A Genealogy of Modernity* (Berkeley: University of California Press, 2004), 189n4.

4. Jacob Katz, *Tradition and Crisis: Jewish Society at the End of the Middle Ages* (New York: New York University Press, 1993), 199.

5. Solomon Maimon, *An Autobiography* (Champagne: University of Illinois Press, 2001), 34.

6. Ibid., 154.

7. Immanuel Kant, *Correspondence*, trans. Arnulf Zweig (Cambridge: Cambridge University Press, 1999), 311–12, 476.

8. Maimon, *An Autobiography*, 147.

9. Ibid., 76.

10. Ibid., 189.

11. Ibid., 216.

12. Abraham Socher, *The Radical Enlightenment of Solomon Maimon* (Palo Alto, CA: Stanford University Press, 2006), 7.

13. Maimon, *An Autobiography*, 229.

14. Ibid., 230–31.

15. Ibid., 231.

16. Hayim of Volozhin, cited in Etkes, *Rabbi Israel Salanter*, 52.

17. Israel Salanter, cited in Etkes, *Rabbi Israel Salanter*, 289–90.

18. Lucy S. Dawidowicz, ed., *The Golden Tradition* (Syracuse, NY: Syracuse University Press, 1996), 173–74.

19. Lawrence Kaplan, "The Hazon Ish: Haredi Critic of Traditional Orthodoxy," in *The Uses of Tradition: Jewish Continuity in the Modern Era*, ed. Jack Wertheimer (New York: Jewish Theological Seminary of America, 1992), 145–74.

20. Friedrich Schleiermacher, *On Religion* (New York: Cambridge University Press, 1996), 23.

CHAPTER 7

THE TRANSFORMATION OF TRADITION AND
THE INVENTION OF JEWISH CULTURE

1. For a comprehensive account, see Benjamin Nathans, *Beyond the Pale: The Jewish Encounter with Late Imperial Russia* (Berkeley: University of California Press, 2002).

2. Judah Leib Gordon, cited in Michael Stanislawski, *For Whom Do I Toil? Judah Leib Gordon and the Crisis of Russian Jewry* (New York: Oxford University Press, 1988), 226.

3. Sholem Yankev Abramovitsh, "The Mare," in *Yenne Velt: The Great Works of Jewish Fantasy and Occult*, trans. Joachim Neugroschel (New York: Simon and Schuster, 1976), 231.

4. Ibid., 234–35.

5. Ibid., 273.

6. Ibid., 199.

7. Ibid., 201.

8. Sholom Aleichem, "On Account of a Hat," in *The Best of Sholom Aleichem*, ed. Irving Howe and Ruth Wisse (New York: New Republic Books, 1979), 108–9.

9. Ibid., 105.

10. Cited in Albert S. Lindemann, *The Jew Accused: Three Anti-Semitic Affairs (Dreyfus, Beilis, and Frank)* (New York: Cambridge University Press, 1992), 174.

11. Sholom Aleichem, "On Account of a Hat," 104.

12. David G. Roskies, "Inside Sholem Shachnah's Hat," *Prooftexts* 21, no. 1 (Winter 2001): 44.

CHAPTER 8

THE REJECTION OF JEWISH RELIGION AND
THE BIRTH OF JEWISH NATIONALISM

1. Perez Smolenskin, cited in Isaac Barzilay, "Smolenskin's Polemic against Mendelssohn in Historical Perspective," *Proceedings of the American Academy for Jewish Research* 53 (1986): 12.

2. Theodor Herzl, cited in Ernst Pawel, *The Labyrinth of Exile: A Life of Theodor Herzl* (New York: Farrar, Straus and Giroux, 1992), 214.

3. Moses Hess, *Rome and Jerusalem: A Study in Jewish Nationalism*, trans. Meyer Waxman (New York: Bloch Publishing, 1918), 64.

4. Ibid., 112–13.

5. Ibid., 48.

6. Karl Marx, *The Essential Writings* (Boulder, CO: Westview Press, 1986), 42.

7. Hess, *Rome and Jerusalem*, 64.

8. Shlomo Avineri, *The Making of Modern Zionism: The Intellectual Origins of the Jewish State* (New York: Basic Books, 1981), 41.

9. Leon Pinsker, *Auto-Emancipation*, trans. D. S. Blondheim (New York: Macabaean Publishing Company, 1906), 8.

10. Ibid., 3.

11. Theodor Herzl, *Zionist Writings: Essays and Addresses*, trans. Harry Zohn (New York: Herzl Press, 1973), 2:112.

12. Theodor Herzl, *The New Ghetto*, trans. Heinz Norden (New York: Theodor Herzl Foundation, 1955), 85.

13. Herzl letter to Mortiz Benedik, dated December 27, 1892, translated and cited in Pawel, *The Labyrinth of Exile*, 181–82.

14. Theodor Herzl, *The Jewish State* (New York: Dover, 1989), 29.

15. Ibid., 38.

16. Ibid., 145.

17. Ibid., 146.

18. Ibid.

19. Ibid., 147.

20. Seventh Zionist Congress Anti-Uganda Resolution (July 30, 1905), in Paul Mendes-Flohr and Jehuda Reinharz, eds., *The Jew in the Modern World: A Documentary History*, 2nd ed. (New York: Oxford University Press, 1995), 548.

21. Ahad Ha'am, *Selected Essays by Ahad Ha'am*, trans. Leon Simon (Philadelphia: Jewish Publication Society of America, 1912), 193.

22. Ahad Ha'am, *Al Parashat Derakhim* (Tel Aviv: Dvir, 1946), 3:30.

23. Ahad Ha'am, *Nationalism and the Jewish Ethic*, ed. Hans Kohn (New York: Schocken Books, 1962), 79.

24. Ahad Ha'am, *Selected Essays by Ahad Ha'am*, 130.

25. Ahad Ha'am, *Al Parashat Derakhim* (Berlin: Jüdischer Verlag, 1930), 1:6.

26. Ahad Ha'am, *Selected Essays by Ahad Ha'am*, 284.

27. Hayim Nahman Bialik, "Ha-sefer ha-'ivri," in *Devrei sifrut* (Tel Aviv: Hotsa'at Devir, 1965), 29.

28. Hayim Nahman Bialik, "Halakhah and Aggadah" (1917), translated in Nahum N. Glatzer, ed., *Modern Jewish Thought: A Source Reader* (New York: Schocken Books, 1977), 55.

29. Michah Josef Berdichevsky, cited in Avner Holtzman, "The Red Heifer," in *Reading Hebrew Literature: Critical Discussions of Six Modern Texts*, ed. Alan Minz (Hanover, NH: Brandeis University Press, 2003), 57.

30. Michah Josef Berdichevsky, "In Two Directions," in *The Zionist Idea: A Historical Analysis and Reader*, ed. Arthur Hertzberg (Philadelphia: Jewish Publication Society of America, 1997), 295.

CHAPTER 9

JEWISH RELIGION IN THE UNITED STATES

1. Mary Antin, *The Promised Land* (Boston: Riverside Press, 1912), xi.

2. Emma Lazarus, *The Poems of Emma Lazarus* (Boston: Riverside Press, 1889), 1:202–3.

3. For these figures, see Samuel Joseph, *Jewish Immigration to the United States from 1881–1910* (New York: Columbia University Press, 1914), 173.

4. The Orthodox Jewish Congregational Union of America (June 8, 1898), in *The Jew in the Modern World: A Documentary History*, ed. Paul Mendes-Flohr and Jehuda Reinharz, 2nd ed. (New York: Oxford University Press, 1995), 371–72.

5. Cited in Neil Gillman, *Conservative Judaism* (Springfield, NJ: Behrman House, 1993), 36.

6. The Columbus Platform, in Mendes-Flohr and Reinharz, *The Jew in the Modern World*, 518.

7. Cited in Frank Julian Warne, *The Tide of Immigration* (New York: D. Appleton, 1916), 359.

8. Ibid., 278–79.

9. Mordecai Kaplan, *Judaism as a Civilization* (Philadelphia: Jewish Publication Society, 1981), 345.

10. Ibid., 125, 159, 166.

11. Ibid., 521–22.

12. Ibid., 223.

13. Ibid., 250.

14. Ibid., 43.

15. Ibid., 242.

16. Leo Strauss, *Spinoza's Critique of Religion* (Chicago: University of Chicago Press, 1965), 1.

17. Ibid., 6.

18. Ibid., 3.

19. Leo Strauss, *Jewish Philosophy and the Crisis of Modernity*, ed. Hart Green (Albany: State University of New York Press, 1997), 34.

20. Strauss, *Spinoza's Critique of Religion*, 6.

21. Kaplan, *Judaism as a Civilization*, 521–22.

CONCLUSION

1. Michael K. Silber, "The Emergence of Ultra-Orthodoxy: The Invention of a Tradition," in *The Uses of Tradition: Jewish Continuity in the Modern Era*, ed. Jack Wertheimer (New York: Jewish Theological Seminary of America, 1992), 23–84.

2. Moses Sofer, "A Reply concerning the Question of Reform (1819)," in *The Jew in the Modern World: A Documentary History*, ed. Paul Mendes-Flohr and Jehuda Reinharz, 2nd ed. (New York: Oxford University Press, 1995), 169–72; Paul Mendes-Flohr and Jehuda Reinharz, "Emerging Patterns of Religious Adjustment," in *The Jew in the Modern World: A Documentary History*, 156–57.

3. 512 U.S. 687 (1994), 683.

4. "Religion, Establishment of," in Thurston Greene, *The Language of the Constitution* (Santa Barbara, CA: Greenwood Press, 1991), 665–72.

5. Ibid., 691.

6. Matt King, "KJ Highest US Poverty Rate, Census Says," *Times Herald-Record*, January 30, 2009.

7. 512 U.S. 687 (1994), 706.

8. Ibid., 740.

INDEX

CPSIA information can be obtained
at www.ICGtesting.com
Printed in the USA
LVHW041925120322
713152LV00005B/213